"Perhaps a meadow exists between dogmatism and skepticism, a fruitful space for cultivating beautiful truth. Perhaps Origen, Augustine, and Edwards can converse there with Flannery O'Connor and Cormac McCarthy. Perhaps instead of rehearsing or debunking information, we can foster theological imagination. Perhaps Joshua McNall's wit and wisdom has pointed the church toward a better future. Perhaps we should listen."

Matthew W. Bates, author of *Gospel Allegiance* and associate professor of theology at Quincy University

"Drawing on the best insights from believers, thinkers, and artists of the past, *Perhaps* demonstrates that the brightest future of the church will be cultivated through the kind of theological imagination modeled here. Such an imagination—robust and inviting, informed and inquisitive—encourages a confidence in Christian belief that, paradoxically, can come only with a willingness to wonder what might be. *Perhaps* is one of the most faith-building books I've read in a long time."

Karen Swallow Prior, author of *On Reading Well: Finding the Good Life through Great Books* and *Booked: Literature in the Soul of Me*

"In a polarized world with the rigidity of fundamentalisms on the one hand and the nihilism of skepticisms on the other, McNall enters to sketch a way forward for the holiness of intellectual humility. This is a creative book that not only argues winsomely from Scripture, theology, and literature, but also invites the reader into a narrative that portrays how the weight of its claims press on everyday life. *Perhaps* will be especially helpful for the student wrestling with the challenges of Christian orthodoxy, and all looking for breathing room to wonder, hope, and ultimately, trust."

James M. Arcadi, associate professor of biblical and systematic theology at Trinity Evangelical Divinity School

"Faith is not knowing all truth. And faith is not making it up as you go along either. McNall presents faith as an expedition into the unknown led by a known God. This is a hope-filling book that intentionally does not give you all the answers. Pilgrims: take this book with you on your journey."

Nijay K. Gupta, professor of New Testament at Northern Seminary

Perhaps

Reclaiming the Space Between

Doubt and Dogmatism

JOSHUA M. McNALL

ivp
Academic

An imprint of InterVarsity Press
Downers Grove, Illinois

InterVarsity Press
P.O. Box 1400, Downers Grove, IL 60515-1426
ivpress.com
email@ivpress.com

InterVarsity Press® is the book-publishing division of InterVarsity Christian Fellowship/USA®, a
movement of students and faculty active on campus at hundreds of universities, colleges, and schools
of nursing in the United States of America, and a member movement of the International Fellowship
of Evangelical Students. For information about local and regional activities, visit intervarsity.org.

All Scripture quotations, unless otherwise indicated, are taken from The Holy Bible, New International
Version®, NIV®. Copyright © 1973, 1978, 1984, 2011 by Biblica, Inc.™ Used by permission of Zondervan.
All rights reserved worldwide. www.zondervan.com. The "NIV" and "New International Version" are
trademarks registered in the United States Patent and Trademark Office by Biblica, Inc.™

The publisher cannot verify the accuracy or functionality of website URLs used in this book beyond
the date of publication.

Cover design and image composite: David Fassett
Interior design: Jeanna Wiggins
Image: white paper surface: © Nenov / Moment Collection / Getty Images

ISBN 978-0-8308-5520-9 (print)
ISBN 978-0-8308-5521-6 (digital)

Printed in the United States of America ♾

Library of Congress Cataloging-in-Publication Data
Names: McNall, Joshua M., 1982- author.
Title: Perhaps : reclaiming the space between doubt and dogmatism / Joshua
   M. McNall.
Description: Downers Grove, IL : IVP Academic, [2021] | Includes
   bibliographical references and index.
Identifiers: LCCN 2021020486 (print) | LCCN 2021020487 (ebook) | ISBN
   9780830855209 (paperback) | ISBN 9780830855216 (ebook)
Subjects: LCSH: Faith. | Thought and thinking—Religious
   aspects—Christianity. | Uncertainty—Religious aspects—Christianity. |
   Dogmatism.
Classification: LCC BT771.3 .M43 2021 (print) | LCC BT771.3 (ebook) | DDC
   230—dc23
LC record available at https://lccn.loc.gov/2021020486
LC ebook record available at https://lccn.loc.gov/2021020487

| P | 25 | 24 | 23 | 22 | 21 | 20 | 19 | 18 | 17 | 16 | 15 | 14 | 13 | 12 | 11 | 10 | 9 | 8 | 7 | 6 | 5 | 4 | 3 | 2 | 1 |
| Y | 37 | 36 | 35 | 34 | 33 | 32 | 31 | 30 | 29 | 28 | 27 | 26 | 25 | 24 | 23 | 22 | 21 |

For Penelope, our exclamation point.

To believe in providence often
means saying "perhaps."

N. T. Wright

Contents

Preface

TOWARD THE BEGINNING of Joseph Conrad's *Heart of Darkness*, the narrator, Charles Marlow, recounts a memory from boyhood. As a child, he had traced a finger over an early and unfinished map of Africa. "At that time," he states, "there were many blank spaces on the earth." But as the modern era lumbered forward, those spaces would be filled—not just with ink but with blood and steel and change. This filling brought both progress and loss: The globe ceased to be a "delightful mystery" and became "a place of darkness." Nonetheless, Marlow admits that he was always drawn to the blank spaces.[1]

This book is like that.

It is a strange work because it fuses disciplines that are normally kept safely separate: theology, fiction, apologetics, and cultural analysis. It may also be controversial for at least two reasons: First, it levels a rebuke against the fractious tribe called *evangelical* while stubbornly refusing to defect in sheer embarrassment. Second, it endorses a word that is anathema to many theologians: *speculation*. The term almost always functions as a shame word in theology, even if it is not always clear what it entails (more on that later). To be speculative is invariably a bad thing. Or so a host of theologians tells us.

My claim is that they are wrong. Or more precisely, my claim is that they are not *always* correct. Sacred speculation (or what I call the ability to say perhaps) is sometimes required as we stand on the foundation of

---

[1]Joseph Conrad, *Heart of Darkness*; cited in *The Norton Anthology of English Literature*, vol. F, *Twentieth Century and After*, ed. Stephen Greenblatt, 9th ed. (New York: Norton, 2012), 1957.

Scripture and the shoulders of the saints. From this perch we peer into the blank spaces on the map. The importance of what I define as "faith seeking imagination" increases in a cultural moment when the church is torn by two unsavory extremes: the force of crippling secular doubt and the zealotry of partisan religious dogmatism. Rekindling a gracious theological imagination—rooted in orthodoxy, Scripture, tradition, community, and great works of art—is essential to confront the "resounding gong[s]" (1 Cor 13:1) of our day with something better than pervasive skepticism or abrasive certainty. In this blank space between unchecked doubt and dogmatism, Christians must relearn how to say "perhaps."

Acknowledgments

Let me give thanks.

As with much of my work, Jerome Van Kuiken made this book immeasurably better through his gracious and thoughtful feedback. Stephanie Leupp and Cheryl Salerno tracked down numerous sources for me. Spenser White and the team at InterVarsity Press helped with the indexing. Dalene Fisher offered Shakespearean insights on chapter ten, Jon Ensor applied his New Testament expertise to chapter eleven, K. M. West gave advice on the fictional story of Eliza, and Caleb Dunn read the whole manuscript to offer wisdom from a pastoral perspective. Thanks to you all!

Since my book blends theology with fiction (interspersed in several vignettes), I've benefited from auditing classes in our university's English department. And because I have now published something with fiction in it, I think I should be allowed to teach literature courses despite my total lack of academic credentials in that area. Make it so, Dr. Fisher!

A huge thanks to the entire team at InterVarsity Press. I want to express gratitude to Dan Reid for his initial interest in the project and to David McNutt for shepherding it at each step along the way. David has been the model editor with sharp insights and warm encouragement. Thanks, David.

Oklahoma Wesleyan University is my employer, but the school feels more like family. President Jim Dunn especially has worked tirelessly to lead a university in what are challenging times for Christian higher education. In so doing, he has managed to remain unapologetically committed to Christian orthodoxy without succumbing to the shrill winds of dogmatism that I critique throughout this book. Here's to that sacred middle space, and here's to OKWU!

I am grateful to my parents, Greg and Bonita McNall, for their constant love and faithful Christian service. And I am deeply indebted to Brian and Janette Maydew for welcoming me to their family fifteen years ago, and for turning the phrase "in-laws" into a cause for rejoicing in my vocabulary.

My wife, Brianna, deserves a thousand thanks and a million dollars for lovingly wrangling our children so I could write, and for proofreading my work both to smooth the grammar and to prevent me from saying things I will regret. I love you, Babe.

Our four kids are the joy of our life. I hope eventually to dedicate a book to each of them. In this one, the fictional character of Wilbur the tortoise is for Teddy Brian. But everything else is for Penelope Elspeth. She is our exclamation point and one of the most joyful, kind, and feisty daughters a dad could ever have.

Do not smile at me that I boast her off,
For thou shalt find she will outstrip all praise
And make it halt behind her. (Shakespeare, *The Tempest*, 4.1.9-11)

Abbreviations

AB	Anchor Bible
ANTC	Abingdon New Testament Commentaries
BECNT	Baker Exegetical Commentary on the New Testament
ICC	International Critical Commentary
NIB	New Interpreter's Bible
NICNT	New International Commentary on the New Testament
NICOT	New International Commentary on the Old Testament
NIGTC	New International Greek Testament Commentary
PG	Patrologia Graeca [= Patrologiae Cursus Completus: Series Graeca]. Edited by Jacques-Paul Migne. 162 vols. Paris, 1857–1886.
PL	Patrologia Latina [= Patrologiae Cursus Completus: Series Latina]. Edited by Jacques-Paul Migne. 217 vols. Paris, 1844–1864.
WBC	Word Biblical Commentary
WJE	Perry Miller, gen. ed. *The Works of Jonathan Edwards*. 26 vols. New Haven, CT: Yale University Press, 1957–2008.
WUNT	Wissenschaftlich Untersuchungen zum Neuen Testament

Introduction

Farewell, Pangaea

Latitude: 64° 15′ 17.40″ N
Longitude: -21° 07′ 18.00″ W

THE REYKJANES RIDGE, ICELAND

ACCORDING TO THOSE strange creatures called geologists, all of Earth's continents were once united as a single landmass: Pangaea. But over time, they drifted. In the oft-quoted words of the poet: "Things fall apart; the centre cannot hold."[1] In some cases this incremental sliding of tectonic plates brought new unions for the torn-asunder landforms. There were "remarriages," as when the Indian subcontinent sidled up to what is now called Asia. The two became one. Their bond birthed the mighty Himalayas, now home to the world's highest peaks, still inching upwards.

But in most cases, the drift put added distance between landforms. And the separation is ongoing. At present, North America and Europe continue to retreat from one another across the Mid-Atlantic Ridge at a rate of approximately one inch per year. Despite the evidence for this division, I have never once felt it. It is possible for the ground to move

---

[1] W. B. Yeats, "The Second Coming," in *The Norton Anthology of English Literature*, vol. F, *Twentieth Century and After*, ed. Stephen Greenblatt, 9th ed. (New York: Norton, 2012), 2099.

beneath your feet without you ever noticing. The Mid-Atlantic Ridge is hidden under several thousand feet of water, and the only portion that is not submerged bisects the tiny country of Iceland at the Reykjanes Ridge. I have never been there. Hence, the physical scar of continental fragmentation continues to escape my view.

More visible is the fragmentation in our human tribes. For we too have our fault lines. This book details one such split within the fractured family known as "evangelical." Specifically, it notes the common move toward one of two extremes:

1. The land of unchecked DOUBT, and

2. The land of strident DOGMATISM.

My claim is that neither of these alluring postures best characterizes a Christian attitude toward the vexing questions of the faith. And my goal is to set forth a third space by which to reclaim the sacred ground between *certainty* and *skepticism*. I call this middle ground *perhaps*. And in this way, the book is about retrieving a form of sacred speculation.

To many theologians, my task will sound quite strange. After all, to refer to one's theology as "speculative" is rarely (if ever) a compliment. At conferences and in book reviews for academic journals, the label is invariably a kind of putdown. Take, for example, the claim of Scott R. Swain in a recent work on theological method: "We should be 'anti-speculative' in our theology," he writes. For to be otherwise "closely approximates the vice of 'curiosity.'" Speculative theology is contemplation cast into its "vicious mode."[2] Swain takes this colorful phrase from the late John Webster, who had himself borrowed it from Augustine.[3] From this vantage point, curiosity is a vain, wicked, prideful, and idolatrous defect that stretches beyond divine revelation in a hankering to know as only God knows.[4] Translation: It's bad. And many others concur.

---

[2]Scott R. Swain, "Dogmatics as Systematic Theology," in *The Task of Dogmatics: Explorations in Theological Method*, ed. Oliver D. Crisp and Fred Sanders (Grand Rapids, MI: Zondervan, 2017), 57-58n33.
[3]See N. Joseph Torchia, "Curiosity," in *Augustine Through the Ages: An Encyclopedia*, ed. Allan D. Fitzgerald (Grand Rapids, MI: Eerdmans, 1999), 259-61. For Augustine, *curiositas* is associated with an excessive appetite for knowing things other than God; it is the tool of the serpent in Genesis 3.
[4]John Webster, *The Domain of the Word: Scripture and Theological Reason* (London: T&T Clark, 2012), chap. 10.

Friedrich Schleiermacher (1768–1834), for all his theological revisions, wanted "nothing to do with any concept of God reached by way of speculation"[5] since to do so would allow philosophical reasoning to usurp the feeling of absolute dependence. Schleiermacher vowed that if he were to find a single speculative proposition in his monumental work, *The Christian Faith*, he would "strike it out."[6] Karl Barth (1886–1968), while leveling the charge of speculation against Schleiermacher, agreed entirely with its vicious nature. Barth defined speculation as a kind of natural theology that proceeds from some other basis than God's concrete revelation in Christ.[7] Finally, Kevin Vanhoozer says flatly that "Christian dogmatics is not a speculative discourse that begins from or limits itself by means of an abstract concept of infinity. It is rather a response to a prior divine communicative initiative."[8]

Virtually everyone agrees that speculation is a very naughty thing,[9] even if we now have several different definitions for what it is:

1. Indulging the idolatrous "vice" of prideful curiosity (Webster and Swain)

2. Replacing the feeling of absolute dependence with philosophical reasoning (Schleiermacher)

3. Usurping God's concrete revelation in Christ with natural theology (Barth)

4. Starting from an abstract concept of infinity rather than the prior divine Word (Vanhoozer)

Not every one of these ideas is mutually exclusive, and I agree with several of their points. Still, I confess that *curiosity* and *speculation* seem

---

[5]Friedrich Schleiermacher, *The Christian Faith*, trans. and ed. H. R. Mackintosh and J. S. Stewart (Edinburgh: T&T Clark, 1989), 730.

[6]Friedrich Schleiermacher, *On the Glaubenslehre: Two Letters to Dr. Lücke* (Chico, CA: Scholars Press, 1981), 87; cited in James Gordon, "A 'Glaring Misunderstanding'?: Schleiermacher, Barth, and the Nature of Speculative Theology," *International Journal of Systematic Theology* 16, no. 3 (2014): 315.

[7]Karl Barth, *Church Dogmatics*, ed. G. W. Bromiley and T. F. Torrance, vol. I.1 (Edinburgh: T&T Clark, 1958), 301.

[8]Kevin J. Vanhoozer, "Analytics, Poetics, and the Mission of Dogmatic Discourse," in *The Task of Dogmatics: Explorations in Theological Method* (Grand Rapids, MI: Zondervan, 2017), 26.

[9]For a rare exception, see Katherine Sonderegger, *Systematic Theology*, vol. 2, *The Doctrine of the Holy Trinity: Processions and Persons* (Minneapolis: Fortress, 2020). She classifies her doctrine of the Trinity as a form of "speculative realism" (261).

to have joined a host of other theological terms that are sometimes hurled more as weapons than as clear and useful descriptors.[10]

So at the risk of taking a "vicious" and unpopular position, allow me to quote the wizard Dumbledore against the Christian theologians: "Curiosity is not a sin. . . . But we should exercise caution with our curiosity."[11] My book defends a form of speculation in theology and in the Christian life, albeit with some important cautions. All elements of Christian doctrine require a certain stretching forth into the "dazzling darkness" that lies beyond our view—if only to encounter Light.[12] So while this kind of speculation is not always a virtue, neither is it automatically a vice. The proof is in the pudding and the praxis. In the coming chapters, I argue that a certain form of "faith seeking imagination" is essential, especially in a climate of polarization and partisan infighting.[13] Both evangelicals and their opponents need to relearn the word *perhaps*.

But before exploring this supposed island between doubt and dogmatism, I must first address a growing problem.

Farewell, Pangaea

Like Pangaea, evangelicals are fragmenting.[14] And it does not take a PhD in sociology to recognize the splintering. In the words of one commentator, many who once claimed the label are in the position of a married couple that has grown apart and now wonder whether divorce is the only option.[15] Others have already filed the paperwork, being driven in some

---

[10]James Gordon seems right to note, "Further work needs to be done on defining the concept of speculation." Gordon, "'Glaring Misunderstanding?,'" 330.

[11]J. K. Rowling, *Harry Potter and the Goblet of Fire*, illus. ed. (New York: Scholastic, 2019), 363.

[12]For reference to the "dazzling darkness," see Sarah Coakley, *God, Sexuality and the Self: An Essay "On the Trinity"* (Cambridge: Cambridge University Press, 2013), 96.

[13]My phrase provides a twist on the traditional Christian motto of "faith seeking understanding" (*fides quaerens intellectum*), espoused by Anselm of Canterbury. See Anselm, *Monologion and Proslogion with the Replies of Guanilo and Anselm*, trans. Thomas Williams (Indianapolis, IN: Hackett Publishing, 1995), 93.

[14]While evangelicals are, of course, a global community, my focus here is more specifically on the North American segment of this population since that is the part that I know best.

[15]Mark Galli, "After Trump, Should Evangelical Christians Part Ways?," *Christianity Today*, November 10, 2016, www.christianitytoday.com/ct/2016/november-web-only/should-evangelicals-part-ways.html. This statement came before Galli's own move to Roman Catholicism.

cases by a much-cited (if slippery) statistic: the 81 percent of self-identifying White evangelicals who supported Donald Trump within the 2016 general election. In the years that followed, many younger Christians especially concluded that this political alliance proved the reality of irreconcilable differences.[16]

Evangelicals, of course, were never monolithic. And the current tension mirrors divides within the broader culture.[17] As we hear on a daily basis, Americans are polarized across a number of fault lines: liberal and conservative, Black and White, urban and rural, millennial and boomer, social justice warriors (SJWs) and the gleefully politically incorrect. "The culture is divided," says the clichéd soundbite, and the lost world of evangelical Pangaea is no different.[18]

My job provides a front-row seat to this division. I am a theology professor at a Christian university near the very buckle of the Bible Belt. I am also a pastor. In these two roles, I have the privilege of interacting daily with both younger students and older Christians. I love my work. But it is not difficult to spot the drift toward one of the aforementioned "continents"—the lands of unchecked (1) doubt and (2) dogmatism. Yeats, it seems, was right: "The centre cannot hold."

While this polarization could easily be illustrated with a mountain of survey data—"death by Barna" one might call it—the better option may be to *feel* the separation by way of narrative. With that in mind, I will revert occasionally throughout this book to fiction and imaginative storytelling to unearth realities that cannot be fully appreciated by detached analysis. In the words of Flannery O'Connor, "A story is a way to say something that can't be said any other way, and it takes every word in the story

---

[16]See, for instance, the many *New York Times* op-eds of Ross Douthat, who claims that evangelicalism has fractured along basically Trumpian lines. The 81 percent statistic is made slippery by the bastardization of "evangelical" as a coherent label by both pollsters and its self-identified "parishioners" (many of whom do not even attend church). See Ryan P. Burge, "The 2016 Religious Vote (for More Groups Than You Thought Possible)," *Religion in Public*, March 10, 2017, https://religion inpublic.blog/2017/03/10/the-2016-religious-vote-for-more-groups-than-you-thought-possible/.

[17]See Thomas S. Kidd, *Who Is an Evangelical?: The History of a Movement in Crisis* (New Haven, CT: Yale University Press, 2019).

[18]See, for instance, Kenneth J. Collins, *Power, Politics, and the Fragmentation of Evangelicalism: From the Scopes Trial to the Obama Administration* (Downers Grove, IL: IVP Academic, 2012).

to say what the meaning is. You tell a story because a statement would be inadequate."[19] To cite James K. A. Smith, "We're less convinced by arguments than moved by stories; our being in the world is more aesthetic than deductive, better captured by narrative than analysis."[20] Stories matter.

We need not go far to find personal accounts of evangelical fragmentation. The dismemberment of the American church—torn and abused like the Levite's concubine by unfaithful "priests" and intertribal wars (Judg 19)—is playing out before our eyes. It is happening in youth groups, on social media, and in (Christian) universities. Thus, while the following narrative is fictitious, it is also an amalgam of the many true stories I have heard from students as they sit within my office.

ELIZA

Inside her college dorm room, Eliza Johnson glared down at the New Testament homework that lay on the quilt that draped her bed. "They will be divided," Jesus prophesied in Luke's Gospel, "father against son and son against father." *Well, he nailed that one,* she thought. Through her laptop speakers came music that served to drown out noise that came perpetually through wafer-thin walls.

The quilt had been a gift from her grandmother. Eliza received it just before departing for the Christian university, eight hours from the factory town where she grew up in Ohio. She would be driving back there soon for Thanksgiving. She was dreading it, even more than the mandatory "spiritual reflections" on her Bible homework.

Her father would be there, watching television as he had been since the factory closed last fall. With his hearing dulled by hours on the line, the TV would be blaring. On it, the prophets of Cable News would pour forth their daily apocalypse in tones to make Christ's words seem tame. "Do you think I came to bring peace on earth!? No, I tell you, but division!"

Her brother Jeremy would be there too. He was a senior at a large state school in Michigan. She hadn't seen him since their mother's

---

[19]Flannery O'Connor, *Mystery and Manners: Occasional Prose*, ed. Sally Fitzgerald and Robert Fitzgerald (New York: Farrar, Straus, and Giroux, 1957), 96.
[20]James K. A. Smith, *Imagining the Kingdom: How Worship Works* (Grand Rapids, MI: Baker Academic, 2013), 108.

funeral. Three years prior, at this same November break, he had con-fided to Eliza that he was gay. "Don't tell Dad," he told her. Eliza hadn't. Still, she knew her father knew. *He blames himself*, she thought. "Not enough male role models these days." Isn't that what the "doctor" on the Christian radio had said? Too many double shifts. Too tired after work to hunt, and fish, and play football. *That's ridiculous*, Eliza thought—*the world is more complex than that.*

But she knew her father didn't only blame himself. "This country is going to hell!" he would interject from his recliner while the pundits barked in the background. "Just look at what they're teaching them in school!" By "them" Eliza knew he meant her brother. While Jeremy had not told his dad that he was gay, he had been more open about what he had learned about religion, and especially Christianity. "A pretext for op-pression; a power play; a social construct to perpetuate the patriarchy."

Eliza had no idea about such schools, but it was around this time that her dad started bringing up the conservative Christian university where she now sat. At the time, she remembered thinking the idea was strange. Her father had never been very religious. He was just "old school." And their family had been strapped for cash since the factory closed and Eliza's mother had come down with cancer. The Christian school was expensive.

But her father made it work. He mortgaged the house; he used money from her mother's life insurance policy; he sold scrap metal. He loved Eliza. She knew that—even if she knew little else for certain. The irony, of course, was that Eliza had been sent to the school because it promised to provide "a Christian worldview" to all its students. As evidence, they had strict policies against all sorts of vices—far more than the Bible, ac-tually. And the university's president had been one of the first to endorse a philandering billionaire as the one to "restore America to its Christian heritage." They were "taking a stand," he said. Though Eliza was hard-pressed to say what some of this partisan rhetoric had to do with Jesus. Then again, there was this passage: "Not peace, but a sword."

The truth was, Eliza was losing her faith—and never faster than the past three months. While she couldn't articulate it fully, few things

brought more disillusionment in the midst of doubts than to be sur-
rounded by those who *seemed* so blissfully certain. Her roommate,
Claire, certainly fit the latter category. At least Eliza thought so: pretty
smile, pastor's daughter, perfect life.

Eliza felt alone.

The night before, beneath the same quilt, she had dreamed she was
adrift on a vast sea, in a boat no bigger than her bed. She felt about to
capsize. Waves lapped over the edges of her vessel, soaking her socks.
In the distance were two islands. They seemed to be receding from
each other as if driven by some underwater eruption. Was she moving,
or were they? On the isle to her right she saw a beach with people on
it. There was her father, the university president, and the talking heads
of Cable News. They were gesturing forcefully. On the other island
were her brother and a great crowd moving toward the setting sun.
Both groups were beckoning—asking her to join them—but she
couldn't. She was marooned somewhere between, and she didn't
have an oar to row.

Deep down, Eliza wanted to believe in God. She wanted to know
the Jesus that her mother had worshiped. He seemed a very different
Savior from the one now on display in some segments of the church.
In years past, her childhood faith had been the thing that gave her
hope as her mother battled cancer and endured the chemotherapy.
"Jesus heals," proclaimed the man on Christian Cable. But her mother
wasn't healed. Nor, as Eliza now recalled, was she on either shoreline
in the dream.

I will return to Eliza's story periodically through a series of short vignettes. So please don't be thrown off when you encounter her again. The
reason for the move is simple: form should match content. And since
the book is about reclaiming a sacred imagination, the fictional narratives will work like leaven sprinkled in with the dough of theological
argument (Lk 13:21).

Eliza's tale could end, of course, in many ways. Though, to disclose
one spoiler, my version will not involve a brilliant young theology

professor who rides in to save the day. My vanity has limits. And her fictitious university is not my own. Even so, some will note that Eliza's tale seems somewhat gerrymandered to fit a certain trope of American Christianity. It is. Undoubtedly. But this fact does not negate the reality that many (former) evangelicals feel a bit like Eliza in her tiny boat— caught between two divergent options that both seem terribly distasteful: the lands of crippling doubt and angry dogmatism. Now to define those terms.

The Sea of Doubt

Recent decades have brought what some claim to be a tectonic defection among younger and former Christians toward increased uncertainty, skepticism, and disillusionment. To return to Yeats, the temptation is to believe "The best lack all conviction, while the worst / Are full of passionate intensity."[21] Religious doubt is on the rise, the pollsters tell us, and with deconstruction comes an upswing of the "Nones"—the label now attached to those who claim no religious affiliation, despite (often) being raised within the confines of a spiritual tribe.[22] The road to None-ville leads through probing doubt.

According to some surveys, Christianity is declining in the United States, and this includes the evangelical variety, though at a somewhat slower rate than Catholics and mainline Protestants.[23] At the same time, we millennials (yes, I too come from this oft-disparaged "Nazareth" of demographics) and our Gen-Z successors are growing more honest about our questions. Hence, parts of the church are even moving to name and claim pervasive doubt as a virtuous step toward growth and new discovery. The topic is in vogue, as evidenced by books and podcasts. In book titles, doubt is described as a "benefit," while certainty is named as both an "idol"

---

[21]Yeats, "Second Coming," 2099.

[22]See Ryan P. Burge, *The Nones: Where They Came From, Who They Are, and Where They Are Going* (Minneapolis: Fortress, 2021).

[23]See the massive 2014 study conducted by the Pew Research Center. Michael Lipka, "A Closer Look at America's Rapidly Growing Religious 'Nones,'" Pew Research Center, May 13, 2015, www.pewresearch.org/fact-tank/2015/05/13/a-closer-look-at-americas-rapidly-growing -religious-nones/.

and a "sin."[24] Yet this move also raises questions: Does the valorization of doubt mesh with biblical passages that proclaim its pitfalls? James, for instance, says that "the one who doubts is like a wave of the sea, blown and tossed by the wind" (Jas 1:6). This certainly does not sound like an endorsement.

Some doubts are healthy, particularly when they attach to false or unexamined assumptions. In such cases, a collapse of confidence may mean a move from naivety to maturity. It may be a chance to consider what one actually believes, or it may be a steppingstone to a more well-grounded orthodoxy. In the latter case, time spent in the fire of consuming questions may be the refining force that brings forth faith as pure as gold (e.g., 1 Pet 1:7).[25]

It would also be wrong to portray all doubts as mere choices that we dispassionately make along the buffet line of belief: *"I'll take the broccoli casserole, the fruit medley, and some soul-crushing uncertainty."* It doesn't work like that. In many cases, doubts choose us—and especially in the wake of trauma. Who, after all, could not question the benevolent sovereignty of God after the drowning of a toddler in a backyard pool, the horror of the Holocaust, or the blood-dimmed tide of a Southeast Asian tsunami? We are ambushed by uncertainty. We do not select the moments when the cognitive dissonance of an old assumption will overflow and wash us out to sea. Tsunamis often come with little warning. For this reason, Jude bears this reminder: "Be merciful to those who doubt" (Jude 22).

To struggle with doubt is almost assumed within modernity. "We're all Thomas now," writes James K. A. Smith, since a secular age involves the unavoidable sense that the Christian faith is "fraught" and our confession "haunted" by its contestability.[26] Thomas may be our patron saint, but as Charles Taylor argues, this same haunting plagues the

---

[24]See, for instance, Gregory A. Boyd, *Benefit of the Doubt: Breaking the Idol of Certainty* (Grand Rapids, MI: Baker Books, 2013); Peter Enns, *The Sin of Certainty: Why God Desires Our Trust More Than Our "Correct" Beliefs* (New York: HarperOne, 2016); and Anthony C. Thiselton, *Doubt, Faith, and Certainty* (Grand Rapids, MI: Eerdmans, 2017).

[25]See A. J. Swoboda, *After Doubt: How to Question Your Faith without Losing It* (Grand Rapids, MI: Brazos, 2021).

[26]James K. A. Smith, *How (Not) to Be Secular: Reading Charles Taylor* (Grand Rapids, MI: Eerdmans, 2014), 4.

minds of atheists and agnostics. Nonreligious people often long for lost transcendence, and they may be tempted to doubt their doubts regarding God.[27] To understand how we got here, some history is needed.

A Brief History of Skepticism

Skepticism is hardly a modern invention. Long before the time of Christ, Socrates (ca. 470–399 BC) ran afoul of the Athenian establishment by asking uncomfortable questions about the local gods. And while the hemlock "cured" his ailment, the issue of pervasive doubt persisted. Pyrrhon of Elis founded a Skeptic school in the third century BC, and the movement was later revived by Sextus Empiricus (ca. third century AD) in a work that, at least in title, echoes a theme that I will later take up: *Against the Dogmatists*.[28] "There is nothing new under the sun" (Eccles 1:9).

Yet, as with Christ, every resurrected body of human thought bears both familiar scars and transformed features. New fads within philosophy can seem both strange and strangely familiar, though we may be hard pressed to recognize the continuity. "Sir, are you the gardener?" (see Jn 20:15).

In the modern era, tales of rising doubt often begin (whether rightly or wrongly) with René Descartes (1596–1650). As the story goes, modernism came to canonize suspicion, as evidenced by a cerebral hashtag: *Cogito, ergo sum*, "I think, therefore I am." The Cartesian creed emerged from a solitary quest "to doubt everything which we find to contain even the smallest suspicion of uncertainty."[29] And while the cogitating Frenchman managed to rebuild the edifice of his belief, later thinkers found the blueprints less persuasive. Hence, in the overly dramatic words of one historian, "There was no way and no hope of ever emerging from the skeptical despair that Descartes had introduced."[30] Or in the idiom of today's pollsters, *Cogito, ergo* None.

---

[27]See Charles Taylor, *A Secular Age* (Cambridge, MA: Belknap Press of Harvard University Press, 2007).

[28]A concise treatment of this history is offered in Thiselton, *Doubt, Faith, and Certainty*, chap. 2.

[29]René Descartes, *Principia Philosophiae*, in *Oeuvres de Descartes*, ed. Charles Adam and Paul Tannery (Paris: J. Vrin, 1964), 6:1.

[30]Richard H. Popkin, *The History of Scepticism: From Erasmus to Spinoza*, rev. ed. (Berkeley: University of California Press, 1979), 199.

After the Enlightenment, the movement called empiricism demanded quantifiable data for every aspect of one's worldview, and many Westerners were swallowed in an ocean of uncertainty. The "Sea of Faith" was fast receding, proclaimed the poet Matthew Arnold (1867), and the recession added acreage to the continent of doubt.[31] A generation later, the godfather of American fundamentalism, William B. Riley (1861–1947), decried what he called the "awful harvest of skepticism" in the American church, and he knew exactly whom to blame: Darwinian evolution, biblical higher criticism, and ethical concerns over the Bible's claims on slavery, women, and sexuality.[32]

Still, orthodoxy's "long, withdrawing roar" (as Arnold put it in his poem) was less apparent on this side of the Mid-Atlantic Ridge—and the Bible Belt is hardly a coastal community. So while places like Europe, Boston, and Seattle became more obviously post-Christian, parts of America held more publicly to faith. Battle lines were drawn between modernists and fundamentalists. And, beginning in the 1950s, there was an upswing in church attendance as leaders like Billy Graham cobbled together (neo-)evangelicalism as an attempted third way between theological liberalism and what was seen as the backward bigotry of fundamentalism.[33]

But today is not the 1950s. A variety of forces have brought increased skepticism inside evangelicalism so that this continent too is fragmenting. While a full discussion of these trends awaits later chapters, it will suffice to say that a trifecta of forces pertaining to (1) science, (2) politics, and (3) sexuality have had much to do with it. The result has been a flux that is celebrated by some and lamented bitterly by others. For every action there is an equal and opposite overreaction—which brings us to our second landmass.

The Land of Dogmatism

While one chunk of evangelical Pangaea drifts with the winds of secular doubt, another tips violently on the tides of zealous dogmatism. The

---

[31]See Arnold's famous poem, "Dover Beach."
[32]Cited in Frances Fitzgerald, *The Evangelicals: The Struggle to Shape America* (New York: Simon & Schuster, 2017).
[33]On evangelical complicity with racism during this era, see Jemar Tisby, *The Color of Compromise: The Truth About the American Church's Complicity in Racism* (Grand Rapids, MI: Zondervan, 2019).

relationship, as with many in our polarized environment, is reciprocal. Yet, before devoting too much time to exploring this symbiosis of certainty and skepticism, a dogmatic definition is in order.

By *dogmatism*, I do not mean the mere adherence to orthodox theology in the face of mounting secularism. Nor do I mean a steadfast commitment to evangelical principles like the saving work of Christ, conversion by grace through faith, the authority of Scripture, evangelism, and the necessity of a transformed life.[34] I myself hold these commitments. So while the confession of these ideas may make one an evangelical, it need not imply a strident dogmatism, much less the dreaded F-word: fundamentalism.

The dogmatism I describe has two features: (1) a shrillness of tone and (2) presumption of certainty on positions that are far from obvious.[35] On the matter of tone, it is not, as John Wesley called it, the "heart strangely warmed" but the face strangely flushed.[36] Dogmatism carries an anger that types in ALL CAPS, replaces listening with loudness, and comes with an extra side of exclamation points. In fairness to the dogmatists, prophetic indignation may seem warranted within a fallen culture. But that does not always make it helpful. In describing a shift toward strident rhetoric within American evangelicalism, Rick Warren details the danger: "The Bible calls the church the body of Christ," yet "what's happened in the last 100 years is that the hands and feet have been amputated and the church has just been a mouth, and primarily it's been known for what it's against."[37]

Religious dogmatism often stems from what I call the Elijah heresy. This is the fear that all God's people are abandoning truth, while "I alone am left a prophet of the LORD" (1 Kings 18:22 NKJV). In the end, however,

---

[34]These points are part of George M. Marsden's definition of the evangelical tradition, in *Understanding Fundamentalism and Evangelicalism* (Grand Rapids, MI: Eerdmans, 1991), 4-5. Kidd defines the movement as "born-again Protestants who cherish the Bible as the Word of God and who emphasize a personal relationship with Jesus Christ through the Holy Spirit." Kidd, *Who Is an Evangelical?*, 4.

[35]I will define *dogmatism* more fully, along with different varieties of certitude, in part 2 of the book.

[36]John Wesley, "Journal entry, May, 1738," in *The Works of John Wesley*, 3rd ed., vol. 1, *Journals from October 14, 1735 to November 29, 1745* (Grand Rapids, MI: Baker Book House, 1986), 103.

[37]Rick Warren, "Myths of the Modern Megachurch," speaking at a 2005 Pew Forum conference, cited in Fitzgerald, *Evangelicals*, 545.

the irony is that Elijah himself ends up uttering false prophecy by exaggerating the extent of his lonely fidelity and the apostasy of everyone else. Today's dogmatism rallies frenzied support from "the base" (a political term that betrays evangelicals in its very usage) by approaching problems in a way that undermines the sovereignty of God and the breadth of his strange family. In so doing, we hover near the position of the early Donatists—that rigorist sect that attempted to exclude all but the "purest" (read: Whitest?[38]) from ecclesial communion. In response, Saint Augustine's words are as important now as ever. In the face of God's diverse kingdom, "these frogs sit in their swamp and croak, 'Christians? None but us!'"[39]

The second part of my dogmatic definition involves a form of prideful presumption (or what I call false certainty) in the face of complex questions. While this attitude can be off-putting, it is also understandable. We all face the temptation of an overconfident certitude on a wide variety of subjects—whether eschatology, economics, or the epidemiology of viruses and vaccines. Armchair presumptions lead to firm pronouncements on things that should probably be held more loosely. After all, in theology especially, we are talking about a mysterious and unseen God, not plotting the schematics for a circuit breaker. As Cornelius Plantinga writes, "Besides reliability, God's other name is Surprise."[40] We see now "through a glass, darkly"; we know "in part" (1 Cor 13:12 KJV).[41]

Where then does this leave us? While the valorization of doubt threatens to drown us in a sea of skepticism, religious dogmatism (in both its shrillness and its certitude) confuses the human knower with the final Judge.[42] The irony between these apparent opposites is this:

---

[38]The "White-washing" of evangelicals is perpetuated by outsiders as well. See Kidd's point that pollsters often exclude those evangelical respondents who are non-White. Kidd, *Who Is an Evangelical?*, 1.

[39]Augustine, *Enarrationes in Psalmos*, 95.11 (PL 36:1234).

[40]Cornelius Plantinga Jr., *Reading for Preaching: The Preacher in Conversation with Storytellers, Biographers, Poets, and Journalists* (Grand Rapids, MI: Eerdmans, 2013), 96. Plantinga credits this observation to Dale Cooper, former chaplain of Calvin College.

[41]Joshua McNall, "Christian, Learn to Say, 'Perhaps,'" April 27, 2016, https://joshuamcnall .com/2016/04/27/christian-learn-to-say-perhaps.

[42]And as the late Robert Jenson once quipped of Hegel, "That is quite a fault." Cited in Colin E. Gunton, *Revelation and Reason: Prolegomena to Systematic Theology*, ed. P. H. Brazier (London: T&T Clark, 2008), 151.

doubt and dogmatism often share a common core. They are locked in a symbiotic embrace, producing offspring in our churches and our college campuses. For, in different ways, both bow before the idol of proof and make their sacrifices. And in the middle, sitting quietly, is perhaps.

Christian, Learn to Say "Perhaps"

Inspiration for this book came in a single pregnant line from N. T. Wright. Tucked away on page 1351 of *Paul and the Faithfulness of God*, the reader finds this gem: "To believe in providence often means saying 'perhaps.'"

It is just a snippet. Wright is speaking of the fact that for Paul moments of unambiguous divine revelation were somewhat rarer than we might guess. Even for Paul certainty was often elusive. Whereas pagans believed in divination, consulting the entrails of animals, and any number of other techniques, for Paul it was different.

> As often as not, Paul sees the divine hand only in retrospect. For the present, the attempt to discern divine intent carries a "maybe" about with it. Maybe, he writes to Philemon about Onesimus, this is the reason he was separated from you. To believe in providence often means saying "perhaps."[43]

Of course, one could locate faith or trust as the midpoint between doubt and dogmatic claims to certitude.[44] And this would be correct. Yet, I take faith to be more the believing allegiance of the will (or heart) whereas perhaps is more an exercise of imagination. Imagination puts things together in our minds; analysis tends to pick them apart.[45] Both are necessary, but the saying of perhaps (which includes the dreaded shame word *speculation*) involves a venturing forth into the unknown, with an intermingling of boldness and humility.

---

[43]N. T. Wright, *Paul and the Faithfulness of God* (Minneapolis: Fortress, 2013), 1351.

[44]Though as I will note later, the meaning of the New Testament *pistis* is far broader than mere "faith" or "trust." See especially, Matthew W. Bates, *Salvation by Allegiance Alone: Rethinking Faith, Works, and the Gospel of Jesus the King* (Grand Rapids, MI: Baker Academic, 2017).

[45]See Alan Jacobs, *How to Think: A Survival Guide for a World at Odds* (New York: Currency, 2017), 43.

As I define it, sacred speculation should function in at least two ways. First, one may use the grammar of *perhaps* as a way of reaching forward from a place of doubt to the hope of gospel truth (read: orthodoxy). In this form, speculation becomes a way of imagining how the basics of Christianity are coherent and compelling, even if they seem unlikely at the moment. This contemplative and apologetic move involves a humility that is not usually found among the resounding gongs of certitude (1 Cor 13:1).

Second, my language of *perhaps* can and should flow forth from basic Christian presuppositions in order to inquire about matters of adiaphora—questions of indifference with respect to orthodoxy and heresy. By *indifference*, however, I do not mean these speculative possibilities are unimportant; indeed, such "perhapsing" may help one remain a Christian in the face of doubt. Regardless, these matters of adiaphora are still located within the broad "hall" of historic Christian belief, as C. S. Lewis described it.[46] Whereas faith says yes to core convictions of the creed(s), the perhaps of sacred speculation stands further out on this scaffolding in order to peer into uncharted territory: the blank spaces on our maps. In both instances, however, it offers a hopeful, humble, and biblically informed "What if?"[47]

Defining the Perhaps of Sacred Speculation

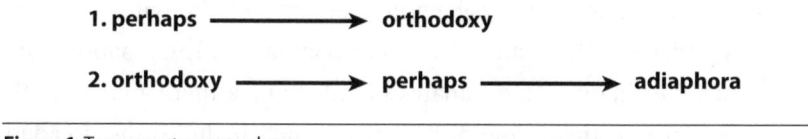

Figure 1. Two ways to say perhaps

To be clear, there are times when *perhaps* is not helpful. Thus, it is not a panacea for our fractured Pangaea. If misapplied, the language can be used to indulge heresy, absurdity, and unbridled speculation—"what-iffery" run

---

[46]For the metaphor of orthodoxy as a broad hall with adjoining rooms (specific traditions), see C. S. Lewis, *Mere Christianity* (New York: Macmillan, 1952), preface.

[47]Further unpacking of this twofold usage of *perhaps* awaits part 1 of the book.

amok.[48] *Perhaps, as some say, the earth sits on the back of a giant turtle.* I doubt it. My suggestion, then, is that our use of sacred speculation should have boundaries (more on this in chap. 3) since the ancient cartographers were right to claim of some blank spaces: "There be dragons."

As one whose heart has been taken captive by the gospel, I choose not to mull over endlessly the perhaps of questions that have already been decided in more foundational (albeit sometimes mysterious) ways. I do not agonize continually over the possibility that "perhaps God is not Love," "perhaps Christ did not conquer death," or "perhaps morality is just an evolutionary adaptation." Although these questions are quite real for many people, the anchor of my own faith and past experience keeps me from endlessly rehearsing them. Yet, in other instances, entertaining new possibilities is crucial. So, you might be asking, when is this kind of hopeful imagining appropriate and helpful?

A Thought Experiment

Consider the following scenario: You are a first-century Jew who has been taught that Yahweh is "One" (Deut 6), that God alone can forgive sins, and that no human should be worshiped. Then a traveling Rabbi visits your village and starts uttering oddities that seem to rub against all this:

> Before Abraham was born, I am! (Jn 8:58)
> I and the Father are one. (Jn 10:30)
> [I have] authority on earth to forgive sins. (Mk 2:10)

What do you do? Apart from God's Spirit, and a profound ability to say perhaps, the answer seems clear: You reject the strange Rabbi; you join the throng of confident doubters; and you cite Bible verses to show that you are justified. "Crucify him!" (Mk 15:13; Lk 23:21).

None of the earliest Christ-followers (especially Jewish ones) could hold onto both monotheism and the worship of the risen Jesus without

---

[48]Thomas H. McCall uses this word to describe speculation sans evidence. McCall, *Against God and Nature: The Doctrine of Sin* (Wheaton, IL: Crossway, 2019), 401.

some fairly thorough reimagining. At some point, they had to say something like the following: "Well . . . this doesn't seem to fit at all with what we've been taught, but perhaps God is doing something we had not expected." For my own part, this thought experiment is unsettling. I am a theology professor. Had I lived in ancient Israel, I would likely have been one of the "teachers of the law" (e.g., Mt 7:29) who frequently interrogated Jesus. What would my response have been to this strange Rabbi? I know myself. And I am not optimistic. I too have trouble remembering that God's other name is Surprise.

Conclusion

In the Gospels, doubt and dogmatism join hands to crucify the Son of God. So while the logic of perhaps is not without pitfalls, its recovery is essential for the Christian faith in a world of conflicts and questions. Both evangelicals and New Atheists need to reclaim the humble middle ground between crippling doubt and angry dogmatism. We need this sacred space, even if it is precarious to stand here shoeless in the wilderness by the bush that burns (Ex 3:2-5).

Unfortunately, to reside between the extremes of doubt and dogmatism will mean fielding fire from both sides. It will mean being called a wishy-washy liberal by one camp and a narrow-minded conservative by another. Yet the motivation for reclaiming this sacred middle rests not in the false assumption that the via media is always right. It is not. After all, if one child confidently shouts that two plus two equals four and another that it equals six, one should not split the difference and proclaim that two plus two equals five. Middle is not always most in line with truth.[49]

---

[49]A reminder of this reality involves the ministry of Billy Graham. In the 1950s, Graham made a difficult choice to stake out a middle ground between a backbiting fundamentalism on one hand and a theologically deficient liberalism on the other. In so doing, he dropped the fundamentalist label and began to speak of the resurgent tribe simply as evangelicals. Yet, on the subject of civil rights and desegregation, Graham's quest for middle ground was less praiseworthy. Though remaining ahead of many White Christian leaders, he criticized the civil rights movement for wanting to go "too far too fast." And while Martin Luther King Jr. languished in a Birmingham jail, Graham advised his "good friend" to "put on the brakes a bit." The idea here is not to look down our noses at a leader who modeled grace and truth far better than most. Rather, the point is that the search for a via media between two opposing positions is not always best. See Fitzgerald, *Evangelicals*, 205.

The motive to reclaim a holy maybe between doubt and dogmatism must be biblical and not just conciliatory. It cannot simply stem from the strong (if somewhat dismissive) sense of "clowns to the left of me, jokers to the right."[50] In the end, the Bible must support my claim that a rekindling of sacred speculation is warranted; otherwise, the premise is baseless. Having now defined the concept of perhaps between the poles of doubt and dogmatism, I move next to examine whether this approach is rooted in the biblical narrative. What did Abraham, our forefather, discover on this matter? To answer that question, we turn to one of the most difficult texts in the whole canon of Scripture.

---

[50]Stealers Wheel, "Stuck in the Middle with You."

Part 1

Understanding Perhaps

You have been given questions
to which you cannot be given answers.
You will have to live them out—
perhaps a little at a time.

WENDELL BERRY,
JAYBER CROW: A NOVEL

1

What Abraham Discovered

Faith Seeking Imagination

> *God reveals himself by an appeal*
> *to our capacity for imagination.*
>
> TREVOR HART

THE AIM OF THIS CHAPTER is to explore whether my attempt to re-claim perhaps as a middle ground between doubt and dogmatism is sup-ported by a careful reading of the Scriptures. To do so, I will repeat a question posed by the apostle Paul: "What then shall we say that Abraham, our forefather . . . , discovered in this matter?" (Rom 4:1). By focusing on the *Aqedah* (or "binding" of Isaac in Gen 22), I will note how Abraham ventured forth in faithful speculation when it mattered most. By faith, Abraham learned how and when to say perhaps. Yet, before I argue this conclusion, I must first frame what was at stake in Abraham's story by looking at the faith narrative that is the *Aqedah*'s dark doppelgänger.

THE HOMECOMING

As the bedraggled warrior crested the hill outside Mizpah, he could see the thin trail of smoke streaking down the sky toward his beloved home. *They must be cooking dinner now,* he thought. He had doubted that he would see this place again. Thankfully, the god to whom he had prayed had proven faithful to their bargain. Enemies had fallen by the warrior's hand, and he had felt a strange strength coursing through him. It was the only explanation for how his band of ruffians had sacked those twenty towns. *I guess some gods can be trusted,* he thought; *I must remember this one.* The victory had been a sign that the warrior must keep his promise. This was the reason he was squinting at the trail of smoke that led down toward the open doorway of his house.

Who was that standing there? He knew before he asked the question. The asking was a weak attempt at denial—an effort to delay the images that flooded his imagination: the altar and the blood. Every father knows his child from a distance. There is something unmistakable in the gait and posture—a mark of Cain now terribly inverted.

Through tears, the warrior saw her racing toward him, dancing, ecstatic, her curls bouncing. She looked like her mother. In one hand she held a tambourine, and with the other she girded up her garments so to speed her coming. She cried with joy as she embraced him. And he wished for all the world that he had died in battle.

Father Jephthah

It is an offense that Jephthah has the gall to appear alongside the likes of Abraham in faith's "hall of fame" (Heb 11). But we cannot understand one man without the other. Jephthah is what happens if Abraham stops listening upon Moriah. He is Abraham with wires crossed. Jephthah is a cautionary tale of what happens when zealous devotion coincides with frightful theological ignorance.[1] In our day, Jephthah is jihad. He is the faith healer who turns down medicine for his sick child. He is the

---

[1] The most influential account of Jephthah's story, in my own life, came from a sermon by the late Haddon Robinson. Given Jephthah's unsettling appearance in Hebrews 11, Robinson preached (in his inimitable fashion) about the danger of a strong faith and bad theology.

militant fringe of the religious Right (or Left). Or more likely, in an age of biblical illiteracy, Jephthah is the church at large.

Born (most likely) to a Hebrew father, Jephthah should have learned the Mosaic prohibitions against human sacrifice. But the period of judges was not a time of much inductive Bible study within Israel's history. Not much Deuteronomy, we may guess, was recited around the table in Jephthah's broken home, much less fastened to the doorposts. His mother was a prostitute. His brothers drove him out to live among the pagans. His father did not stop them. How much, then, could Jephthah have known of Yahweh living with the bandits in the land of Tob? He returned, years later, because his kin needed "muscle" to defeat their enemies. And after haggling, they were willing to make him leader in exchange for his unique skill set (Judg 11:8-10). Jephthah had a knack for bargaining. And like some other sons of prostitutes, he turned youthful scorn into a frightful male aggression. Such was Jephthah's "gift."

But even tough guys say Hail Marys in a pinch. So when Jephthah sought the help of Israel's God before his mercenary fighting, he did it in the only way he knew: he bargained like a pagan. He haggled with God just as he had with his brothers:

> If you give the Ammonites into my hands, whatever comes out of the door of my house to meet me when I return in triumph from the Ammonites will be the LORD's, and I will sacrifice it as a burnt offering. (Judg 11:30-31)

Apparently, he never expected that his little girl would be the one to greet him. What was he hoping for? A slave? A goat? Regardless, if there was one thing he had learned in Tobite Sunday school, it was that warrior-gods hate nothing more than those who renege on promises. Jephthah was a man of his word. And besides, if he broke his vow, would his brothers still keep theirs? It would set a precedent. And Jephthah did not have that much faith. So the book of Judges ends his tale with a sad post-script: "He did to her as he had vowed. And she was a virgin" (Judg 11:39).

Between Mizpah and Moriah

What does Jephthah have to do with Abraham? According to the Torah, what Jephthah did in slaughtering his child was "detestable" (e.g., Deut 12:31; 18:9-10). It was abominable and ignorant. He is a cautionary tale. Yet Hebrews lists him as a man of faith.[2] After all, Abraham too was willing to sacrifice his child out of obedience to God. So how exactly are the two men different?

The most obvious answer is that God actually commanded Abraham to kill his child while Jephthah only thought this action was required. The trouble for Jephthah was that he had misunderstood Yahweh; the trouble for Abraham was that he understood perfectly. Yet, a further difference is that Abraham had more time and opportunity to get to know this God of promises and high demands. While neither man had (much) access to the Torah to provide an anti-Molech memory verse, Abraham had experienced a longer history with Yahweh. And Abraham remained open to a last-minute course correction.[3] Alongside these differences, however, I will now move to a point that is often missed: Abraham had learned how to say perhaps.

●   ○   ●

In Genesis 22, we are presented with the *Aqedah*—a Hebrew word that refers to the "binding" of Isaac upon an altar of burnt offering. Like the later narrative of Jephthah, this tale seems ghastly to modern readers. What kind of deity demands a child's murder, regardless of an eventual reprieve? The late atheist Christopher Hitchens implied (perhaps rightly) that if the story were to happen today, we would chalk it up to schizophrenia, or worse: "All three monotheisms . . . praise Abraham for being willing to hear voices and then to take his son Isaac for a long and gloomy

---

[2]One way around the conundrum is to claim that Hebrews mentions Jephthah merely for his military exploits (alongside those of Gideon, Barak, and Samson) and not for his fateful vow and follow-through. Still, child sacrifice would seem to be an apparent disqualifier, rising above even the sins of men like Samson.

[3]Did the Spirit ever whisper stop within the soul of Jephthah? After all, this same Spirit had quite recently come upon him (Judg 11:29). Did Jephthah quell the still, small voice with a masculine assumption that a man must always keep his vows? One might find both cultural and biblical justifications for such logic (Deut 23:21; cf. Num 30:2).

walk. And then the caprice by which his murderous hand is finally stayed is written down as divine mercy."[4]

Despite the force of Hitchens's claim, there are certain points that he gets wrong. In the Bible, they are not voices heard by Abraham but a voice (singular)—and its accent belongs to the same promise-keeping, womb-reviving God that Abraham had come to know as powerful and trustworthy. Abraham, we might say, had a history with this voice. So when the angel halts the hand of sacrifice, the point is not capriciousness (*"See how nice I am, old man!? I didn't make you do it!"*) but a "severe mercy."[5] The test is God wringing the incipient idolatry from Abraham's heart for the good of future generations. Despite its horror, the trial is teaching him to value the Giver over even his most precious gifts.[6]

But these points hardly trim the *Aqedah* of its rough edges. The tale resists our taming—and especially when we place ourselves in Abraham's position. Generations of readers have wondered what went through the old man's mind as he ascended Mount Moriah. In most cases, the attempts to psychologize such ancient persons yield dubious results.[7] "The past is a foreign country," says the adage. "They do things differently there."

Genesis 22 is also rather sparse for conversation. There are clues to Abraham's thoughts, but only that. With Moriah looming in the distance, the old man tells the servants that both he and the boy will return after having worshiped (Gen 22:5). And in response to Isaac's question regarding their lack of animal accompaniment, Abraham assures him, "God himself will provide the lamb for the burnt offering" (Gen 22:8). Are these words polite deceptions or prophetic hope? Either way, it is Isaac wriggling on the altar just one verse later. What did Abraham expect to happen next?

---

[4]Christopher Hitchens, *God Is Not Great: The Case Against Religion* (London: Atlantic Books, 2007), 53.

[5]The phrase comes from C. S. Lewis, spoken to Sheldon Vanauken, and inspiring the title of his memoir. See Sheldon Vanauken, *A Severe Mercy: A Story of Faith, Tragedy, and Triumph* (New York: HarperCollins, 1980).

[6]For its intended audience, the *Aqedah* served as a protective reminder that while the gods of other nations might take one's child in human sacrifice, the God of Israel was not like this.

[7]A reality that, of course, problematizes even our earlier account of Jephthah.

Only the book of Hebrews tells us. In Hebrews 11, just prior to the awkward nod to Jephthah, the inspired author gives a window into Abraham's inner world. "By faith," it says, he was willing to kill Isaac. Yet he did not do so in despair. According to the text, the patriarch held fast to Yahweh's prior promise that "it is through Isaac that your offspring will be reckoned" (Heb 11:18; cf. Gen 21:12). How could this be? The unnamed author offers this interpretation:

> By faith . . . Abraham *reckoned* that God could even raise the dead, and so in a manner of speaking he did receive Isaac back from death. (Heb 11:17, 19, emphasis added)[8]

In the NIV translation, Abraham "reasoned" (*logisamenos*) to this bold conclusion. Yet in other English versions, the word is less certain and cerebral. We are told that he merely "considered" that the Lord was able to raise Isaac from the dead (ESV, NASB, and NRSV). Regardless of translation, my claim is that Abraham's *logisamenos*—his ability to "consider" a strange possibility—serves as a model for what this book proposes. The *logisamenos* points to his ability to say perhaps.

Faith Seeking Imagination

My thesis is that between *certainty* and *skepticism* resides *perhaps*—and the reclaiming of this little word is crucial to the life of faith. Speculation is not always unwarranted in theology. Nor is it always useless. Moriah proves this.

For Abraham, the process of hopeful imagining rested on the foundation of his prior faith in God. Hence, the ability to say perhaps does not supplant faith; it builds on it. By faith Abraham "considered" the possibility that God could raise the dead. By faith he "reasoned" that even a bloody death would not keep Isaac from fathering descendants. Another astonishing point is that Abraham's "reckoning" required a resurrection from the ash heap underneath the altar! This raises a serious question. Wounds can be sutured, and CPR may start a heart, but how does one heal ash?

---

[8]The language of "having reckoned" is used by Gareth Lee Cockerill, *The Epistle to the Hebrews*, NICNT (Grand Rapids, MI: Eerdmans, 2012), 556.

Whatever the answer, it bears noting that this same God had already twice conquered death in Isaac's conception. This point must not be missed. We learn elsewhere that both (1) Abram's flesh and (2) Sarai's womb were "as good as dead" prior to Yahweh's intervention (Heb 11:12; Rom 4:19). Hence, Abraham's thinking, according to Hebrews, seems to be that if God had twice overcome death in the boy's conception, why not again? After all, the best predictor of future capability is past action. The ability to conquer death was already on God's résumé. There was a certain logic to Abraham's apparently ridiculous deduction. Still, the words "as good as" would cast a pall over even the most trusting parent. A barren womb is different from a burned-up body.

For Abraham, this speculative venturing forth from faith's foundation gave him the courage to obey. In other words, saying perhaps changed how he lived. It was not the equivalent of irrelevant speculation about how many angels may dance on the head of the pin. Abraham's *logisamenos* mattered. Yet it also stands distinct from completely unfounded or unbridled speculation (what I have previously dubbed "what-iffery").

Though later theological tradition would rightly make much of "faith seeking understanding" (*fides quaerens intellectum*), my own project involves "faith seeking [a redeemed] imagination"—*fides quaerens imaginationem*.[9] I am interested in a faith that learns how and when and why to say perhaps.[10]

While Abraham's consideration stands apart from skepticism, it also stands distinct from certainty. Unlike a presumptuous façade ("Don't worry Isaac; I know how this will all play out!"), *logisamenos* only ventures one possible way in which the promise may hold true. And, indeed, the story plays out differently than Abraham had reasoned. In the end,

---

[9]This idea connects to a question by James K. A. Smith: "What if the primary work of [Christian] education was the transforming of our imagination rather than the saturation of our intellect?" Smith, *Desiring the Kingdom: Worship, Worldview, and Cultural Formation* (Grand Rapids, MI: Baker Academic, 2009), 18.

[10]Hence the epigraph that frames this chapter: "God reveals himself by an appeal to our capacity for imagination." Trevor A. Hart, "Imagination," in *T&T Clark Companion to Atonement*, ed. Adam J. Johnson (London: Bloomsbury, 2017), 551.

God does not allow the killing of the boy; hence, Isaac was received back from the dead only "figuratively speaking" (Heb 11:19 ESV). Yet from another angle, Abraham's reckoning toward resurrection is absolutely right. As Christ reveals, Yahweh *did* one day keep his promise through the death and raising of the beloved Son.

For these reasons, Abraham is the model for my remaining chapters. Given my view of Scripture, it matters not whether a concept like perhaps can help us steer a middle course between the poles of doubt and dogmatism if indeed the Bible contradicts it. Middle is not always most in line with truth. And even an elegant metaphor is baseless without biblical roots. With my reading of the *Aqedah* now briefly outlined, I must now consider an objection to it.

The Kierkegaard Contention

The most famous alternative to my account of Abraham's *logisamenos* comes from the "melancholy Dane"—the Christian existentialist, poet, and social critic—Søren Kierkegaard (1813–1855). His great work on Abraham and Isaac is *Fear and Trembling* (1843).[11] The haunting pathos of the book remains palpable. And it is a stinging indictment of a cultural Christianity that sees faith as either a naive preoccupation to be moved past in one's maturity or a concept that must be redefined to fit the ruling form of modern reason. In the view of Kierkegaard's pseudonymous alter ego, John of Silence,[12] Abraham knew better.

Fear and Trembling throws down the gauntlet before those who would dismiss the faith of the ancients without understanding its true depth and difficulty. In those olden days,

---

[11]Søren Kierkegaard, *Fear and Trembling: A Dialectical Lyric* and *The Sickness Unto Death*, trans. with introduction and notes by Walter Lowrie, rev. ed. (Princeton, NJ: Princeton University Press, 1945), 12. Subsequent citations are from the Lowrie translation unless otherwise noted.

[12]There is debate over the extent to which such pseudonyms may be said to speak for Kierkegaard. Still, the practice fits his method of "indirect communication"—a technique by which he communicates ideas without directly arguing for them. This approach allows the audience to embrace truth on its own merits, rather than accepting or rejecting it based on Kierkegaard's authorial testimony. See Kenneth D. Boa and Robert M. Bowman Jr., *Faith Has Its Reasons: Integrative Approaches to Defending the Christian Faith*, 2nd ed. (Downers Grove, IL: InterVarsity Press, 2005), 347. For ease of reference, I sometimes speak of Kierkegaard as the author of the work, yet with the caveat that the voice of John of Silence may not always be synonymous with his own.

faith was a task for a whole lifetime, not a skill thought to be acquired in either days or weeks. When the old campaigner approached the end, had fought the good fight, and kept his faith, his heart was still young enough not to have forgotten the fear and trembling that disciplined his youth. . . . Where these venerable figures arrived our own age begins, in order to go further.[13]

In the cross hairs was the Christendom of nineteenth-century Denmark, where one's status as a believer was assumed by birth and breeding.

Fear and Trembling also levels a denunciation of the modern myth that one can find a harmony between religion and human-centered reason. The chief foil here is Georg W. F. Hegel (1770–1831). In spectacular fashion, Hegel had constructed a vast and abstract system in which the ugly ditch between reason and revelation was to be bridged by virtue of his own brilliance.[14] In response to Hegel's hubris, John of Silence makes clear that his own account will be different. "This is not the System," he shouts. "It has nothing whatever to do with the System"—which he likens to a tower that has the marks of Babel's shaky bricks.[15] While Kierkegaard took issue with many parts of Hegelian philosophy, the crucial point has to do with Hegel's confidence that he had reduced faith to an abstract system of rational philosophy now explicated exclusively by him. In contrast, Kierkegaard viewed faith as a form of "divine madness" that "begins precisely where thinking leaves off."[16]

For this reason, Kierkegaard is often set forth as the prime example of fideism—the idea that faith and rationality are mortal enemies. But the charge that Kierkegaard is a full-fledged fideist is controversial.[17] What

---

[13]This passage is from the Alastair Hannay translation of Kierkegaard's *Fear and Trembling* (London: Penguin Books, 1985), 42. As Ronald M. Green notes, "To go further" was a jab at the Hegelians of the day, who had adopted the motto "one must go further" as a way of presenting faith as an early phase of intellectual development that must now be transcended. See Green, "'Developing' *Fear and Trembling*," in The *Cambridge Companion to Kierkegaard*, ed. Alastair Hannay and Gordon Daniel Marino (Cambridge: Cambridge University Press, 1997), 260.

[14]For the proverbial "ugly, broad ditch" between reason and the revealed truths of history, see G. E. Lessing (1729–1781), "On the Proof of the Spirit and of Power," in *Lessing's Theological Writings*, ed. Henry Chadwick (Stanford, CA: Stanford University Press, 1956), 53-55.

[15]Kierkegaard, *Fear and Trembling*, 24-25.

[16]Kierkegaard, *Fear and Trembling*, 37.

[17]Along these lines, Myron Penner argues that Kierkegaard is rejecting not reason per se but rather the modern conception of reason. Myron Bradley Penner, *The End of Apologetics: Christian Witness in a Postmodern Context* (Grand Rapids, MI: Baker Academic, 2013), 11. Beyond this, Boa

matters for my investigation, however, is only Kierkegaard's treatment of Abraham and the *Aqedah*.

"Though Abraham arouses my admiration," says John of Silence, "he at the same time appalls me."[18] The reason for the shock involves the patriarch's willingness to suspend the ethical mandate against slaughtering one's child.[19] And yet, says John of Silence, this is precisely what makes Abraham a man of faith. True faith involves the "teleological suspension of the ethical."[20] For Abraham, the priority is the command of God, a word that seems utterly irrational and even diabolical in light of prior promises and moral prohibitions. In the *Aqedah*, Abraham leaped past the ethical into the paradox of the absurd, albeit with fear and trembling. Kierkegaard's takeaway is that sin's opposite "is not virtue but faith."[21]

To its credit, *Fear and Trembling* is well aware that Abraham was hardly the only one to believe he must sacrifice his child. History gives examples like Agamemnon (from Greek mythology) and, yes, Jephthah, who did likewise. The difference, says Kierkegaard, is that these men were not truly "knights of faith." They were merely "tragic heroes" or "knights of infinite resignation." They stayed within the realm of the ethical whereas Abraham transgressed this border. While stranded by the sea, Agamemnon learned that the gods had been offended and that unless he offered up his daughter, everyone would die. His choice was excruciating, but it was both rational and ethical by a certain standard of ancient judgment. Like a pagan Caiaphas, Agamemnon's conclusion was a simple calculation of the greater good: it is better that one girl should die than for the whole boatload to perish (cf. Jn 11:50).[22]

---

and Bowman note that Kierkegaard still employs reason in the form of *indirect* arguments for the gospel's truth; this includes the argument that the gospel must be true because no one would make up such an absurd set of claims. See again, Boa and Bowman, *Faith Has Its Reasons*, 347.

[18]Kierkegaard, *Fear and Trembling*, 71.

[19]"He did it for God's sake because God required this proof of his faith; for his own sake he did it in order that he might furnish the proof." *Fear and Trembling*, 70.

[20]See esp. Kierkegaard, *Fear and Trembling*, 64-65.

[21]Søren Kierkegaard, *The Sickness unto Death: A Christian Psychological Exposition for Upbuilding and Awakening*, ed. and trans. Howard V. Hong and Edna H. Hong (Princeton, NJ: Princeton University Press, 1980), 213.

[22]Slightly different versions of the tale exist in the Greek tragedians, Sophocles and Aeschylus.

So too with Jephthah. As some ancient prooftexter might have argued, the Torah is clear that vows to God must always be kept (Deut 23:21; cf. Num 30:2)! And Jephthah's failure to maintain a solemn bargain might have set a dangerous precedent for him if his brothers chose to follow suit. In these ways, both the pagan Agamemnon and the Hebrew Jephthah remain (however tenuously by modern standards) within the realm of the ethical. Oh, and one more thing: Jephthah and Agamemnon killed their girls. In a deeply patriarchal setting, this detail might also add a note of sinful rationality to their actions.

Yet *Fear and Trembling* also sees a final difference between Abraham, the knight of faith, and these tragic figures: Abraham never relinquished hope in God's prior promise that it would be through Isaac that his off-spring would be numbered.[23] Of course, these two statements from the Lord appear to stand in utter contradiction:

1. Isaac will one day father offspring.

2. Kill Isaac.

Somehow, Abraham held to both ideas. In the words of *Fear and Trembling*, he weathered the "concussions of existence" and leaped into the void.[24] Kierkegaard saw such faith as "the paradox that does not permit of mediation." It is a "miracle"[25] and "madness."[26]

"If Only I Knew Hebrew[s]!"—A Response to Kierkegaard

I disagree with one aspect of this powerful interpretation. The difference between Kierkegaard's reading and my own has to do with the extent to which Abraham had reasonable warrant for "considering" that God might keep his promise. Kierkegaard says that he had none. I say that he had a certain (speculative) logic—rooted in evidence but still falling far short of certainty. Now to explain.

In the prelude to *Fear and Trembling*, we hear of a man from Denmark who has always been captivated by the story of Abraham and Isaac

---

[23]See Kierkegaard, *Fear and Trembling*, 46-47.
[24]Kierkegaard, *Fear and Trembling*, 73.
[25]Kierkegaard, *Fear and Trembling*, 77.
[26]Kierkegaard, *Fear and Trembling*, 37.

though he admits being "less and less able to understand it." Pseudonyms aside, the man bears an unmistakable resemblance to Kierkegaard. And in the prelude's closing line, we read, "That man . . . didn't know Hebrew, if he had known Hebrew, he perhaps would easily have understood the story [of the *Aqedah*] and Abraham."[27]

I would add only a single letter (*s*) to that final line. While the Hebrew language may not have done much to aid Kierkegaard's understanding, Hebrews (the New Testament book) could have changed key aspects of his exegesis. After all, it is in Hebrews that we gain the crucial insight into Abraham's resurrected rationality. By faith, Abraham "reasoned" that God could even raise the dead (Heb 11:19).

The closest Kierkegaard comes to grappling with the *logisamenos* of Hebrews is in the following passage, which must be quoted at length:

> All that time [Abraham] believed—he believed that God would not require Isaac of him, whereas he was willing nevertheless to sacrifice him if it was required. He believed by virtue of the absurd; . . . even at the instant when the knife glittered he believed . . . that God would not require Isaac. . . . He did not believe that some day he would be blessed in the beyond, but that he would be happy here in the world. God could give him a new Isaac, could recall to life him who had been sacrificed. He believed by virtue of the absurd; for all human reckoning had long since ceased to function.[28]

The passage gets some things right: Abraham's hope was not for some heavenly reunion with Isaac's ghost but for blessed happiness in this world.

But *Fear and Trembling* misses two key points: First, it assumes too much continuity between the ethics of modern Denmark and the ethics of the ancient Near East. Second, it fails to grapple with my point regarding God's long track record of overcoming death in Abram's story. When taken together, these two insights move Abraham away from a fideism that embraces faith's utter irrationality and toward a middle ground in which *perhaps* is the result of faith seeking (a redeemed) imagination: *fides quaerens imaginationem.*

Now to illustrate these two points.

---

[27]Kierkegaard, *Fear and Trembling*, 26.
[28]Kierkegaard, *Fear and Trembling*, 46-47.

First, in contrast to Kierkegaard's description of the *Aqedah* as "the teleological suspension of the ethical," John Walton argues that, in the culture of the day, it would hardly have been viewed as absurd or unethical to claim that a god might demand so costly a sacrifice:

> The command to sacrifice his son would not have been as shocking to Abraham as it is to us. In the Canaanite worldview, the god who provided fertility (El) was also entitled to demand a portion of what had been produced. This was expressed in sacrifice of animals and grain and in the sacrifice of children. . . . Abraham's compliant acquiescence, as much as it reflects the power of his faith, also suggests that human sacrifice is familiar to his conceptual worldview. However saddened he may have been, he is not dumbfounded by the macabre or peculiar nature of Yahweh's demand. It was culturally logical, despite being emotionally harsh, and only baffling in light of the covenant promises.[29]

The story of Jephthah proves this point.[30] The past, once more, is a foreign country.

Second, Abraham's experience with Yahweh as a God who conquered death—both in Sarai's womb and in his withered body—gave birth to a certain kind of reasoned speculation that God might keep his promise regarding Isaac's offspring. In this way, his faith did not begin "where thinking leaves off." The great gift of Kierkegaard is to show the massive gulf between Christianity and a rational pursuit of certainty. By modern standards, Abraham's actions do seem like a divine madness. (Just ask Hitchens.) Still, Kierkegaard's failure—like that of many others in our polarized and fragmented culture—was to miss the possibility of a middle ground between rational certainty and the absurd.

---

[29]John H. Walton, *Genesis*, NIV Application Commentary (Grand Rapids, MI: Zondervan, 2001), 511. Walton never mentions Kierkegaard and does not seem to be explicitly responding to his position.

[30]What's more, because Abraham lived long before the reception of the Mosaic law (not to mention the ethical assumptions of modern Denmark), it is anachronistic to say that God's command required him to ponder the teleological suspension of "the ethical" as a universally acknowledged boundary. Jerome Van Kuiken suggests that it would be better to view the *Aqedah* in terms of the "teleological *permission* of the ethical" (emphasis added). Van Kuiken, "Why Protestant Christians Should Not Believe in Mary's Immaculate Conception: Response to Mulder," *Christian Scholars Review* 46, no. 3 (2017): 238n26.

In this no man's land resides the *logisamenos* of the book of Hebrews. It is a baptized form of reasoning that allowed Abraham to say perhaps in a way that motivates hopeful obedience. If only Jephthah had been able to engage in such a Spirit-guided form of thoughtful speculation. How might his story have been different? Now for a final (speculative) word on that.

A BETTER SACRIFICE

As the warrior crested the hill outside Mizpah, he could again see a trail of smoke as it streaked down toward his beloved home. Thankfully, the God to whom he had prayed had once more proven faithful. The girl was beside him. But, unlike her father, she did not glance back to see the burning home.

So much for brothers, thought the warrior. This was the second time his siblings had driven him away while citing "legal" reasons. Still this was a better sacrifice than the one he had narrowly averted.

How had he averted it? The swirl of events was fuzzy. It had been an unquestioned assumption, in his time, that one must always pay one's vows. After all, if one should break a bargain, what motive would others have to keep theirs? The system would collapse they told him. *Well, this is not the system!* It felt like a leap into the void.

They would say that Jephthah had grown soft, that he had given over to emotion like a woman. But that was not quite right. He had intended to fulfill his vow, until the voice had stayed his hand: "'Grant me this one request' it said. 'Give me two months to roam the hills and weep with my friends because I will never marry.'" A lot can happen in two months. The words tugged at his mind like a ram caught in a thicket. They gave time for the Spirit to work—the Spirit that still clung to Jephthah like a scent slowly evaporating. And while it did not overpower his ability to resist, it did make him capable of contemplating new ideas about the ethical and God's will. On some nights, during that two-month stay of execution, he could almost hear a child's voice: "Take up and read."

And so he did. Jephthah may have lived in Tob, but he was not completely oblivious to Torah. He had referenced parts of it when haggling with the king of Ammon. Anyone can be an expert when one wants to justify something. But this was different. The motive now was something more than power. For the first time, he was listening more than bargaining. At least he thought so. It was impossible to know. Yet, in the morning he heeded the voice; he sent for the one old man in all of Gilead who was said to have memorized the words of the great book.

When the old scribe finally arrived, Jephthah didn't haggle. He just listened—to Genesis, Exodus, Leviticus, and so on. There were passages on keeping vows. But there were other passages too—about the "detestable" practice of human sacrifice and about an angel who had stayed the hand of Abraham. How should one make sense of seemingly opposing commands?

Always keep your vows. Never sacrifice your child.

Even with the Spirit heavy on him, certainty was absent.

Perhaps, thought Jephthah, there is a sin worse than the breaking of one's vow. Perhaps the request of two months to mourn virginity was the angel moving in to stay his hand. There was no proof. There rarely is. Nevertheless, after days of listening, Jephthah went—up from his country, from his people, and from his father's household. He went up to the mountains, where she had gone to weep and wander.

And on the way, the warrior could not resist one final bargain. "If you let me find her, Lord, among the rocky crags and greening valleys, I will break my prior promise and throw myself upon your mercy." It took four days. But he found her. And this time it was the warrior who was running. In this way, the Scripture was fulfilled in a way that few expected.

She returned to her father, and he did to her as he had vowed. And she was a virgin.

From this comes the Israelite tradition that each year the young women of Israel go out for four days to commemorate the daughter of Jephthah the Gileadite.[31]

---

[31]For biblical citations and allusions, see Judges 11.

"Perhapsing" Church Tradition

Origen, Julian, and Jonathan Edwards

So memory pulls us forward [and] prophecy
is only brilliant memory.

MARILYNNE ROBINSON, *HOUSEKEEPING*

IDEAS CRY OUT FROM THE GROUND, like Abel's blood—even if we fail to trace their ancestry. They never really die. "What has been will be again" (Eccles 1:9). For this reason, one danger in a theology of imagination is that it would fail to listen to specific ways past thinkers put speculation to use in helpful and unhelpful ways. After all, while Abraham said perhaps in the *Aqedah*, he also did so in the impatient incident of Ishmael's conception (Gen 16). It is necessary, therefore, to embark on a selective sounding of Christian tradition. This chapter will survey a trio of theologians from past centuries to note how they said perhaps for good or ill.

Since my treatment of Abraham focused almost exclusively on the benefits of faith seeking imagination, the present chapter provides some balance by highlighting its dangers. The result is not, however, an invalidation of my thesis that believing in providence means learning how to say perhaps. The contention is rather that we can learn insights about faithful speculation by observing how it has been done imperfectly. In this way, a look backward will provide raw materials for the erection of some constructive "guardrails" (or principles) that I will undertake in the next chapter.

For sake of space, I will limit my historical exemplars to three figures, each representing a different part and period of the tradition:

1. Origen of Alexandria, a Greek speaker from the patristic era who lived in Africa and Asia

2. Julian of Norwich, a medieval mystic from what we now call England

3. Jonathan Edwards, a modern Puritan with revivalistic tendencies from North America

The trio also nods to the three major "houses" of Christianity. For while Origen was not technically Eastern Orthodox, he was heavily influential in that tradition, Julian was Roman Catholic, and Edwards was a Protestant of the Calvinist variety. In some ways, these thinkers could not be more different; yet I will also note points at which their imaginations converge.

Origen of Alexandria

For some students, all they know of Origen of Alexandria (AD 186–254) is that he allegedly cut off his testicles out of zeal for Jesus, muddied Scripture by allegorical interpretation, and was condemned for teaching universal salvation. But Origen's life and legacy are more complex than that. To Saint Jerome—who had few kind words for anyone!—Origen was the greatest teacher after the apostles.[1] He suffered torture rather than recant his faith; he studied philosophy under a master of his day (Ammonius Saccas), spoke boldly against heresy,[2] and sought to reverence Scripture by seeing every passage as pointing to Christ.

---

[1]Jerome's views soured as Origen's theology came under critique. Toward the end of his life, however, he maintained that one could mine Origen selectively to great benefit.

[2]He writes in one passage that "we must watch out for ourselves lest we be caught up by the specious arguments of heretical doctrine and fall away from the mystery of the church." Origen, *Homily on Job*, 20.15. This translation is from Hans Urs von Balthasar, ed., *Origen: Spirit and Fire;*

My interest in Origen, however, has to do with his propensity for speculation. "Where Origen was good," the saying went, "no one is better; where he was bad [there is] no one worse."[3] Separating these extremes is made more difficult, however, by the fact that many of Origen's writings were destroyed in the wake of controversy, and those that survive (especially *On First Principles*) show signs of alteration by opponents and apologists alike.[4] The consensus was that Origen was worst when he gave full vent to speculative theories. But while his willingness to say perhaps got him into trouble, it also aided orthodoxy, as seen in eternal generation (the idea that the Son is eternally begotten from the Father so he is neither a created being nor a separate god as claimed in polytheism).[5] When considering where to begin with Origen, however, it is best to start with his great passion: the Bible as the perfect pointer to the Son of God.

"The one, perfect body of the Logos"—Origen and Scripture. Origen was obsessed with Scripture. Ironically, it was a literal interpretation that supposedly led him to self-castration after reading in Matthew that some "have made themselves eunuchs for the kingdom of heaven's sake" (Mt 19:12-13 NKJV).[6] Later, Origen disagreed with this reading

---

A *Thematic Anthology of His Writings*, trans. Robert J. Daly (Washington, DC: Catholic University of America Press, 1984), 172.

[3]The saying goes back to Cassiodorus (ca. 485–ca. 585), if not further. Cited in Michael J. McClymond, *The Devil's Redemption: A New History and Interpretation of Christian Universalism* (Grand Rapids, MI: Baker Academic, 2018), 1:235.

[4]Rufinus (ca. 344–ca. 411) admits, for instance, that his Latin translation of *On First Principles* has altered passages that might give offense, allegedly because of prior changes by Origen's opponents. Jerome also supplies translations of Origen that may be more reliable, and other smaller fragments exist in the Greek original.

[5]Origen, *On First Principles*, 1.2.4. In what follows, I will quote from both the Butterworth and Behr translations depending on the ease of reading and the reliability of the passage in question. In each case, I will note the specific translator in the footnote. For the Butterworth translation, see Origen, *On First Principles*, trans. G. W. Butterworth (Notre Dame, IN: Ave Maria Press, 2013).

[6]The question of Origen's self-castration remains disputed. Both Behr and McGuckin reject it as a likely smear by Origen's opponents while Crouzel and Trigg are among the majority of scholars that accept it. See Behr's introduction, in Origen, *On First Principles: A Reader's Edition*, trans. John Behr (Oxford: Oxford University Press, 2019), xv; John Anthony McGuckin, ed., *The Westminster Handbook to Origen* (Louisville, KY: Westminster John Knox, 2004), 6; Henri Crouzel, *Origen: The Life and Thought of the First Great Theologian*, trans. A. S. Worrall (San Francisco: HarperCollins, 1989), 9; and Joseph W. Trigg, *Origen* (New York: Routledge, 1998), 14.

as he opted for a more "spiritual" exegesis.[7] "The letter kills," he never tired of saying (2 Cor 3:6). After all, he bore on his body the marks of biblical literalism.

Origen found warrant for allegory in the New Testament. There, Christ proclaimed that the Old Testament had been pointing to him (Lk 24:27, 44). Paul spoke of Hagar and Sarah as two covenants taken "figuratively" (Gal 4:24); he identified a wilderness rock with the Messiah (1 Cor 10:4); and he responded with contempt for a strictly literal interpretation of a command about unmuzzled oxen (Deut 25:4; 1 Cor 9:9-10). All these passages led Origen to believe that Christ's words included not only those given when he "dwelt in the flesh" but also those handed down when the Word was in Moses and the Prophets. In the end, the Bible itself led Origen to speculative interpretations.[8]

Admittedly, some of these allegories led to seemingly bizarre conclusions. Origen read Song of Songs as speaking of the life-giving "wine" that flows from Christ's ample breasts: "for your [breasts are] more delightful than wine" (Song 1:2).[9] Such imagery would give Freud a field day, but the insight was Origen's attempt to follow Paul in finding Christ, not just in gushing "rocks" (1 Cor 10:4) but in nourishing "breasts" within the Scriptures.[10]

In addition to his love of Scripture, Origen remained a staunch adherent to the "rule of faith" that outlined Christianity's core convictions. And on topics like the Trinity, it is unfair to criticize him on the basis of a consensus that was yet to be established. He desired to be "a man of the church," not "some founder of a heresy."[11]

---

[7]See Origen, *Commentary on Matthew*, 15.1, available in a new translation by Ronald E. Heine, *The Commentary of Origen on the Gospel of St Matthew*, 2 vols. (Oxford: Oxford University Press, 2018).

[8]See Origen, *On First Principles*, preface.

[9]While most modern translations read "your love is better than wine," the Septuagint plausibly translated it as *mastoi* (breasts). See Bryan Litfin, "Origen," in *Shapers of Christian Orthodoxy: Engaging with Early and Medieval Theologians*, ed. Bradley G. Green (Downers Grove, IL: IVP Academic, 2010), 130n61.

[10]Origen likened the threefold sense of Scripture (literal, moral, and spiritual) to the three-part division of the human being into body, soul, and spirit. Elsewhere, he added a fourth sense, the anagogical, that pertained to the eschaton. *On First Principles*, 4.2.4.

[11]Origen, *Homily on Luke*, 16.6 (von Balthasar, 155).

Before the beginning: Origen on origins. But on what happened prior to or after history, Origen felt free to speculate since "no clear statement on this is set forth in the ecclesiastical teaching."[12] Into this formless void of unsettled doctrine, he spoke a very loud "Perhaps!" He suggested that prior to the physical world, God had generated a number of spiritual beings (*logika*) that existed without mortal bodies. Some of these clung closely to God (the angels) while others (demons and humanity) turned away by varying degrees and cooled in their love for God.

In response to this rebellion, the human soul was placed in its embodied state.[13] Still, Origen did not see materiality as a mere penalty for sin.[14] Some rational beings came down "to offer service to those below them" in a foreshadowing of Christ's incarnation.[15] And even those who fell because of sin were sent into the physical world for a redemptive purpose, to understand the error of their ways so they might be saved and restored.[16]

A true academic, Origen viewed the cosmos as a classroom in which fallen natures might learn their faults and return to God by the same free will by which they fell. In this way, (1) God's good justice and (2) creaturely freedom remained the enduring poles of this thought. Like Irenaeus before him, Origen was a vocal opponent of the Gnostics, with whom he had firsthand experience in Alexandria.[17] But unlike Irenaeus, Origen's focus was on the Gnostic smear about the perceived unfairness of differing human lots in life rather than their hatred of materiality.[18] The Gnostic question was as follows: If the Creator is just, powerful, and

---

[12]*On First Principles*, pref. 7 (Behr).

[13]*On First Principles*, 2.8.3; also, 1.5.1.

[14]After all, the demons erred more fully than humanity, yet they were not laden with bodies like our own. Somewhat confusingly, Origen claimed that even angels and demons were always united to a certain kind of body. Only God is truly immaterial. See Stephen R. Holmes, *The Quest for the Trinity: The Doctrine of God in Scripture, History and Modernity* (Downers Grove, IL: IVP Academic, 2012), 75.

[15]*On First Principles*, 2.9.7 (Behr); see also, 3.5.4.

[16]See Trigg, *Origen*, 28.

[17]On specific (so-called) Gnostic schools as they relate to Origen and Alexandria, see Ronald E. Heine, *Origen: Scholarship in the Service of the Church* (Oxford: Oxford University Press, 2010), 51-55.

[18]Origen also objected strongly to other parts of Gnostic doctrine, most notably the claim that the capricious creator-god of Israel was a different deity than the good God of Jesus Christ.

loving, why do we inherit such disparities in intelligence, health, and creaturely capacity?

Origen attributed these differing lots, in an apologetic move, to our differing degrees of pretemporal rebellion.[19] In answer to the question of "Who sinned, this man or his parents?" (Jn 9:2), his reply would apparently be "both"—although the *logika* of blind men apparently cooled more thoroughly than others. This speculative theory led Origen to read almost all of Genesis 1–3 as referring to the prematerial fall of human and demonic natures. Even the "garments of skin" given to Adam and Eve (Gen 3:21) were symbols of the bodies we must wear until we make it back to a purely spiritual existence.

It was fundamental for Origen that "the end is always like the beginning."[20] Hence, the world must have a conclusion similar to its inception.[21] Then "all things shall be restored to their original state."[22] It would be impossible to overstate the importance of this idea to Origen's speculative theology.

"The end is like the beginning": Origen's eschatology. Since the beginning was without matter, time, or punishment, so too the end. After all, did not Paul proclaim that God would then be "all in all" (1 Cor 15:28)? Based on this passage, Origen may have taught that the distinction between the Creator and creatures would eventually be blurred. To this end, Jerome quotes him as writing that "the whole of bodily nature may be resolved into . . . the divine nature."[23] The end shall be (like) the beginning.[24]

In the translations we have, Origen often cloaked his eschatological speculations in cautiousness. When speaking, for instance, of the demons'

---

[19]See Origen, *On First Principles*, 2.1.1.

[20]Origen, *On First Principles*, 1.6.2 (Butterworth).

[21]See Origen, *On First Principles*, 2.1.3 (Butterworth).

[22]Origen, *On First Principles*, 2.1.1 (Behr); see also 3.5.4; 3.6.3; 3.6.8. See also Peter W. Martens, *Origen and Scripture: The Contours of the Exegetical Life* (Oxford: Oxford University Press, 2012), 228-29.

[23]Jerome, *Letter* 124.10 (to Avitus), in *Opera, Epistularum Pars III*, 112 (ed. I. Hilberg), cited in McClymond, *Devil's Redemption*, 1:266.

[24]A close reading of the parallels in Genesis 1–2 and Revelation 21–22 reveals that the dictum itself is not flatly wrong, so long as we retain the "like" rather than assume the end must simply "be" the beginning in a cyclical fashion. See William J. Dumbrell, *The End of the Beginning: Revelation 21–22 and the Old Testament* (1985; repr., Eugene, OR: Wipf & Stock, 2001).

possible salvation, he asks readers to judge if this is possible or if "deep-rooted wickedness turns at last from a habit into a kind of nature."[25] In introducing eschatology more generally, Origen notes his "caution" while clarifying that he is merely "discussing and investigating rather than laying down fixed and certain conclusions."[26] Is that true?

In other places, Origen is definite. Divine wrath is merely restorative as opposed to retributive. And when Scripture speaks of a "punishment of fire,"[27] this is only a refining for ultimate redemption. What are consumed are only wicked thoughts, evil actions, and sinful desires.[28] "Whenever we read of the anger of God, whether in the Old or the New Testament, we do not take such statements literally, but look for the spiritual meaning in them, endeavoring to understand them in a way that is worthy of God."[29] What is deemed "worthy" is however somewhat subjective, as is the interpretive dilemma of which principles (*principiis*) should be made axiomatic and which should be held more loosely. This conundrum (as both Julian and Jonathan Edwards will demonstrate) is a continual question for sacred speculation.

Lessons from Origen's speculative theology. A first lesson from Origen is that no one says perhaps in a vacuum. No one speculates with a blank slate. The (Middle) Platonism imbibed by Origen in Alexandria, his encounters with Gnosticism, and a variety of other factors mean that his creative reworking of creation and eschatology were sometimes indebted to forces that have little to do with either Scripture or the rule of faith. So too today.

Second, Origen's allegorical speculations emerged not from a self-consciously low view of Scripture but (if anything) from an inappropriately high one. The Bible, he proclaims, is "the one, perfect body of the Word."[30] Thus, to engage Scripture faithfully is to encounter Christ.

---

[25]Origen, *On First Principles*, 1.6.3. As I will note in chap. 12, C. S. Lewis asked a similar question of human souls within the afterlife.

[26]Origen, *On First Principles*, 1.6.1 (Butterworth).

[27]Origen, *On First Principles*, 2.10.6 (Butterworth).

[28]See Origen, *On First Principles*, 1.1.2.

[29]Origen, *On First Principles*, 2.4.4 (Butterworth).

[30]Origen, *Homily on Jeremiah, Fragment* (PG 13:554). This translation is that of Robert Daly in von Balthasar, *Origen*, 88.

While appreciating the exalted status Origen ascribes to sacred writ, a proper biblical theology makes clear that the Word's "one, perfect body" is not a book but an embodied Jew who sits enthroned in heaven, even if his body also comes to us in sacramental bread (Lk 22:19) and in the dirt-and-tear-streaked faces of the "least of these" (Mt 25:40). The Bible, for all its inspired and authoritative power, is not the "perfect body" of the Logos. And a high view of Scripture is no automatic safeguard against the dangers of theological speculation.

Third, Origen reveals how a speculative apologetic attempt to confront error (in his case, Gnosticism) can inadvertently veer toward the very monster it seeks to slay. I have noted this already in the tone and tactics of contemporary culture warriors since our opponents tend to "rub off on us." In Origen's case, being conformed to the image of the opposition occurred by accepting certain Gnostic presuppositions.

Some of Origen's allegorical flights came from a desire to refute the Gnostic notion that vast portions of the Old Testament were "unworthy" of God. Origen conceded this critique, but only as it pertained to literal interpretation.[31] He also sought to defend divine justice by pushing back against a form of divine sovereignty that made God responsible for differing lots in life. Yet, in rejecting this branch of Gnostic teaching, he accepted other Gnostic claims: (1) humans fell into bodies; (2) physicality is a burden to be grieved despite redemptive possibilities through knowledge; (3) a vast speculative system must be constructed to account for our predicament; and (4) materiality will pass away when evil is expunged.

Our opponents tend to rub off on us, and especially when we mix perhaps with polemic. By responding to the "cultured despisers" of Judeo-Christian teaching, Origen affirmed ideas that would later be seen as either heretical or highly strange. In his view, both our blessings and our burdens were earned by our pretemporal choices. Even the embryonic John the Baptist would not have leaped in Elizabeth's womb had

---

[31]This too bore a similarity to some Gnostic heretics that Origen sought to correct. The Valentinians, for instance, pulled many strange "jewels" out of the scriptural depths, and they were perfectly happy to affirm the same inspired texts as Origen. See Heine, *Origen*, 53-54.

he not merited the honor before creation.[32] Unfortunately, Origen's defense of God's justice results in a kind of merit-based prosperity theology projected backward to our pretemporal *logika*. It absolutized creaturely freedom and undermined God's sovereignty. In short, the speculative cure caused as many problems as it solved.

Now for a controversial lesson that will reappear throughout my book: while it is often said that heresy is the mother of orthodoxy, it is equally true that apologetics sometimes fathers heresies (or at least errors) when divorced from a proper theological foundation. This happens when speculation seeks to clarify what should remain in mystery. Hence, Origen was called a dogmatist not for an angry or divisive demeanor but for an alleged tendency to invent new dogmas. Not every blank space on the map of theological inquiry should be filled by the speculative cartographer.

Finally, and more positively, Origen's originality led also to emerging orthodoxy. Thus, his example is not entirely cautionary. It was, after all, his speculation regarding the eternal generation of the Son as a distinct person alongside the Father and the Spirit that proved useful for Nicene trinitarianism.[33] Origen therefore demonstrates not only the dangers of sacred speculation but also its promise.[34] To say perhaps need not lead toward only heresy or *adiaphora*; it may also point toward a more robust and rooted orthodoxy. And although our best imaginative intentions can go wrong, even theological misfires can be worked together for good. For every *Aqedah* there is an Ishmael, but Ishmael too receives a blessing (Gen 17:20).[35] Now to the Middle Ages, and a second exemplar of speculative theology.

---

[32]Origen, *On First Principles*, 1.7.4.

[33]Though he had also implied that the whole world of spiritual beings were somehow co-eternal in their generation. See Origen, *On First Principles*, 1.2.10. For a concise treatment of Origen's complex influence on the pro-Nicene tradition, see Khaled Anatolios, *Retrieving Nicaea: The Development and Meaning of Trinitarian Doctrine* (Grand Rapids, MI: Baker Academic, 2011), 16-17.

[34]For a classic treatment, see J. N. D. Kelly, *Early Christian Doctrines*, rev. ed. (New York: HarperOne, 1978), 131. See also, Kevin Giles, *The Eternal Generation of the Son: Maintaining Orthodoxy in Trinitarian Theology* (Downers Grove, IL: InterVarsity Press, 2012), 99-102.

[35]Rebecca Lyman is right to note that Origen's audacious faults "are errors of spiritual zeal as much as intellectual curiosity." Rebecca Lyman, "Origen," in *Early Christian Thinkers: The Lives and Legacies of Twelve Key Figures*, ed. Paul Foster (Downers Grove, IL: IVP Academic, 2010), 124-25.

Julian of Norwich

Julian of Norwich (1342–ca. 1416) stands distinct, not just from Origen but from the vast majority of voices in the histories of Christian theology. She is an "unlettered" commoner (unable to read Latin), a receiver of visions on what she thought was her deathbed, a religious recluse who enclosed herself in a tiny room for over twenty years, and, perhaps most obviously, she is a *she*. Julian is the first woman known to have written a book in English.

But in other ways, Julian and Origen are similar. Both sit somewhat awkwardly alongside the orthodox tradition. Both have been praised and pilloried for statements about divine wrath. Both were ascetics in seemingly odd and extreme ways. Both used maternal imagery for God and spoke of Christ as nursing mother. Both have been accused of universalism.[36] And both lived under plausible threat of death for their writings.

Still, one facet of Julian's work makes her seem ill suited for a survey of speculation. A vision (if it be genuine) is not a conscious act of casting forth one's thoughts and theories. It is something received as gift or interruption. So why include Julian in this chapter? The answer has nothing to do with the tokenism of trotting out a lone female to complement the lettered males of history. On the contrary, the recent critical edition of Julian's work identifies her as "one of the great *speculative* theologians of the Middle Ages."[37] And, indeed, she is both rare and radical. Bernard McGinn notes how she minimized and even broke with many teachings of late medieval thought and mysticism. So while other female mystics, like Catherine of Siena, were granted a formal role in the tradition, Julian was "too original" for that.[38]

---

[36]In Julian's case, this notion stems from her disbelief in divine wrath, and from her famous statement that "alle shalle be wele." McClymond sides with Bernard McGinn in concluding that Julian did *not* believe in universalism. See McClymond, *Devil's Redemption*, 1:395. See also Bernard McGinn, *The Varieties of Vernacular Mysticism: 1350–1550*, vol. 5 of *The Presence of God: A History of Christian Mysticism* (New York: Herder & Herder, 2012), 456.

[37]Nicholas Watson and Jacqueline Jenkins, eds., preface to *The Writings of Julian of Norwich: A Vision Showed to a Devout Woman and a Revelation of Love* (University Park: Pennsylvania State University Press, 2006), ix (emphasis added).

[38]Bernard McGinn, *The Varieties of Vernacular Mysticism*, 470.

Unlike other mystics who minimized positive speech and imagery to honor God's transcendent mystery,[39] Julian was more open to the place of reasoned analysis, visual depiction, and imaginative conclusions.[40] More importantly, her decades of prayerful reflection reveal a distinction between what Julian "saw" and what she came to "understand" after years of contemplation.[41] In this gap sits a daring, prayerful speculation. But I am getting ahead of myself.

Julian's life and times. On May 8, 1373, an East Anglian woman lay dying for a span of seven days. She was only thirty years old. Still, the fact that Julian had lived this long was probably considered fortunate. The Black Death had ravaged Norwich when she was six, claiming half its population.[42] But while young Julian (if that was her original name) survived the pestilence, her present illness was so dire that last rites were given and a crucifix was brought in for her to gaze upon. Julian's arms fell limp, her breathing labored, and she recalled a light enveloping the cross. Instantly her pain was gone and she felt completely whole. Then, on recalling a prayer she had once made to experience the Lord's passion, she watched as Jesus came to life upon the cross.

Sixteen visions ("shewings") followed. They are described by Julian in two texts: the Short Text (*A Vision Showed to a Devout Woman*) is a more personal account while the Long Text (*A Revelation of Love*) was written twenty years later, when Julian was enclosed as an anchorite until her death around the age of seventy-four.[43] Although the longer *Revelation*

---

[39]See especially Pseudo-Dionysius (6th cent.) or the unnamed author of *The Cloud of Unknowing* (14th cent.).

[40]Veronica Mary Rolf, *An Explorer's Guide to Julian of Norwich* (Downers Grove, IL: InterVarsity Press, 2018), 15.

[41]Watson and Jenkins (*Writings of Julian*, 7) draw attention to the distinction between "I saw" in Julian's initial record of her vision (The Short Text), and her "I understood" as it appears in The Long Test, written years later.

[42]Rolf, *Explorer's Guide*, 28.

[43]The Long Text was written between 1393 and 1416. The following translations are my own, based on the critical edition of the Middle English by Watson and Jenkins (*Writings of Julian*), though I am aided by the accessible work of Veronica Mary Rolf, *Julian's Gospel: Illuminating the Life and Revelations of Julian of Norwich* (Maryknoll, NY: Orbis, 2013), and Rolf's introductory *Explorer's Guide*. The Short Text will hereafter be referred to, after the standard fashion, as Julian's *Vision* whereas the Long Text will be cited as her *Revelation*.

retains around 80 percent of the *Vision*, it also expands the account with insights gained during years of prayerful reflection.[44]

That Julian wrote anything reveals her courage, grit, and deep devotion. She was, in her words, "a woman, uneducated, unlettered, feeble, and frail." Yet, the impediments to writing went far beyond gender, class, or language. The Catholic Church was cracking down and even burning certain Lollard followers of John Wyclif (1330–1384), a group condemned, in part, for the "heretical" practice of writing in a vulgar (non-Latin) tongue and for daring to teach despite holding no office in the church.[45] For the unlettered Julian to set forth visions in Middle English for the common people (whom she called *evencristens*) carried clear and present dangers.

The threat may be perceived in the Short Text (*Vision*). After admitting her lowly and uneducated status, Julian nonetheless proclaims that she has received these visions "by the shewing of him who is sovereign teacher." The implication is that while Julian does not have the legal credentials to teach, Jesus does. After all, "because I am a woman should I . . . not tell you the goodness of God, since it is his will that it be known?"[46] A first lesson from her work is therefore a profile in courage. Perhaps, she seems to say, I do have something to offer God's people, despite my lowly status and the prohibitions placed on my gender.

A survey of "shewings." Now to the visions. Julian recounts that "suddenly I saw red blood trickle down from under the garland [of thorns], hot and freshly, plentiously and vividly, exactly as it was at that time that [it] was pressed on his blessed head."[47] The following scenes are, by some distance, the most graphic depictions of Christ's death in all medieval literature. Julian describes, among other things, the four manners of Christ's "drying out" as he was overcome by thirst.[48] The point, however,

---

[44]Rolf, *Explorer's Guide*, 56.

[45]In 1401 a statute titled *De Haeretico Comburendo* ("Regarding the Burning of Heretics") was sanctioned by King Henry IV; and in 1409 the *Constitution Against Gospellers* prohibited unlicensed religious or lay preachers not approved by the Catholic Church.

[46]Julian, *Vision*, 6.35-43.

[47]Julian, *Revelation*, 4.1-3 (p. 135).

[48]Julian, *Revelation*, 16.1, 18, 22 (p. 179): "I saw the sweet face as it were dry and bloodless with pale dying. . . . I saw the sweet flesh dry in my sight, part after part." Rolf notes the scientific accuracy

is not a macabre pity but the revelation of theological truth: "Herewith [by the cross] is the fiende overcome."[49]

The scope of Julian's visions is too vast to summarize here, but an entry into their more speculative elements comes by a question that had long vexed her: "How does God behold us in our sin?" Like other medieval Christians, Julian was well aware of her unworthiness before God. She was beset by guilt and fearful of judgment. Yet this foreboding did not match what she now saw. Here the Trinity was "our everlasting lover" in whom there is not the slightest bit of wrath.[50] The God revealed to Julian loves all that exists, from the worst of sinners to the tiniest hazelnut. All things, including our digestion and excretion, have their being by the triune love. Even the minuscule hazelnut, which is figuratively described as "all that is made," will last forever "for God loveth it."[51] How different this is from Origen's view of matter, creation, and eschatology!

No wrath in God? Julian was confused by the revelation of a wrathless God, and she struggled against it.[52] She was well aware of the earthly judgment ("dome"[53]) pronounced on sin by the church. Recall, for instance, the burning of supposed heretics mentioned earlier. Likewise, the purpose of her *Vision* was to compel readers "to greater hatred of sinne and loving of God."[54] Human sin was, for Julian, "the sharpest scourge that any chosen soul may be smitten with."[55] Nevertheless, Christ's claim in the vision was that sin is actually "behovely."

The Middle English term *behovely* refers to something "useful, necessary, fitting, or possibly advantageous."[56] But how could sin be that? Julian is torn between two apparent contradictions: the "common teaching of the holy church" that "we deserve pain, blame, and wrath for

---

of Julian's description based on a modern forensic study of death by crucifixion. Rolf, *Explorer's Guide*, 97-98.

[49]Julian, *Revelation*, 13.3-4 (p. 169).

[50]Julian, *Revelation*, 4.8, 11 (p. 135).

[51]Julian, *Revelation*, 5.1-13 (p. 139).

[52]See Julian, *Revelation*, 13.14 (p. 169). A key line reads, "In God there *may* be no wrath," but she clearly means to say that such a thing cannot be (emphasis added).

[53]The Middle English word connects to the "doom" associated with many judgments.

[54]Julian, *Vision*, 6.39-40 (p. 75).

[55]Julian, *Revelation*, 39.1 (p. 239).

[56]This definition is that of Rolf, *Explorer's Guide*, 61.

our sins," and her visionary experience in which sin is "behovely." In the vision, she saw clearly: "Our Lord was never wroth nor never shall be. For he is God, he is good, he is truth, he is love, he is peace. And his might, his wisdom, his charity, and his unity do not permit him to be wroth. . . . God is that goodness that may not be wroth, for God is nothing but goodness."[57]

Christianity had long claimed that God does not experience the fluctuation of bodily passions (including anger) as fallen creatures do. Yet the Scriptures also speak of God's "wrath," not merely in the past but in the present and the future.[58] Julian rejects this possibility. And her view places wrath in contradiction to God's true attributes.[59] It is important, therefore, to ask how she defines such wrath.

Julian claims that wrath is "a rebelliousness and a contrariousness to peace and to love." Wrath therefore comes from a failure of strength, wisdom, or goodness.[60] If defined like this, then Julian seems safe in disavowing wrath in God. But her definition is hardly the biblical one. Even worse, it leads Julian to say that with respect to himself God "may not forgive." For what is forgiveness except the merciful setting aside of wrath? She claims that if God were wroth "even a touch," we would have "neither life, nor home, nor being."[61] Julian remains conflicted by this teaching, and its consolation comes only through a parable that she did not include in her initial *Vision*.

The parable of the Lord and his servant. In her later *Revelation*, Julian describes a scene that played out in her imagination. She saw a "lord" (or master) sitting solemnly in peace. She then saw a servant standing

---

[57]Julian, *Revelation*, 46.16, 23, 24-29 (p. 263).

[58]Tony Lane offers a helpful survey of how various theologians have critiqued the concept of divine wrath throughout the tradition. See Lane, "The Wrath of God as an Aspect of the Love of God," in *Nothing Greater, Nothing Better: Theological Essays on the Love of God*, ed. Kevin J. Vanhoozer (Grand Rapids, MI: Eerdmans, 2001), 138-67.

[59]When dealing with the relation between God's love and wrath, Jordan Wessling suggests that various theologies can be separated into "divergent" versus "unitary" accounts. In the divergent paradigm, love and wrath must be balanced against one another. In the unitary paradigm, God's wrath is simply an outflow of his love when it confronts evil. See Wessling, "How Does a Loving God Punish?: On the Unification of God's Love and Punitive Wrath," *International Journal of Systematic Theology* 19, no. 4 (2017): 421-43.

[60]Julian, *Revelation*, 48.5-7 (p. 267).

[61]Julian, *Revelation*, 49.2-14 (p. 269).

by obediently. The lord sent forth the servant, and the servant ran joyfully to do his lord's will. On leaving, however, the servant fell into a ditch and experienced "great soreness." The servant groaned and writhed in agony, but he was unable to help himself.[62] Julian then claims that the lord looked on the servant with tenderness and "double cheer," knowing that he would be rewarded more than he would have been if he had never fallen.[63] Then, with no explanation, the parable vanished from her sight.

Julian pondered this "ghostly" exemplum for some twenty years, though she did not include it in her initial *Vision* because she says she did not understand it. At first, she thought the servant must be Adam, but this identity did not fit the servant's perfect obedience.[64] Then, after years of prayer and contemplation, Julian felt that she was shown the double meaning. She was applying Origen's speculative exegesis not merely to the Scriptures but to mystical experiences.[65] The servant was both Christ and Adam. In his divinity, he was God's Son, who was "sent out" in the incarnation. Yet, in his humanity, he was Adam (or rather, all humanity), dirty and threadbare from the fall and suffering. "When Adam fell, God's Son fell. Because of the perfect union [between Christ and humanity] which was made in heaven, God's Son might not be separated from Adam, for by Adam I understood all humankind."[66]

This mystical "oncing" of Christ and Adam—that is, their union by way of the human soul—led Julian to understand how God beholds us lovingly in our sin. It explained how there could be no wrath in God toward humanity. And it explained how sin could be "behovely." For Julian, "our good lord Jesus [has] taken upon himself all our blame, and therefore our father [will not] assign any more blame to us than to his

---

[62]Julian, *Revelation*, 51 (pp. 273-77).

[63]Julian, *Revelation*, 51.47-48 (p. 275).

[64]For the servant, "only his good will and his great desire [to please his master] was the cause of his falling." Julian, *Revelation*, 51.31 (p. 275).

[65]This point is made by Robert Sweetman, "Sin Has Its Place, but All Shall Be Well: The Universalism of Hope in Julian of Norwich," in *"All Shall Be Well": Explorations in Universalism and Christian Theology, from Origen to Moltmann*, ed. Gregory MacDonald (Eugene, OR: Cascade, 2011), 72-73.

[66]Julian, *Revelation*, 51.185-87 (p. 283).

own dearworthy son, Jesus Christ."[67] Sin is indeed terrible in its own right, but it is behovely insofar as it necessitates so great a redemption and brings us to full recognition of God's goodness. In this way, Julian's view of sin mirrors somewhat the *"O felix culpa"* of the Catholic *Exsultet*: "Oh happy fault that earned for us so great, so glorious a Redeemer."[68]

Julian's understanding of this redeeming love was linked to motherhood.[69] And, like Origen, she used the metaphor of Christ as nursing his church.[70] Just as a loving mother will "give her child to suck her milk, [so] our precious mother Jesus" feeds us "most tenderly with the blessed sacrament."[71] Julian's maternal imagery was not merely eucharistic but also connected to the idea that we have nothing to fear from God. Like a frightened child, we can run to "mother Jesus" and admit our faults while knowing that we shall be welcomed.[72]

By the cross, "our gracious mother has brought us up to our father's bliss." And it was in this context that the most famous words of her vision should be understood, "'Alle shalle be wele . . . alle manner of thing shalle be wele.'"[73] In an age beset by warfare, papal schism, plague, and the burning of so-called heretics, Julian encountered a different Christ than the one depicted in segments of the church. This Lord had "one'd" himself to her in the midst of suffering, and proclaimed that it was his great joy to suffer and secure salvation for her. The vision so affected Julian that she dedicated her life to its contemplation, transmission, and communication to the pilgrims who came to her for spiritual direction. But what should we think of it?

---

[67]Julian, *Revelation*, 51.197-99 (p. 283).

[68]The logic of the *felix culpa* can be traced as far back as Ambrose and Augustine.

[69]"Mercy is a pitteful properte, which [be]longeth to moderhode in tender love." Julian, *Revelation*, 48.23–34 (p. 267).

[70]Lest this nursing image seem too strange or unorthodox, one should recall that Paul employs the motherly metaphor to speak of himself and his ministry (see 1 Cor 3:1-3). See Beverly Roberts Gaventa, *Our Mother Saint Paul* (Louisville,KY: Westminster John Knox, 2007), chap. 3.

[71]Julian, *Revelation*, 60.25-32 (p. 313).

[72]Veronica Mary Rolf supposes that Julian must have been a mother herself. Her suggestion is rooted partly in Julian's claim that heaven will allow "our motherhood in Christ" to begin anew. Rolf, *Explorer's Guide*, 148, citing Julian, *Revelation*, 63.40-42 (p. 321). Watson and Jenkins disagree, arguing in their introduction to *Writings* (4) that Julian's references to pregnancy and mothering are theological, and that she was likely a nun.

[73]Julian, *Revelation*, 63.36-40 (p. 321).

"Every shewing is full of privities"—a response to Julian. While there is no time for a full response to Julian's mystical theology, it is important to ask how she relates to the saying of perhaps between doubt and dogmatism. Julian, in fact, admits to doubt. Immediately after her revelation, she dismissed the occurrence to a nearby minister as mere madness: "I said I had raved today." The friar laughed heartily, but when Julian mentioned the bleeding crucifix, he turned serious and marveled at the miracle. Ashamed, Julian wondered how this man could take seriously her vision when she had momentarily denied it.[74]

In her *Revelation*, she insists that she believes the vision, despite the fact that such "shewings" never returned, and despite the fact that Christ left her with "neither sign nor token" to serve as proof.[75] While Saint Francis received the stigmata, and other mystics claimed to have been given relics to hold as evidence (a thorn from Christ's crown or a droplet of his blood), Julian had only the "prophecy" of "brilliant memory" to pull her forward.[76]

What of us? Should we view Julian's visions as mere ravings? One tendency when dealing with such claims may be to accept or reject them completely. Either the telling is entirely a revelation from God, or it is a sham of delusion or deception. But why must it be all one or the other?[77] The apostle Paul was open about the remaining uncertainties that accompanied his rapturous mystical experiences. "Whether it was in the body or out of the body I do not know"; the experience was "inexpressible" (2 Cor 12:2, 4). Likewise, Julian reveals that she is not entirely certain, either of the vision or of her later interpretation of it. "Every shewing," she proclaims, "is full of ['misty'] privities."[78]

One may easily poke holes in some of Julian's claims. For instance, the New Testament reveals numerous examples of divine "wrath" (*orge*)

---

[74]Julian, *Revelation*, 66.12-17 (p. 331).

[75]Julian, *Revelation*, 70.3 (p. 343).

[76]Thus the epigraph for this chapter: "So memory pulls us forward [and] prophecy is only brilliant memory." Marilynne Robinson, *Housekeeping: A Novel* (New York: Picador, 1980), 192.

[77]Some will automatically reject such claims as they rub against cessationist presuppositions. Yet this too strikes me as rather speculative given the scant support for cessationism in both Scripture and the wider Christian tradition.

[78]Julian, *Revelation*, 51.59-62 (p. 277).

directed at both sin and evildoers.[79] The book of Revelation speaks of the "wrath of the Lamb" (Rev 6:16) as a future reality. And there is no hint that sin is ever behovely. Biblically speaking, it is best to view divine wrath not as an explosion of unrighteous rage or weakness but as God's just opposition to the evil that afflicts his beloved creation. And, by this account, divine wrath should be viewed as an outflow of holy love.[80]

Sadly, this was not a God with which Julian had been familiar. She inhabited a violent period in which the church burned "heretics" for the offense of translating Scripture into a "vulgar tongue." Likewise, she was told that everything from the Great Pestilence to the death of children was the product of God's wrathful judgment. With this in mind, Julian was reaching, however imperfectly, for a God who might be found between the poles of doubt ("I raved") and dogmatism ("burn them!"). When put this way, it is hardly worth asking which account of sacred speculation (Julian's or that of those who burned Bible translators) stands in need of more revision.

If Origen's speculation came from philosophical "first principles," Julian's flowed from "first sight"—a vision of Christ upon the cross. Both were Christocentric in their own ways. And both had related tendencies with regard to divine wrath, eschatological optimism, and the near deification of the human soul.[81] In contrast with Origen, however, Julian was far more concerned with the physical world of blood and bone and hazelnuts. The fact that she was dealing with a vision also serves as a reminder that imagination is often tied to images alongside words or principles. Both Origen and Julian desired to stay true to "mother church," yet both pushed the bounds of the established orthodoxy.[82] It is behovely, therefore, that my final historical exemplar provides a counterbalance.

---

[79]For a brief sampling from the New Testament, see Mt 3:7; Lk 3:7; 21:23; Jn 3:36; Rom 2:5, 8; Eph 5:6; Col 3:6; 1 Thess 2:16.

[80]See, for instance, Lane, "Wrath of God as an Aspect of the Love of God," 138-67.

[81]While Origen appears to flirt with the re-deifying of the *logika* (which are not quite synonymous with "souls") in the eschaton, Julian sometimes seems to see the human soul as possessing an unfallen bit of "divine stuff" within us. As she writes, "In each soul that shall be saved is a godly will that never assented to sinne, nor never shall." *Revelation*, 53.9-10 (p. 293).

[82]In almost the same breath as Julian rejects the ideas of divine wrath and divine forgiveness, she proclaims that she yields herself, as a simple child, "to my mother church." *Revelation*, 46.41 (p. 263).

Jonathan Edwards

It is hard to imagine a view of God more different from Julian's than that displayed in "Sinners in the Hands of an Angry God." In the sermon, Jonathan Edwards (1703–1758) proclaimed to unconverted churchgoers that God "holds you over the pit of hell, much as one holds a spider, or some loathsome insect, over the fire." He "abhors you, and is dreadfully provoked."[83] The imagery was so terrifying that parishioners wailed for Edwards to stop, and it is unclear if he ever finished preaching the sermon.[84] Yet, the portrait of a dour Puritan belies the sense in which Edwards belongs alongside Origen and Julian as a speculative and adventuresome figure.

Locating Edwards alongside Origen and Julian. Like Origen, Edwards was a philosophical theologian of the highest caliber.[85] He read Latin, Greek, and some Hebrew by the age of twelve, despite growing up on the relative frontier of colonial New England. Like Julian, he was a mystic who experienced rapturous visions of Jesus.[86] And his love of nature makes some view him as a "colonial John Muir."[87]

Like Origen, Edwards wrote effusively, with the complete edition of his works running to seventy-three volumes online.[88] He was an exegete enthralled with Scripture in both its literal and typological sense.[89] Like

---

[83]Citations from Edwards will come from Perry Miller, gen. ed., *The Works of Jonathan Edwards* (*WJE*), 26 vols. (New Haven, CT: Yale University Press, 1957–2008). See also, The Works of Jonathan Edwards Online, 73 vols., http://edwards.yale.edu. This free database contains the full twenty-six volumes of the printed editions plus much additional material.

[84]Michael J. McClymond and Gerald R. McDermott, *The Theology of Jonathan Edwards* (Oxford: Oxford University Press, 2012), 31. Marsden cautions readers that the sermon is often misunderstood, for to be in the "hands" of the angry God is to be upheld, by his grace, from the fires of hell that our sins deserve. See George M. Marsden, *Jonathan Edwards: A Life* (New Haven, CT: Yale University Press, 2003), 222.

[85]Perry Miller, in his introduction to *WJE*, 1:viii. Bruce Kuklick notes that "the foundation stone in the history of American philosophy is Jonathan Edwards." Kuklick, "Jonathan Edwards and American Philosophy," in *Jonathan Edwards and the American Experience*, ed. Nathan O. Hatch and Harry S. Stout (New York: Oxford University Press, 1986), 246.

[86]See Marsden, *Jonathan Edwards*, 185

[87]So say McClymond and McDermott, *Theology of Jonathan Edwards*, 72.

[88]See McClymond and McDermott, *Theology of Jonathan Edwards*, 10–11.

[89]While Edwards clearly had no trouble with God's literal, retributive wrath, he took after Origen in allegorizing (or typologizing) rather freely, as when he asserted that the "great hail out of heaven" in Revelation 16 should be viewed not as literal stones but as "strong reasons and forcible arguments" provided by apologists such as himself. *WJE*, 5:114.

both Origen and Julian, he had a strong ascetic streak, which included a strict diet and a ban on Sunday humor.[90] Like Origen and Julian, Edwards's mysticism and his biblical interpretation were Christocentric since "all the beauties of the universe do immediately result from the efficiency of Christ"[91] as "emanations" of his "sweet benevolence."[92] Like Origen and Julian, he was accused of pantheistic implications,[93] and he went beyond Origen in extending his christological typologies past Scripture to nature.[94]

But in a thousand other ways, Edwards was unique. He was an English Puritan in New England, a conservative churchman, a missionary to the Mohicans in Massachusetts, and a revival preacher who used hellfire to help ignite the Great Awakening. He could be stridently dogmatic, and even used the word *dogmaticalness* to describe his propensity for ego, scorn, and criticism.[95] Still, it would be wrong to view Edwards as an angry partisan who lacked joy and deep relationships. He was enthralled by beauty. And his dying words, when his body reacted violently to a smallpox serum, were for his beloved wife. Edwards asked the physician to tell Sarah that their union was of such a "spiritual" nature that he hoped it would continue forever.[96]

God of glory and delight. My concern is with Edwards's theological imagination. A first example involves his ability to make fresh connections between previously held beliefs. In *The End for Which God Created the World*, he started with a long-accepted truth of the Reformed tradition: God does all things for the glory of his name. Yet Edwards went

---

[90]See Marsden, *Jonathan Edwards,* 107; also, McClymond and McDermott, *Theology of Jonathan Edwards*, 64.

[91]*WJE*, 13:330.

[92]*WJE*, 13:279.

[93]Most notably by Charles Hodge, *Systematic Theology* (Grand Rapids, MI: Eerdmans, 1986), 2:220. Hodge claims that Edwards's views result in "essentially pantheistic" consequences.

[94]To Edwards, the whole universe was "full of images of divine things, as full as a language is of words." *WJE*, 11:152. Despite making use of both typology and allegory in his biblical interpretation, Edwards was also critical of those who were "turning all into nothing by allegory and not having it be true of history." *WJE*, 11:151.

[95]*WJE*, 16:769.

[96]See Marsden, *Jonathan Edwards*, 494.

on to argue to his first congregation that, for God, the pursuit of glory intersects with the human longing for joy. "God created man for nothing else but happiness."[97]

Young Jonathan's creative contention was that these two ideas (God's pursuit of his own glory and his desire to delight his creatures) were "not different" since God created humanity so he might glorify himself by making humans blessed by God's goodness.[98] Centuries later, one of Edwards's popularizers would refer to this argument under the provocative label of "Christian Hedonism"—the idea that God is most glorified in us when we are most satisfied in God.[99] Rather than set these goals in opposition, Edwards united them.[100]

This may not seem like a particularly speculative move. After all, it has deep roots in both the Calvinist tradition and biblical theology. Nevertheless, it bears reminding that what is often called imagination is not so much the invention of something completely new but the making of connections between established truths that have not been adequately linked. Creativity comes by connecting dots that are already there.

This aspect of Edwards's work provides a lesson for today. In rejecting a false dichotomy between divine glory and creaturely delight, we find a praiseworthy "non-contrastive impulse."[101] Edwards refuses the false choice between God's passion for glory and the divine grace that results in the glorification of creatures. For the Creator to be God-centered is good news for fallen creatures because it is through saving sinners and renewing creation that God receives praise. In the words of Crisp and Strobel, "God being glorified does not require, necessarily, for creatures to lose glory; rather, God's glorification entails within itself the glorification of his people."[102]

---

[97] *WJE*, 14:145.

[98] *WJE*, 14:145-46.

[99] See John Piper, *Desiring God: Meditations of a Christian Hedonist* (Downers Grove, IL: InterVarsity Press, 2004).

[100] *WJE*, 8:440-41.

[101] This is the phrase used by Oliver D. Crisp and Kyle C. Strobel, *Jonathan Edwards: An Introduction to His Thought* (Grand Rapids, MI: Eerdmans, 2018), 106.

[102] Crisp and Strobel, *Jonathan Edwards*, 205.

But this is hardly the most speculative part of Edwards's theology. In his philosophical commitments, Edwards can be both daring and profoundly odd.[103] These aspects of his thought are often little known to those sporting "Edwards is my Homeboy" t-shirts. They exist in (1) his immaterialism, (2) his occasionalism, and (3) his belief in continual creation. Now to explain those high-flying terms.

Immaterialism, occasionalism, and continual creation. Strange as it sounds, Edwards did not believe in the full existence of materiality. He was an idealist who went to great lengths to distinguish himself from the materialism of Thomas Hobbes (1588–1679), who had claimed that God must be material since matter was all that existed. Edwards took the opposite approach: the world exists only as an "idea" in the divine mind; thus matter is illusory. God alone is "Being in general," and all else exists as a mere "shadow" of God's life.[104] Rather than claim that everything (including God) is made of matter, Edwards concluded that God is immaterial, and that "no matter is, in the most proper sense, matter."[105] Herein lies Edwards's radical immaterialism.[106]

Edwards largely hid this belief from his congregants. In his journal, he cautions himself on the subject, noting that "a prudent man concealeth knowledge" (Prov 12:23 KJV).[107] Yet his metaphysical speculation only gets stranger. He also affirmed a doctrine of "continual creation." This meant that God repeatedly recreates the universe from nothing each instant. It is "most agreeable to the Scripture," he claims, "to suppose creation to be performed new every moment."[108] Since God alone has true being, his assumption was that our world cannot endure across time. And since God alone causes things to be, natural things are "only occasions" (hence "occasionalism") rather than

---

[103]This fact has caused two Edwards scholars to refer to him as a "deviant" and "exotic" Calvinist. See Oliver D. Crisp, *Deviant Calvinism: Broadening Reformed Theology* (Minneapolis: Fortress, 2014); also, Crisp and Strobel, *Jonathan Edwards*, 106.

[104]See *WJE*, 6:206.

[105]*WJE*, 6:235.

[106]See McClymond and McDermott, *Theology of Jonathan Edwards*, 107, 165. "Immaterial antirealism" is the label given by Crisp and Strobel, *Jonathan Edwards*, 72.

[107]"Diary," January 10, 1724; cited in Marsden, *Jonathan Edwards*, 80.

[108]*WJE*, 14:418; cf. 6:241.

"proper causes."[109] At each moment, the universe passes out of existence, only to be replaced by a slightly different version in God's mind a moment later.[110]

The analogy of a flipbook helps explain occasionalism.[111] On each page, suppose an artist (God) draws a slightly altered stick figure. The artist then turns the pages to produce the illusion of a person dancing on the page across a span of seconds. In actuality, each page contains a completely different entity, drawn from scratch.[112] The figure's movement and its sustained existence across a time are only appearances.

These aspects of Edwards's theology dovetail with his strong view of divine sovereignty. "God is the sole causal agent of all that comes to pass."[113] Freedom of the will (in God and humans) is not therefore the ability to act otherwise but the ability to act on the basis of one's strongest desires.[114] Since human desires are irrevocably evil after the fall, salvation comes only by God's all-determining sovereignty and grace. From beginning to end, these aspects of Edwards's speculation are rooted in the sovereignty of God.

Learning from Edwards on sacred speculation. It is hard to find anything in Scripture that implies that God recreates an illusory and immaterial world each moment.[115] Nonetheless, Edwards professed certainty: "'Tis certain with me that . . . the existence of things every moment ceases and is every moment renewed."[116] On the subject of God as "being" itself, he was heir to a long history that flowed backward through Christian theology, Greek philosophy, and the "I

---

[109] *WJE*, 18:157.

[110] See also *WJE*, 3:402.

[111] This explanation is also used by Crisp and Strobel, *Jonathan Edwards*, 207.

[112] My analogy breaks down since the flipbook exists prior to the drawing whereas Edwards's doctrine of continual creation is ex nihilo in each successive instant.

[113] Crisp and Strobel, *Jonathan Edwards*, 119.

[114] Herein lies Edwards's famous account of "compatibilism" (the notion that divine determinism and human freedom coexist); see Edwards, *Freedom of the Will*, in *WJE*, 1:135-63.

[115] Biblical support for this view was sought (however unadvisedly) in Isaiah: "I am the Lord, . . . there is none beside me" (45:5-6 KJV). Although Edwards's claim that "God is, and there is none else" sounds blatantly pantheistic (*WJE*, 6:345), McClymond and McDermott (*Theology of Jonathan Edwards*, 106) argue that he was attempting to connect his view to Scripture.

[116] *WJE*, 13:288.

AM" statements of Scripture (e.g., Ex 3:14).[117] Yet these were hardly his only influences.

A deeper motive for these speculative conclusions exists in a phenomenon that will show up again in this book: apologetics as the father of (near) heresy. Like Origen (and perhaps Julian), Edwards's strangest claims seem driven by well-intentioned attempts to ward off perceived threats. Across the span of his life—or, from one "occasion" to another—he strove to distance Christianity from what he saw to be a trio of errors: (1) deism, (2) materialism, and (3) "Arminianism."[118] Yet, at each point, Edwards's knee-jerk reactions produced new dangers.

Against Hobbes and the materialists, he sided with the breadth of classical theism in arguing for the immateriality of God as a perfect being who is utterly "simple" (not composed of parts) and outside time. Yet the apologetic move caused Edwards to go much further than Origen in denying materiality, not only "in the beginning" or the "end" but ever! Against deists who believed that God had set creation moving and walked away, Edwards located the whole of creation within God. Yet in overcoming the detachment of the deist God, he embraced a form of panentheism (the belief that all things exist within God, though God's being is not exhausted by creation). For Edwards, the world exists as an idea in God's mind,[119] and God is the "space" that we inhabit.[120]

Finally, against so-called Arminians, Edwards embraced an extreme account of divine sovereignty that was so severe that it appears to make God the author of evil. A recent introduction to his thought therefore concludes that "the cost of Edwards's vision of God is that human agency appears to be a very meagre thing indeed, and God appears to be morally responsible for sin."[121] Thomas McCall goes further, saying

---

[117]For a critical account of this history, see Stanley J. Grenz, *The Named God and the Question of Being: A Trinitarian Theo-Ontology* (Louisville, KY: Westminster John Knox, 2005), chaps. 1–2.

[118]Edwards used the label "Arminian" to describe a variety of non-Calvinist beliefs, none of which were technically identical to the theology of James Arminius (1560–1609).

[119]While Hodge accused Edwards of pantheistic tendencies, Crisp and Strobel (*Jonathan Edwards*, 100, 103-5) argue that panentheism is a more accurate description of Edwards's view of God and creation.

[120]*WJE*, 3:304; the claim that "space is God" comes from *WJE*, 6:339-40.

[121]Crisp and Strobel, *Jonathan Edwards*, 120.

that Edwardsean occasionalism means that no human actually endures long enough to do anything. "Thus God—indeed, only God—is the cause of the first sin, and of all subsequent sins as well."[122] This is, to put it mildly, a problem.

In these areas of sacred speculation (immaterialism, occasionalism, an all-determining divine sovereignty), Edwards lacks an appreciation for the particularity of material creation as something that stands distinct and yet related to God by virtue of the Son and Spirit.[123] Despite God-glorifying motives, the result is like trying to praise an artist by denying that her painting exists. As with Origen and Julian, the outcomes of the Edwardsean imagination are mixed. He provides not just examples of how and why theologians say perhaps but also lessons to be learned before we venture into blank spaces ourselves.

Conclusion

This chapter has sought to understand both the possibilities and the pitfalls of saying perhaps by looking to a trio of representatives: Origen, Julian, and Edwards. The results of these imaginative theologies were mixed, and the driving forces were diverse: whether a particular system of philosophy (Origen), a flash of spiritual experience (Julian), or an amalgamation of factors as seen in Edwards's forays into immaterialism, occasionalism, and continual creation. Since no one says perhaps in a vacuum, we would do well to ponder our influences. For every *Aqedah* there is an Ishmael. And in the heat of the moment, it is not always easy to determine which prompting "voice" is that of God (Gen 16:2).

None of this means, however, that one should denounce the saying of perhaps in life or in theology (as if we could). Like Abraham upon Moriah, fidelity to God sometimes requires faith seeking imagination, even when the stakes are high. Even imperfect utterances of perhaps can

---

[122]Thomas H. McCall, *Against God and Nature: The Doctrine of Sin* (Wheaton, IL: Crossway, 2019), 190-91.

[123]For a treatment of this kind of particularity, see Colin E. Gunton, *The One, the Three and the Many: God, Creation and the Culture of Modernity*, 1992 Bampton Lectures (Cambridge: Cambridge University Press, 1993), chaps. 6-7; likewise, Gunton, *The Triune Creator: A Historical and Systematic Study* (Grand Rapids, MI: Eerdmans, 1998).

be worked together for good, whether that involves a musing about an eternally generated creation that inspires Nicene trinitarianism, a courageous writing of visionary experience, or a connection of dots between God's glory-seeking purpose and the pursuit of human happiness. Once again, as Genesis reminds us, Ishmael too receives a blessing.

Both positive and negative examples provide reasons to look back at history before looking forward to our own time, beset by different forms of doubt and dogmatism. "What has been will be again," proclaims the teacher (Eccles 1:9). Ideas cry out from the ground to instruct us, and brilliant memory pulls us forward.

3

Guardrails on Moriah

How (Not) to Say Perhaps

Are you carrying the fire?

CORMAC MCCARTHY, *THE ROAD*

IT'S TIME TO MOVE TO APPLICATION. Having surveyed some examples of sacred speculation in both Scripture and tradition, the task now is to cobble together some tentative barriers to theological oversteering when we exercise a hopeful imagination. How do we say perhaps in faithful ways while avoiding crippling doubt and arrogant dogmatism?

Every mountain roadway needs some guardrails. On sharp curves especially, these devices offer a measure of protection to travelers, even if it is still possible to go careening off a cliff. My aim is to set forth some tentative "commandments" (ten seems fitting) to prevent sacred speculation from going awry. My goal with these guardrails is not to create a comprehensive guide to speculative theology but to highlight a few basic principles to aid the journey. After all, one would hate to fall off a precipice on Mount Moriah while carrying up the fire.

My incandescent metaphor ("carrying the fire") comes not only from the *Aqedah* (Gen 22:6) but from a work of fiction: Cormac McCarthy's postapocalyptic novel, *The Road*. Despite McCarthy's status as an atheistic guide ("There is no God and we are his prophets"),[1] *The Road* is a tale of fathers and sons, mountains and fire, sacrifice and post-Pangaea "maps and mazes."[2] I will return to the story periodically in this chapter, not just for artistic flavor but as a way of bridging the gap between Moriah and the "roads" we take today. Throughout the rest of the book, I will move increasingly to show how inspired works of fiction can ignite the Christian imagination when read with eyes of faith. But for now, some guardrails for the road ahead.

1. Be Clear About the Unclear

A first guide to sacred speculation is the need to be crystal clear about the unclear.[3] Theologians from Origen to Edwards demonstrated the temptation to claim certainty for perhapses in a way that sometimes damaged credibility and outstripped supporting evidence. "'Tis certain with me," claimed Edwards on continuous creation,[4] despite that fact that the position has little backing in Scripture or tradition. In times of polarization, this temptation grows more insistent; yet it is always present in the human psyche.

There is a need to reclaim theological modesty as something that requires neither a surrender to the lazy demons of "Who knows!?" nor a slide toward the false certainty that is used to cover fears that we are losing an argument, or that the discussion is more complex than we would like to admit. Feigned certitude can be a form of dogmatism. Hence, to say perhaps in honest and careful ways means making the decision to leave some spaces—if not blank—then at least not colored in with permanent ink. Be clear about the unclear.

2. Mean Your Maybes

On the opposite side of the roadway, it is important to "mean your maybes" since some versions of "What if?" are disingenuous. This

---

[1]Cormac McCarthy, *The Road* (New York: Vintage, 2006), 170.
[2]McCarthy, *Road*, 286-87.
[3]I first heard this point in a lecture by theologian Sarah Coakley.
[4]*WJE*, 13:288.

happens when one wants to avoid the repercussions of a conclusion by sheltering under the umbrella of "Hey, I'm just asking questions!" In these moments, one should remember a lesson that we learn from Eden's serpent: not all questions are benign.

Perhaps should not be used as a mere hedge against critique. To cite one example, it is possible to discern a dishonest *maybe* in the work of Origen (or at least his sympathetic translator). At points, he seems to have reached a clear conclusion on a given topic—say, divine wrath or universal salvation—only to profess a "great fear and caution" while repeatedly clarifying that he is merely "discussing and investigating rather than laying down fixed and certain conclusions."[5] In some cases, this may well be true (see guardrail #1), but in other moments the reader suspects that Origen is seeking shelter under a false maybe.

3. Consider Thy Source

A third guardrail to errant speculation is the need to consider the extrabiblical sources of our supposals. No one says perhaps in a vacuum. Thus, Christians must consider the unstated presuppositions that may be driving our theological proposals.

When we evaluate the work of others, these sources can seem obvious. We pronounce confidently that Origen was guided by Platonic presuppositions, Anselm was working with a feudal view of wounded honor, and Barth's reading of natural theology was conditioned by the Nazism of his day. We are adept at deconstructing the ancestry of other people's ideas, but we can maintain a striking ignorance of our own influences. In the words of Wittgenstein, "Nothing is so difficult as not deceiving yourself."[6] Thoughtful Christians must develop a self-critical attitude that is willing to consider a variety of sources that may be driving our perhapses.

Unstated drivers for belief go far beyond the academic books that line one's shelf. The influence of parents, upbringing, nationality, race, health,

---

[5]Origen, *On First Principles*, 1.6.1.
[6]Ludwig Wittgenstein, *Culture and Value*, ed. Georg Henrik von Wright, rev. ed. (London: Wiley-Blackwell, 1998), 39.

wealth, politics, age, and geography must be considered. The death of a baby sister in one's youth, the church tradition that fired a beloved professor, the divorce, the disability. These factors shape us as sources alongside Scripture, tradition, and rational analysis.

To recognize these drivers is not necessarily to fall victim to the genetic fallacy: the false notion that to have discovered a prior source for a position is to have disproven it. Nor should it be equated with a flippant "nothing but-ism" that reduces all opinions to an algebraic outflow of demographics, genetic heritage, or party politics. Our shared humanity and the image of God can provide a counterbalance to this brand of identity politics, with the obvious caveat that our backgrounds surely shape us in important ways. There is no view from nowhere, and for this reason, we should be open to acknowledging the underlying sources of our speculative suggestions. Consider thy source.

4. Beware the "Heresy" of Apologetics

A key theme in the last chapter was the extent to which apologetic moves can spawn unintended consequences. For Origen, his rebuttal to Gnostic smears about the Old Testament and the unfairness of differing lots in life led to the adoption of some quasi-Gnostic conclusions. Likewise, Jonathan Edwards's attempt to ward off deism, materialism, and a loosely defined Arminianism led to a panentheistic denial of material existence, and a God who (seemingly) authored evil. The warning is clear: though heresy is often called the mother of orthodoxy, apologetics sometimes fathers further errors by responding in a flailing fashion to opponents.[7]

This does not mean that apologetic concerns have no place. A preemptive safeguard (although not a foolproof one) is to ask, What unintended problem might I be fostering by an effort to refute error? How might my attempted correction be an overcorrection that sends people careening toward the ditch? Could this rebuttal to postmodern

---

[7]This is not to say that apologetics is unnecessary, or that the discipline must always take the form of gladiatorial combat. For an alternative vision, see Justin Ariel Bailey, *Reimagining Apologetics: The Beauty of Faith in a Secular Age* (Downers Grove, IL: IVP Academic, 2020).

relativism and leftist identity politics mask the extent to which I too have been taken captive by a truth-decaying propaganda? Could my concern to avoid anti-intellectual fundamentalism lead to conclusions that fly in the face of Scripture and orthodox tradition? The list of possibilities goes on and on.

One way to avoid the consequences of apologetic overreach is to consider not only ideas and beliefs but resulting practices as well. The Christian imagination differs from other intellectual programs in its commitment to practice over mere analysis. To channel Karl Marx, "The philosophers have only *interpreted* the world; the point, however, is to *change* it."[8] Unfortunately, as the cruel history of Marxism demonstrates, attempts to change the world can lead to calamity, since they often proceed with a stunning ignorance of our ability to make things worse.

Nonetheless, true doctrine demands to be lived. Theology, to cite Kevin J. Vanhoozer, "takes not a village but a body: the church."[9] The point of theological imagination should be embodied worship, not just knowledge or interpretation. Demons acknowledge Jesus as Lord, but they do not "confess" and follow him with joy.[10] A further guardrail to unbridled speculation is therefore the reminder that the true test of a theology is how it plays out in the field of worship and obedience. What kind of praxes does it foster?

Of course, not all unintended consequences can be avoided. To live in a web of post-Babel relationships—as we all do—is to risk both misunderstanding and a certain "butterfly effect" by walking down the street. In the words of E. M. Forster, "There's never any knowing . . . which of our actions, which of our idlenesses won't have things hanging on it forever."[11] This realization can lead to anxiety. But lest we take Forster's words too pessimistically, the gospel interjects that even Roman crosses

---

[8]Karl Marx, "Thesis 11," in *Theses on Feuerbach*; cited in Karl Marx with Friedrich Engels, *The German Ideology* (Amherst, NY: Prometheus Books, 1998), 571 (emphasis original).

[9]Kevin J. Vanhoozer, "Analytics, Poetics, and the Mission of Dogmatic Discourse," in *The Task of Dogmatics: Explorations in Theological Method*, ed. Oliver D. Crisp and Fred Sanders (Grand Rapids, MI: Zondervan, 2017), 46.

[10]See Mt 8:28-29; Mk 1:23-24; 5:2-7; Jas 2:18-19; also, Vanhoozer, "Analytics, Poetics," 45.

[11]E. M. Forster, *A Room with a View / Where Angels Fear to Tread* (New York: Knopf, 2011), 347.

may have things hanging on them in a way that conditions eternity itself. Beware *haeresis apologetica* (the "heresy of apologetics"). But don't let this warning cow you into silence.

5. Don't Go Alone

A justifiable critique of speculative theology is its willingness to cast off centuries of wisdom in order to go it alone. For instance, one might criticize Julian of Norwich for implicitly elevating her vision over the judgment handed down in church tradition. The speculative claim to have heard a voice that proclaims some strange, new truth is rightly seen as dubious. Yet we must remember that people do hear voices in the Scripture, including Abraham on Mount Moriah.

Even on Moriah, however, one needs traveling companions. In the *Aqedah*, these come not just in Isaac and the servants, but in the angelic presence that provides a guardrail to Abraham's obedient faith. Loneliness is the first "not good" in God's creation (Gen 2:18), and after the fall that reality becomes more acute. In the wasteland of *The Road*, Cormac McCarthy highlights our universal human need for company: "The one thing I can tell is that you won't survive for yourself," proclaims a weary traveler. "A person who had no one would be well advised to cobble together some passable ghost. Breathe it into being and coax it along with words of love."[12]

Christian theology has little need for ghosts. Across centuries, our dead cry out from the ground and from their writings. "By faith," not only Abel but Augustine and Aquinas speak, though dead (Heb 11:4). To hear these voices, however, we must cultivate a temporal bandwidth that reads dispatches from the past in a culture pathologically obsessed with the present.[13] Today the rush of "hot takes" and "Twitter journalism" threaten to drown out anything that happened more than five minutes ago. So while the book of Judges speaks of a forgetfulness between generations (Judg 2:10), we face the possibility of forgetting what was dubbed

---

[12]McCarthy, *Road*, 57.

[13]See Alan Jacobs, *Breaking Bread with the Dead: A Reader's Guide to a More Tranquil Mind* (New York: Penguin, 2020), 10-13.

outrageous just last week. Going together requires cultivating not just community in a generic sense but community of a kind that spans centuries, cultures, and continents. Make friends with "passable ghosts."

Of course, you need some living friends as well. A. J. Swoboda highlights the importance of community for those trying to maintain Christian faith through seasons of doubt and deconstruction. He draws on the passage in Matthew's Gospel when Jesus sees the faith of a paralyzed man's *friends* and then says to the man, "your sins are forgiven" before healing him (Mt 9:2). Swoboda's claim is that "we all need a group around us [that] believes for us when we struggle to believe on our own."[14]

In the academy, not going alone involves listening to other disciplines in an age of silos. What might I, a theologian, have to learn from my colleagues in biblical studies, philosophy, psychology, science, or history? Expanding spatial bandwidth means listening to other traditions too. It requires being enmeshed in a local church rather than sequestered in an ivory tower. And it will mean saying no to a version of church that is a Sunday morning simulacrum—a drive-thru lane of big-box-style, anonymous, consumer Christianity.

On this subject, Russell Moore laments:

> One of my former students, who came to Christ after years in a street gang, tells me he is happy to give up the violence and the drugs but says he misses every day the community and the sense of belonging that came with his gang membership. I've heard much the same from those who have come to Christ out of everything from the pornography industry to the Ku Klux Klan. They do not, for a minute, look longingly back at their former sin, but they have found no comparable sense of camaraderie, of belonging, of family.[15]

To not go alone in one's theological imagination means reclaiming a life that clashes with the ethos of suburbia. *The garage door goes up; the garage door goes down. "And there was evening, and there was*

---

[14]A. J. Swoboda, *After Doubt: How to Question Your Faith without Losing It* (Grand Rapids, MI: Brazos, 2021), 89.

[15]Russell Moore, *The Storm-Tossed Family: How the Cross Reshapes the Home* (Nashville: B&H, 2018), 59-60.

morning—[every] day" (Gen 1). It may mean seeking out a spiritual director or designated confessor so that one can be honest about the wrestling match between the poles of doubt and dogmatism. And not going alone will mean reclaiming prayer.

Katherine Sonderegger claims that the proper posture of all great theology is "the intellect, bent down, glorified, in prayer."[16] Across the centuries, some of the most interesting and imaginative bits of Christian theology have come not as the results of lonely, trailblazing geniuses but as answers to prayer.

Consider Anselm. While I have never found his ontological argument convincing as a proof of God's existence, I find it fascinating that this bit of speculative theology comes as an answer to prayer. Unlike the *Monologium*, the *Proslogium* is a supplication. In the first chapter, Anselm confesses his inadequacy, and he invites God's helping presence:

> I do not endeavor, O Lord, to penetrate thy sublimity, for in no wise do I compare my understanding with that; but I long to understand in some degree thy truth, which my heart believes and loves. For I do not seek to understand that I may believe, but I believe in order to understand [*credo ut intelligam*]. For this also I believe—that unless I believed, I should not understand.[17]

One way we refuse to go alone in the cultivation of a theological imagination is by welcoming the presence of "another Helper": God's Spirit within us (see Jn 14:16 NKJV).

Or consider Augustine. Part of the power of the *Confessions* is that some of the more imaginative bits (i.e., its speculative aspects) are seen as coming not from the receptacle of Augustine's quite-obvious genius, but as divine responses to prayer. In book eleven, the author asks after the nature of time itself. What is time's essence, given that the future ceaselessly funnels into the past through an indefinable present? In the face of this enigma, Augustine takes his ignorance to God, and then

---

[16]Katherine Sonderegger, *Systematic Theology*, vol. 1, *The Doctrine of God* (Minneapolis: Fortress, 2015), xxi.

[17]Anselm of Canterbury, *Proslogion, with the Replies of Gaunilo and Anselm*, trans. Thomas Williams (Indianapolis: Hackett, 1995/2001), chap. 1.

moves to cautious speculation. "*Perhaps* what I do not know is how to articulate what I do know."[18] Augustine then proceeds to beg: "Do not shut the door, Lord my God. . . . I beg you, do not shut the door on my longing to understand these things which are both familiar and obscure." He arrives at an imaginative conclusion: In his view, time is merely a "*distention animi*"—a distension or distortion in the human mind.[19]

Even prayerful perhapsing carries risks. With wrong motives, it could fall afoul of Christ's command about long litanies uttered for a human audience (Mt 6:5-6). And since the answer is seen as coming from God, there is the possibility of both mishearing and manipulation (e.g., "God told me to marry you"; or in the case of cult leaders like David Koresh, "God told me to marry lots of you"). I highlight Augustine, therefore, as both a model and a cautionary tale.[20]

Prayerful theology is essential to the Christian life, but prayer is not a panacea. We need other guardrails to fallenness and self-deception, and we need them stacked on top of one another. Like the successive strata of metal and concrete that line our real-life roadways, we need more than one level of protection in our use of the imagination. That brings me to the next commandment.

6. Embrace Voluntary Submission

Submission is a dirty word in many circles, especially since it has been abused. But that does not change the fact that all Christians are called to voluntary submission. "Submit to one another out of reverence for Christ," proclaims Ephesians 5:21. And this goes for the imagination too. When wrestling in the arena between doubt and dogmatism, we need points of voluntary submission.

---

[18]Augustine, *Confessions*, 11.25. This translation is that of Henry Chadwick (New York: Oxford University Press, 1998), 239 (emphasis added).

[19]Augustine, *Confessions*, 11.27.

[20]I have argued elsewhere that Augustine's solution to the conundrum about time seems to have come more directly from Plotinus (the neo-Platonic philosopher) than from God. And in some cases, Augustine's conclusions rub against a robust doctrine of temporal being and goodness. See Joshua McNall, *A Free Corrector: Colin Gunton and the Legacy of Augustine* (Minneapolis: Fortress, 2015), 110-12.

Personally, I submit to the inspiration and authority of Scripture. I do not always understand the Bible, nor do I always like it. But I live under its authority. My biblical submission should not be synonymized, however, with a rigid fundamentalism. It is not an ultra-Protestant biblicism that discounts tradition, context, community, reason, and continued guidance by the Spirit. Submission to Scripture means that when I encounter something in the Bible that I find distasteful, I will not simply conclude that my opinion is correct and Scripture is wicked, backward, or erroneous. It is an attempt to recognize both my limitations and my fallenness.

My second point of voluntary submission involves a decision to think within the great, strange swath of Christian orthodoxy. As a Protestant, I adopt this commitment secondarily to Scripture though the two are related. The bloody aftermath to the Reformation, seen most notably in the Thirty Years' War, made clear that one needs more than an individual brain and a vernacular Bible to produce fruitful theology. Thus, just as I distrust my opinions against Scripture, so also I must question the sovereign rightness of my individual interpretations of Scripture.

Not going alone (guardrail #5) and voluntary submission (guardrail #6) come together in a layering effect. To swim in a sea called Christian orthodoxy is to pray and think and wrestle within a community that names the triune God and pledges allegiance to the Jesus who is fully human and divine. This orthodoxy should be both gracious and capacious. It is not bounded by the sharp fence lines of particular denominations or a given political platform. Nor should the boundaries of orthodoxy be ceded to graceless border agents (heresy hunters) who self-deputize on the internet. If this happens, voluntary submission morphs into dour dogmatism—and abuse.

7. Am I Merely Arguing to Win?

In polarized times, another guardrail (especially on social media) is to ask repeatedly, Am I merely arguing to win? Am I seeking truth, or am I trying to signal my superiority or virtue? Am I trying to point others toward a grace-and-truth-filled Christ, or am I concerned chiefly with defeating them by way of argument?[21]

In *How to Think*, Alan Jacobs highlights the need to move away from the argument-as-war approach to difficult subjects. Jacobs tells the story of the Yale Political Union, a debate society with unusual priorities. Whereas most debates are focused on crowning a winner, the Yale Political Union did not keep score. Instead, they counted converts. The value, however, was not just in converting another person but in being converted: being "broken on the floor." This metaphor refers to the priority placed on a willingness to change one's own mind even in the midst of making an argument. If someone asked you, "Have you ever broken on the floor?" writes Jacobs, the correct answer was yes.[22] The goal was not to win the argument at all costs but to grow toward truth. So too in theology and the Christian life. To wrestle the angel is to commit oneself to what Tolkien called "the long defeat"[23]—and, in losing, to receive a blessing that may look to others like a shameful limp.

To starve the hunger that is arguing to win, one must openly acknowledge weak points in one's own proposals. In all fields, but in theology especially, belief is partly based on presuppositions that cannot be proven. To quote John Webster, theology proper "is oriented chiefly to invisible things, 'things that are unseen'" (2 Cor 4:18).[24] This does not mean, of course, that Christian thought is baseless. It grows in the soil of God's word and is nourished by the blood and bone of tradition. But it is not the same as doing arithmetic. And when venturing into the sacred space of perhaps, a willingness to admit weak points is important.

---

[21]See Richard Hughes Gibson and James Edward Beitler, *Charitable Writing: Cultivating Virtue Through Our Words* (Downers Grove, IL: IVP Academic, 2020).

[22]Alan Jacobs, *How to Think: A Survival Guide for a World at Odds* (New York: Currency, 2017), 52-53. Jacobs draws on the story of Leah Libresco (now Leah Libresco Sargeant) in her interview with *America* magazine. Sean Salai, "My Journey from Atheist to Catholic: 11 Questions for Leah Libresco," *America*, January 14, 2015, http://americamagazine.org/content/all-things /my-journey-atheist-catholic-11-questions-leah-libresco.

[23]J. R. R. Tolkien, *The Fellowship of the Ring*, book 2, chap. 7: "The Mirror of Galadriel." See Tolkien, *The Lord of the Rings*, ed. Wayne G. Hammond and Christina Scull, 50th anniversary, one-volume edition (Boston: Houghton Mifflin, 2004), 357.

[24]John Webster, *God Without Measure: Working Papers in Christian Theology* (London: Bloomsbury T&T Clark, 2016), 1:6.

We live in a cultural moment that heralds the death of expertise.[25] With social media and alternative news sources, almost anyone can assume the mantle of a public intellectual. And because of a widespread sense that the academy and "the establishment" have sometimes abused their power (and funding!), distrusting experts gains traction. This is not all bad. Jesus commissioned apostles not geniuses.[26] And Paul asked openly, "Where is the wise person? Where is the teacher of the law? Where is the philosopher of this age? Has not God made foolish the wisdom of the world?" (1 Cor 1:20).

But Paul's statement does not imply that expertise is useless. (A quick survey of his letters will reveal its utility.) One negative repercussion of a shift away from credentialed expertise is that we have turned to "authorities" more on the basis of their Twitter following than their training. The result is a widespread failure to acknowledge when we are propounding on subjects that we know nothing about. Nowhere was this more apparent than during the Covid-19 pandemic, when it seemed that virtually every voice on the internet suddenly became an authority in medicine and public policy. A better way would be to admit when one is speaking out of one's depth, to admit (up front) potential weak points in one's argument, and to forgo merely arguing to win.

8. Seek Noncontrastive Connections

Another way to avoid a strident dogmatism is to seek noncontrastive solutions. I touched on this terminology earlier, when dealing with the "non-contrastive impulse" in Jonathan Edwards.[27] The virtue came to the fore when he connected two well-established ideas: God's desire for glory and the universal human desire for happiness. Rather than pit these two ends against each other, Edwards united them: God is maximally

---

[25]See Tom Nichols, *The Death of Expertise: The Campaign Against Established Knowledge and Why It Matters* (Oxford: Oxford University Press, 2017).

[26]See Søren Kierkegaard, "On the Difference Between a Genius and an Apostle," in *The Book on Adler*, ed. and trans. Howard V. Hong and Edna H. Hong (Princeton: Princeton University Press, 2009).

[27]See Oliver D. Crisp and Kyle C. Strobel, *Jonathan Edwards: An Introduction to His Thought* (Grand Rapids, MI: Eerdmans, 2018), 106. For a prior emphasis on noncontrastive theological solutions, see the work of Kathryn Tanner, *Christ the Key* (Cambridge: Cambridge University Press, 2010).

glorified when his creatures are maximally satisfied in him. This saying of perhaps was not the invention of some new doctrine but the linkage of two previously existing points.

Yet the connection between established points requires some creative vision. The noncontrastive impulse is an ability to see two points in relation and to say, *What if these two values or ideas are not necessarily at odds?* Imagination is the faculty by which we put things together. And in an age of polarizing doubt and dogmatism, noncontrastive connections are especially needed.

9. Don't Rush the Mystery Card

Every Christian must eventually lay down the mystery card. This constitutes an admission that there are things about God, the world, and ourselves that are beyond us. And on these matters, we have a duty to recall the first guardrail: be clear about the unclear. Yet a problem with the mystery card is that it can be rushed to excuse laziness or contradiction.

Dietrich Bonhoeffer hits upon this danger when describing the conclusion of Goethe's *Faust* after a lifetime of seeking knowledge ("I see that we can know nothing!"). Bonhoeffer remarks that "it is something entirely different . . . when a student repeats this statement in the first semester to justify . . . laziness" than when it is spoken at the end of a life of patient, honest inquiry. "Used as a conclusion, the sentence is true; as a presupposition, it is self-deception."[28] Bonhoeffer's point is that the preemptive IDK ("I don't know") can be a way of avoiding the hard work of thinking, seeking, and acting in obedience.

Mystery should also be distinguished from contradiction. Some positions stand in irreconcilable opposition. Thus, to seek noncontrastive solutions is not to become a flippant "both-ander" (as in, "It's not either-or; it's both-and!").[29] It is crucial to distinguish paradox from poor logic. This point is even more important when emphasizing things like imagination and the rejection of crippling doubt and dour dogmatism. To do

---

[28]Dietrich Bonhoeffer, *Discipleship*, ed. Geffrey B. Kelly and John D. Godsey, trans. Barbara Green and Reinhard Krauss, Dietrich Bonhoeffer Works 4 (Minneapolis: Fortress, 2001), 51.

[29]I borrow the "both-ander" label from Jacobs, *How to Think*, 100.

so could push one into the emotive realm of woo-woo mysticism in an attempt to build a bridge between different landmasses.

In the words of Thomas McCall, "'Mystery' must not be confused with logical incoherence." Nor should we "glorify what is clearly incoherent with the shroud of 'mystery.'"[30] Theology, and speculative ideas specifically, should be bounded not only by Scripture and orthodoxy but also by certain logical commitments like the law of noncontradiction. Coherence matters in theological proposals, even as we strive for clarity and precision.[31] Thus we should not rush appeals to mystery as a cloak for contradictions.

10. Ask a Better Question

One way to bring both clarity and precision to theology is by asking better questions. Jesus modeled this approach better than anyone. In some cases, Christ's questions may seem like mere evasion: "John's baptism—where did it come from?" (Mt 21:25). But his purpose is more likely a refusal to be pigeonholed into the false factions of his day. Christ frequently reminds us that we cannot arrive at the correct answer by asking the wrong question. What does the color blue smell like? Which is better, doubt or dogmatism? "Who sinned, this man or his parents?" (Jn 9:2).

Questions have been encoded in the Jewish tradition through the centuries, and this encoding continues today. The Nobel laureate in physics Isidor I. Rabi was once asked what led him to a career in science. "My mother made me a scientist without ever intending it," Rabi pronounced. "Every other Jewish mother in Brooklyn would ask her child after school: 'So? Did you learn anything today?' But not my mother. She always asked me a different question. 'Izzy,' she would say, 'did you ask a good question today?'"[32] In theology too, the

---

[30]Thomas H. McCall, *An Invitation to Analytic Christian Theology* (Downers Grove, IL: InterVarsity Press, 2015), 19.

[31]See again McCall, *Invitation*, 17-19, for the role that analytic theology can play in this endeavor.

[32]These words of Isidore I. Rabi are quoted by Donald Sheff in a letter to the editor in the *New York Times*, January 19, 1988, www.nytimes.com/1988/01/19/opinion/l-izzy-did-you-ask-a-good -question-today-712388.html.

difference between a question and the right question is crucial. Great questions provide boundaries for our perhapses, like guardrails on a mountain roadway.

Conclusion

At the outset of this book, I set forth Abraham as our biblical exemplar of faithful speculation. By faith, he marched up Mount Moriah "carrying the fire" for God's sacrifice (Gen 22:6). By faith he "considered" that God could even raise the dead (Heb 11:17-19 ESV). And so, by faith, he said perhaps. Yet how do we know that someone (including ourselves) is "carrying the fire" on behalf of God rather than marching Jephthah-like in the wrong direction?

More than once in this chapter, I have referenced the phrase "carrying the fire" in Cormac McCarthy's novel *The Road*. In the story, a boy and his father walk like Abraham and Isaac through an ashy wilderness with death on every side. The reader is never told what caused this annihilation. A nuclear blast? A natural disaster? McCarthy knows the monster is scarier if you don't see it. The focus is on the boy and his father as they walk toward the coast.

In *The Road*—as on Moriah—there is no foolproof, external way to tell whether one is carrying the fire of abiding goodness or simply walking to one's tragic demise. No guardrail can make the road of life completely safe. Nor can any set of rules fully establish how to do the work of sacred imagination. Yet, that doesn't diminish the importance of establishing some basic helps for the saying of perhaps along the way.

Surprisingly, the atheist McCarthy ends his Pulitzer Prize–winning work with talk of God that is simultaneously talk of fathers and sons, mountains and fire, sacrifice and post-Pangaea "maps and mazes." In his epilogue, these broken continents—like the brook trout that once swam in the streams—will "not be put back together. Not be made right again." Yet, even in the lamentation, there is a subtle whisper of perhaps. The boy is taken in, and a surrogate mother tells him "the breath of God" is still moving over the waters, "though it pass from man to man through all time." Hence, the novel's final words speak to a (possibly) still-enchanted world that has long "hummed of mystery."[33] The message is clear: keep walking.

BETWEEN TRENCHES

Latitude: 50° 01′ 23.28″ N
Longitude: 2° 45′ 8.99″ E

THE SOMME

Spring semester. Freshman year.

"I found a water bottle full of rum and drank about half a pint."

Eliza was startled awake by words she'd never expected from a gray-haired history professor at a teetotalling Christian college. The professor, it turns out, was not confessing. He was reading from a book by Robert Graves. The memoir, *Good-bye to All That*, covered Graves's time in World War I. Still, Eliza's internal narrator responded in the pirate accent of Jack Sparrow. *"Why is the rum gone!?"*

She had worked late the night before and hadn't gotten to bed till after midnight. But on the upside, she had slept better. The old nightmare of the ocean and the boat had mostly ceased by spring semester. That meant no more waking with the quilt clutched tightly in her fingers. And no fear that the "sea" would swamp her bed and soak her socks. But the memory was still vivid. She was quoting *Pirates of the Caribbean* after all.

Her roommate's boyfriend, Clay, sat two rows over. He didn't seem to be listening either. Clay had a square-shaped head that reminded Eliza of the mini fridge in their dorm room, with an intellect to match. He was the place kicker on the football team. And Eliza had to fight (when Clay annoyed her) to keep from repeating what her dad muttered when the player for the Steelers cost them a game by shanking a field goal. "Never trust a kicker!"

"Never trust a kicker" also came to mind when Eliza arrived back to the dorm early one night from working at the campus coffee shop. Eliza had opened the door only to be confronted with Clay's naked hindquarters as he lay atop her roommate—Claire. They were on Eliza's bed.

---

[33]McCarthy, *Road*, 286-87.

"Eliza! Knock!" had been Claire's exasperated response.

"It's my room!" Eliza wanted to say. But she just let out a frightened scream, dropped her latte, and shuffled backward into the hallway. Clay hadn't looked her in the eye after that.

Claire.

Claire was the prim and proper preacher's daughter that Eliza had been assigned, no doubt to keep Eliza on the straight and narrow. She didn't care that Claire and Clay were having sex. But the hypocrisy of the whole thing gave her another reason to distrust this Christian "bubble" she now found herself in.

The professor interrupted her daydream with more reading. This portion of the memoir was about an unfortunate British soldier named Samson. After the part about the rum, Graves recounted that "Samson lay groaning about twenty yards beyond the front trench." He had been cut down by machine-gun fire, and three men had been killed in attempts to rescue him. Finally, an orderly managed to make it to Samson, but the wounded man had sent him back with the claim that he was not worth saving. Samson sent apologies to the rest of the company for making a racket.

Then came the line that silenced Jack Sparrow. The professor read how Graves himself had crawled into no man's land at dusk. "The first dead body I came upon was Samson's, hit in seventeen places." He had "forced his knuckles into his mouth to stop himself crying out and attracting any more men to their death."

"Holy crap," Clay muttered.

Holy crap was right.

● ○ ●

Somehow this Samson story resonated with Eliza more than the one about the long-haired judge from the Old Testament. She kept picturing the bloody knuckles jammed between teeth in an extreme attempt at self-silencing. In Eliza's experience, the worst thing about being stuck between two firing lines was not the personal peril but the sense that screaming might lure others to the same predicament.

One felt responsible.

Eliza had felt this fear while sitting between her father and her mother in the cancer ward. How could she tell them she was losing her faith at the very moment Jesus was the only thing sustaining her mom? The only compassionate choice was the Samson option: open mouth; insert knuckles.

Eliza had felt the loneliness of no man's land more recently when sitting between her father and her brother, Jeremy, in the family living room during semester break. Theirs was a cold war. Like the Western Front on Christmas Eve, the two sides exchanging cigarettes and singing carols but with the promise of renewed hostilities.

Hostilities boiled over when Eliza was back in Ohio over Christmas break. Her dad and brother argued bitterly over politics and religion. (Were they separate?) And like poor Samson, Eliza was caught in the crossfire.

What to do?

For Robert Graves, the answer came by way of two sources: desertion and English literature. After signs of shellshock and the Spanish flu, he walked off his post to die somewhere more comfortable. But Graves survived. Soon after, a friend mercifully signed his discharge papers and he enrolled in Oxford. A distinguished career in poetry and fiction followed, with a plaque that bears his name in Westminster Abbey. He was done with England however (or so he thought). Thus the title of the memoir, *Good-bye to All That*, was a farewell to the British Isles and their present culture.

Eliza was done with her "island" too. As if driven by an unseen force, she walked out of class and changed her major. In the registrar's office she picked up a brochure to study abroad. Desertion. *Check*. English literature. *Check*.

* Quotations from Robert Graves, *Good-bye to All That*, rev. 2nd ed. (Garden City, NY: Doubleday, 1957), 157-59.

Part 2

Against Dogmatism

*Sometimes the Bible in the hand
of one man is worse than a whiskey
bottle in the hand of [another].*

Harper Lee,
To Kill a Mockingbird

4

Survival of the Shrillest

What Dogmatism Sounds Like

*I can testify about them that they are zealous for God,
but their zeal is not based on knowledge.*

ROMANS 10:2

PART ONE LOCATED THE LOGIC OF PERHAPS within the biblical narrative (chap. 1), church tradition (chap. 2), and contemporary application (chap. 3). The result was an understanding of both the promise and the pitfalls of sacred speculation and the construction of some guardrails to avoid disaster. My main idea has been that the saying of perhaps is crucial to the life of faith, despite the dangers of a speculative theology. That is what our forefather Abraham "discovered in this matter" (Rom 4:1).

Now it's time to talk about the first of two excesses that must be avoided if we are to employ a gracious Christian imagination: the land of strident dogmatism (part 2). I start with this particular extreme for an important purpose: one reason many (former) evangelicals are sliding toward the land of doubt and deconstruction is that "evangelicalism" has become increasingly synonymous with a brand of narrow, partisan dogmatism. As noted in the introduction, to embrace the kind of dogmatism I describe is not synonymous with affirming Christian dogmas (i.e., orthodoxy). Nor does it preclude deep confidence in gospel truth. Rather, the dogmatism I've come to bury has two elements (1) a posture of combative shrillness and (2) a projection of false certainty. It is a matter of tone and emphasis, form and content. But I begin with what dogmatism sounds like.

The Tone of Dogmatism

What I call "tonal dogmatism" comes across as an abrasive antipathy toward those who fail to see the obviousness of (Christian) truth. It involves the tenor of speech and not merely its truth value. After all, it is possible to be correct in what we believe and yet wrong in the way that we communicate it.

It was not technically wrong to claim—as the religious leaders of John 8 do—that "in the Law Moses commanded us to stone" adulterers (Jn 8:5; cf. Lev 20:10). Yet it is abhorrent to apply a law, in any era, as a weapon to be selectively hurled at others, especially when a woman's life is used as ammunition.[1] As Shakespeare noted, "The devil can cite Scripture for his purposes."[2] And in the words of Miss Maudie in Harper Lee's *To Kill a Mockingbird*, "Sometimes the Bible in the hand of one man is worse than a whiskey bottle in the hand of [another]."[3] Any book can be a projectile. Christians must not merely affirm the words of sacred writ but deliver them with the appropriate spirit. For Václav Havel, "There is only one way to strive for decency, reason, responsibility, sincerity, civility, and tolerance, and that is decently, reasonably, responsibly, sincerely, civilly, and tolerantly."[4] The opposite is dogmatism.

In terms of attitude, our failure shows forth in an unnecessarily combative posture, and a tendency to use an inflammatory rhetoric that

---

[1]Whether this passage was originally part of John's Gospel is of no consequence to my larger argument.

[2]William Shakespeare, *The Merchant of Venice*, 1.3.99.

[3]Harper Lee, *To Kill a Mockingbird* (1960; repr., New York: Harper, 2002), 50.

[4]Václav Havel, *Politics, Morality, and Civility: An Essay* (Washington, DC: Trinity Forum, 2006), 24-25. Cited in Tim Muehlhoff and Richard Langer, *Winsome Persuasion: Christian Influence in a Post-Christian World* (Downers Grove, IL: IVP Academic, 2017), 3.

breeds inflammatory responses. In such cases, religious zealotry is not (as Marx alleged) the opium of the masses, to keep them docile and subservient,[5] but a stimulant of the most potent variety.[6] In this highly amped-up and outraged context, the voices that receive the most attention will invariably be the shrillest.

Social media and dogmatism. Nowhere is this shrillness more apparent than on social media. Alan Jacobs highlights the dangers of digital dogmatism as it relates to what he calls the "Repugnant Cultural Other" (RCO). "Everyone today seems to have an RCO, and everyone's RCO is on social media somewhere. We may be able to avoid listening to our RCO, but we can't avoid the realization that he or she is there, shouting from two rooms away."[7]

Online disinhibition leaves participants unconstrained by face-to-face etiquette. And increased incivility results in what Deborah Tannen dubs an "argument culture": an environment that pushes us to approach the world, and other people, in an adversarial mindset.[8] In many cases, the binary codes that run our social media (all ones and zeros) have infected us.[9] First we craft them, then consume them, like the Israelites' golden calf (Ex 32:20). We are conformed to their electronic image so that we too must be all ones or zeros on every complex issue.

The result is an outrage-induced dogmatism.

To be fair, motivation for this online boldness may be praiseworthy. "I am attempting to shine lights in the darkness," someone might say, "one meme at a time!" Yet, in so doing, we monetize the merchants of outrage so that social-media habits beget a Darwinian survival of the shrillest. The angriest and least-nuanced voices are amplified in a feedback loop

---

[5]See Karl Marx, *Critique of Hegel's "Philosophy of Right,"* trans. Annette Jolin and Joseph O'Malley (1970; repr., Cambridge: Cambridge University Press, 2009), 131.

[6]See Terry Eagleton, *Reason, Faith, and Revolution: Reflections on the God Debate* (New Haven, CT: Yale University Press, 2009), 42.

[7]Alan Jacobs, *How to Think: A Survival Guide for a World at Odds* (New York: Currency, 2017), 27. Jacobs notes that the term Repugnant Cultural Other (RCO) is taken from Susan Friend Harding, "Representing Fundamentalism: The Problem of the Repugnant Cultural Other," *Social Research* 58, no. 2 (1991): 373-93.

[8]Deborah Tannen, *The Argument Culture: Stopping America's War of Words* (New York: Random House, 1998), 3. Cited in Muehlhoff and Langer, *Winsome Persuasion*, 54.

[9]I first heard this analogy from the actor Dax Shephard, on his podcast *The Armchair Expert*.

of self-perpetuating dogmatism. As the saying goes, "We become what we behold. We shape our tools and then our tools shape us."[10]

Yet even now, a clarification is in order. To be against dogmatic shrillness cannot be synonymized with a blanket call for universal niceness—especially as defined by the contemporary czars of political correctness. After all, Jesus was not always nice. He flipped tables, likened friends and enemies to Satan, and ultimately wound up on a Roman cross. These examples are thus frequently cited as justification for inflammatory rhetoric within the public square. "Jesus offended the establishment," one might say. "I'm just following in his footsteps!"

Maybe. Or maybe not. A danger of any ideology (not least religious ones) is the learning of a grammar that enables us to rename vices as virtues. Thus, in a well-known passage, D. A. Carson notes that "people do not drift toward holiness."

> We drift toward compromise and call it tolerance; we drift toward disobedience and call it freedom; we drift toward superstition and call it faith. We cherish the indiscipline of lost self-control and call it relaxation; we slouch toward prayerlessness and delude ourselves into thinking we have escaped legalism; we slide toward godlessness and convince ourselves we have been liberated.[11]

My claim is that Christians often drift toward dogmatic shrillness and rename it prophetic boldness. We must therefore answer a crucial question: How can we tell the difference?

Dancing and weeping > gnashing and tweeting. In his famous treatment of *The Prophetic Imagination*, Old Testament scholar Walter Brueggemann sought to address this issue. How does genuine prophetic discourse differ from angry cavil that masks belligerence under a banner of prophetic boldness?[12]

---

[10]This statement is often attributed to Marshall McLuhan, but the best I can determine is that it emerges from Father John Culkin, a Jesuit priest and friend of McLuhan's. Culkin's statement, however, is meant as an encapsulation of McLuhan's thought. See J. M. Culkin, "A Schoolman's Guide to Marshall McLuhan," *Saturday Review*, March 18, 1967, 51-53, 71-72.

[11]D. A. Carson, *For the Love of God: A Daily Companion for Discovering the Riches of God's Word* (Wheaton, IL: Crossway, 2006), 2:23.

[12]Walter Brueggemann, *The Prophetic Imagination*, 2nd ed. (Minneapolis: Fortress, 2001).

Prophetic speech, claims Brueggemann, is deeply critical of the sin and numbness that afflict God's people. But it is also characterized by an imaginative pathos expressed in two seemingly contradictory dispositions: (1) deep anguish and (2) exuberant hope.[13] In light of this combination, it is tempting (though not quite right) to cite G. K. Chesterton in saying that prophets are the preachers "God made mad / For all their wars are merry, and all their songs are sad."[14] The marriage of lament and joy makes the prophet both more prone to tears and more prone to dancing than is usual among the resounding gongs (1 Cor 13:1) and thought leaders that masquerade as God's mouthpieces.

"If we are to understand prophetic criticism," writes Brueggemann, we must note that its underlying character is "anguish and not anger."[15] The two emotions often coexist, of course, as in the loving parent who is both gutted and exasperated by the rebellion of a child. In this case, righteous anger is but an outflow of brokenhearted love.[16] But even in instances of righteous anger, the crucial distinction comes down to which attribute (or posture) has been given pride of place. Cynics smirk, pundits rant, prophets weep. Brueggemann explains:

> I believe that the proper idiom for the prophet in cutting through the . . . numbness and denial is the language of grief, the rhetoric that engages the community in mourning for a funeral they do not want to admit. It is indeed their own funeral. . . . I believe that grief and mourning, that crying in pathos, is the ultimate form of criticism.[17]

Note how different this sounds from the snarky shrillness that pervades our public discourse—and our social media especially. Can one weep on Twitter? Can a meme lament? Is there an appropriate emoji to express the pathos of Rachel wailing for her children (Jer 31:15)? Dogmatism

---

[13]See Brueggemann, *Prophetic Imagination*, 36, 46, 65.

[14]G. K. Chesterton wrote this of the "Gaels of Ireland" in "The Ballad of the White Horse."

[15]Brueggemann, *Prophetic Imagination*, 81.

[16]See also Tony Lane, "The Wrath of God as an Aspect of the Love of God," in *Nothing Greater, Nothing Better: Theological Essays on the Love of God*, ed. Kevin Vanhoozer (Grand Rapids, MI: Eerdmans, 2001), 138-67.

[17]Brueggemann, *Prophetic Imagination*, 46.

often fails to be prophetic because it loses its love-based grounding in lament. It is the empty husk left over when God's people exchange crying eyes for gnashing teeth and call it prophetic boldness.

Yet anguish alone may be despair. And, indeed, some dogmatism is driven partly by a sense that the war is lost. In our hell-in-a-handbasket despondency, self-styled prophets imitate the biblical Elijah at his lowest and his least prophetic: "I am the only one left, and now they are trying to kill me too" (1 Kings 19:14).[18] Despair morphs into bitter anger as we unwittingly take on the character of Satan, who is "filled with fury, because he knows that his time is short" (Rev 12:12). In such cases, dogmatism springs forth from a lack of hope.

It is important, however, to define Christian hope theologically. Some false hopes are idolatrous delusions. And others betray inflated pride in our innate potential. Christian hope is centered on the resurrection of Jesus, the Messiah (1 Cor 15).[19] Yet, in the history of both Israel and evangelicalism, false hope happens when people transfer confidence to merely human "lords." Hence the psalmist sings, "Do not put your trust in princes, / in human beings, who cannot save" (Ps 146:3). To hope overly in princes (political leaders) is to lose sight of Yahweh, and to risk idolatry. Hence, the psalm's relativizing of all human leaders comes only after a repeated and exultant song of praise:

> Praise the LORD.
> Praise the LORD, my soul.
> I will praise the LORD all my life;
>   I will sing praise to my God as long as I live. (Ps 146:1-2)

Right worship keeps fallen attempts at prophetic boldness from devolving into dour dogmatism. In the words of Brueggemann, "Prophecy cannot be separated very long from doxology, or it will either wither or become ideology."[20]

---

[18]See my prior treatment of Elijah in the introduction.

[19]For an accessible treatment of Christian hope as something distinct from progress, optimism, or "good vibes," see Glenn Packiam, *Worship and the World to Come: Exploring Christian Hope in Contemporary Worship* (Downers Grove, IL: IVP Academic, 2020), chap. 3.

[20]Brueggemann, *Prophetic Imagination*, 17.

Now for a second feature. For those familiar with the customs of the ancient world, it is difficult to picture doxology without a bit of dancing. After all, the first-named prophetess was Miriam. And when she first steps foot on the biblical stage to lead God's people, it is "with timbrels and dancing" (Ex 15:20).

> Sing to the LORD,
>   for he is highly exalted.
> Both horse and driver
>   he has hurled into the sea. (Ex 15:21)

This exultant bodily exercise raises yet another reason to distrust much speech (and even more tweeting) that passes for prophetic boldness. Because when covenantal critique spirals into demagoguery, it "is not a place where much *dancing* happens."[21]

The pirouettes need not always be literal. The metaphor of dance speaks to how genuine prophetic discourse—as opposed to strident dogmatism—is undergirded by a rightly ordered hope and an imaginative poetic energy. It is the domain of the artist more than of the pundit. Brueggemann suggests, therefore, that our conception of prophetic speech "is most often too serious, realistic, and even grim." On the contrary, "the characteristic way of a prophet in Israel is that of poetry and lyric. . . . The *imagination* must come before the *implementation*."[22] At this point, we again see the importance of the word *perhaps*. For if hatred is, as Graham Greene claimed, "a failure of imagination,"[23] prophetic hope is the imagination's fanning.

In the famous example of Archbishop Desmond Tutu, however, the dancing was often literal. As a famous story goes, there was an occasion when the South African leader was meeting with a group of fellow Christians at the very height of the racist apartheid regime. In the midst of the worship service, the back door burst open and White men with guns rushed in to disrupt the gathering. Undeterred, Tutu, with his trademark

---

[21]Brueggemann, *Prophetic Imagination*, 36 (emphasis original).
[22]Brueggemann, *Prophetic Imagination*, 39-40 (emphasis original).
[23]Graham Greene, *The Power and the Glory* (1940; repr., New York: Penguin, 1998), 133.

impish smile, approached the lead officer: "You may have the guns, you may have all this power, but you have already lost. Come, join the winning side." With that, the worshipers burst into jubilant song and uninhibited dance, encircling the stone-faced soldiers in a peaceful but not passive choreography. Trust not in princes! Horse and rider he has thrown into the sea!

If this tub-thumping expression of prophetic hope seems antithetical to anguished lamentation, think again. The two are often married. For in both the grieving and the dancing a common core is the prophetic refusal to settle into numbness. To misspell a refrain from the old gospel song, "joy comes in the *mourning*." For "it is precisely those who know death most painfully who can speak hope most vigorously."[24] Prophetic hope is not the same as naive optimism;[25] nor is prophetic criticism mere "carping and denouncing."[26]

Conclusion

The goal of this chapter has been to separate the posture of perhaps from the cultural extreme of dogmatic shrillness. To do so, Brueggemann helps us to distinguish tonal dogmatism from prophetic boldness. Admittedly, there is still a certain *je ne sais quoi* ("I don't know what") in the distinction. One knows it when one sees it. Thus, the attempt to separate the two postures (prophet or demagogue) must lean more on Spirit-led discernment than a dictionary. Genuine prophets are sometimes killed for their annoying refusal to shut up ("Will no one rid me of this meddlesome priest!?"[27]), just as insufferable agitators are encouraged by fans who are all too willing to confer the digital oil of anointing on their "prophetic" ministries. Even so, true prophets are more likely to be sawn in half (Heb 11:37) than retweeted.

---

[24]Brueggemann, *Prophetic Imagination*, 67.
[25]Brueggemann, *Prophetic Imagination*, 101.
[26]Brueggemann, *Prophetic Imagination*, 11.
[27]This utterance was attributed to Henry II of England (in AD 1170) regarding Thomas Becket, the Archbishop of Canterbury. Taking the statement as an order, four knights rode off and murdered Becket.

5

The Trouble
with Certainty

A Guide to "Knowing Darkly"

The special mark of the modern world is not that it is skeptical,
but that it is dogmatic without knowing it.

G. K. CHESTERTON

ALONGSIDE SHRILLNESS OF TONE, dogmatism's second feature involves a projection of false certainty onto complex questions. This misguided form of certitude now demands to be unpacked if the language of *perhaps* is to be recovered. In the view of Krish Kandiah, "The Bible has more room for doubt, uncertainty and struggle than we have ever allowed ourselves to believe."[1] In keeping with this logic, scholars like Gregory Boyd and Peter Enns suggest that the pursuit of certainty has become an "idol"[2] and a "sin"[3] within contemporary Christianity. "The

---

[1]Krish Kandiah, *Paradoxology: Why Christianity Was Never Meant to Be Simple* (Downers Grove, IL: InterVarsity Press, 2017), 5.

[2]Gregory A. Boyd, *Benefit of the Doubt: Breaking the Idol of Certainty* (Grand Rapids, MI: Baker Books, 2013).

[3]Peter Enns, *The Sin of Certainty: Why God Desires Our Trust More Than Our "Correct" Beliefs* (New York: HarperOne, 2016).

opposite of faith is not doubt," says a common adage; the opposite of faith is "certainty."[4]

But wait a minute. Doesn't the Bible praise certainty? After all, Jesus performed a miracle so that people would "know" (*eidēte*) that he possessed authority to forgive sins (Mt 9:6). Paul spoke of being "convinced" (*pepeismai*) that nothing can separate us from God's love (Rom 8:38), and Luke says the risen Jesus offered many convincing "proofs" (*tekmēria*) of his resurrection (Acts 1:3). These passages seem to elevate certitude as a good thing and as something God desires for his people. So why speak of it as a danger, much less a sign of dogmatism? In response to biblical texts like these, Anthony Thiselton notes that there are different forms of certainty that must now be differentiated.[5]

Psychological Certainty

In the passages above, we encounter what Thiselton calls a "psychological" certainty. This is a feeling of supreme confidence, conviction, and trust in a person or thing—regardless of whether one can marshal irrefutable evidence to back up that belief.[6] Psychological certainty is a deeply personal experience. It is more like the way one knows that he or she is deeply loved than it is like a mathematical or logical proof. This inner confidence appears in Scripture: "I know whom I have believed," says the apostle Paul, "and am convinced that he is able to guard what I have entrusted to him until that day" (2 Tim 1:12).

Psychological assurance is a knowing with the bowels, the gut, the heart. And in salutary forms, it is the product of the Spirit's work. Alvin Plantinga argues that genuine faith in God is a properly basic belief. It is not groundless, yet neither can we reason *to* it on the basis of prior premises; instead, we reason *from* it.[7] This way of knowing comes as gift

---

[4]The earliest reference I can find to this quotation comes from Anne Lamott, *Plan B: Further Thoughts on Faith* (New York: Riverhead, 2006), 256-57. Lamott notes that it was related to her by a man she calls "Father Tom."

[5]Anthony C. Thiselton, *Doubt, Faith, and Certainty* (Grand Rapids, MI: Eerdmans, 2017).

[6]Thiselton, *Doubt, Faith, and Certainty*, 95.

[7]See Alvin Plantinga, *Warranted Christian Belief* (Oxford: Oxford University Press, 2000), chap. 6.

by revelation rather than by the incremental striving of unaided human reason.[8]

To speak of this experience as certainty may sound dodgy. After all, the English empiricist John Locke (1632–1704) long ago pointed out that the sheer intensity of a feeling does not guarantee its truthfulness.[9] Many people feel strongly that the earth is flat, individuals with mental illness have believed that God told them to murder their families, and our social media feeds are glutted with passionate opinions on various absurd beliefs—as evidenced by the worn letters on our collective Caps Lock keys. "Fake news!" we shout, when a claim rubs against our intense feelings. Does this mean that psychological certainty is worthless? Not necessarily. In a moment, I will attempt to reclaim the value of the concept (albeit by another name). But before that, I must turn to another species of certitude.

Absolute Certainty

A second kind of certainty is largely the product of the Enlightenment. It was birthed by modernity's concern to subject all feeling, experience, and tradition to rigorous critique. In the words of René Descartes, "It was necessary, once in the course of my life, to demolish everything and start again."[10] For "the only way to freeing ourselves from these opinions [of others] is to make the effort to doubt everything which we find to contain even the smallest suspicion of uncertainty."[11]

Unfortunately, as Alister McGrath notes, absolute certainty is attainable only for a small class of beliefs—namely, ideas that are capable of being demonstrated by propositions. And, "frankly, the things that

---

[8]For a recent survey of various positions on the relation between reason and faith, see Lara Buchak, "Reason and Faith," in *The Oxford Handbook of the Epistemology of Theology*, ed. William J. Abraham and Frederick D. Aquino (Oxford: Oxford University Press, 2017), 46-63. Also, Colin Gunton, *Revelation and Reason: Prolegomena to Systematic Theology*, ed. P. H. Brazier (London: T&T Clark, 2008).

[9]See John Locke, *An Essay Concerning Human Understanding*, ed. Peter H. Nidditch (1689; repr., Oxford: Clarendon, 1979), 4.19; cited in Thiselton, *Doubt, Faith, and Certainty*, 95.

[10]René Descartes, *Discourse on Method*, in *Oeuvres*, ed. Charles Adam and Paul Tannery (Paris: J. Vrin, 1964), 7:17. Subsequent citations by volume and page number.

[11]Descartes, *Principles of First Philosophy*, in Adam and Tannery, *Oeuvres*, 8:5.

you can know with absolute certainty are actually not that important."[12] Whether one agrees with McGrath's last claim or not, it is clear that anyone who desires to speak of life's biggest questions—questions of meaning, love, morality—must make statements rooted in trust, tradition, and unquantifiable experience.

The irony is that the modern quest for absolute certainty helped pave the way for nihilism and what Lesslie Newbigin described as "an abandonment of the claim to be able to know truth."[13] Immanuel Kant argued in his *Critique of Pure Reason* (1781) that we have no unmediated access to "the thing in itself"—that is, to external reality. We only have access to information passing through the gateway of our minds. And the mind can be an untrustworthy narrator.[14]

Nietzsche argued that claims to certainty and revelation serve as cloaks for power plays to bend others to our will. Thus "truth" must be eternally entombed in scare quotes. It is a soldier of fortune, especially when fortunes can be made. The only person Nietzsche respected in the New Testament, therefore, was Pontius Pilate with his cynical and pragmatic question: "What is truth?" (Jn 18:38). Nietzsche's recent heirs are postmodernists, like Michel Foucault, who assert that even scientific claims are driven by the will to power.[15] What is needed, therefore, is a deconstruction of all truth claims to see what self-interest lies behind them.

In the face of corruption within certain disciplines, the lure of suspicion is strong. In a chastened form, it brings a wakeup call to our naiveté. There are no neutral observers. And our fallen truth claims are sometimes driven by a quest for money, sex, and power. Supposedly

---

[12]Alister McGrath, *Doubting: Growing Through the Uncertainties of Faith* (Downers Grove, IL: InterVarsity Press, 2006), 23.

[13]Lesslie Newbigin, *Proper Confidence: Faith, Doubt, and Certainty in Christian Discipleship* (Grand Rapids, MI: Eerdmans, 1995), 36.

[14]See, for instance, the claims of certain evolutionary biologists that natural selection is concerned not primarily with giving us a completely accurate "read" on the world but with ensuring behavior that accords with the so-called four Fs: feeding, fleeing, fighting, and (ahem) reproducing. See Alvin Plantinga, *Where the Conflict Really Lies: Science, Religion, and Naturalism* (Oxford: Oxford University Press, 2011), chap. 11.

[15]In the wry words of the Catholic postmodernist Alasdair MacIntyre: "Facts, like telescopes and wigs for gentlemen, were a seventeenth-century invention." MacIntyre, *Whose Justice? Which Rationality?* (South Bend, IN: University of Notre Dame Press, 1988), 357.

evidence-based fields like science, medicine, and statistics can be driven by ulterior motives. So inquiring minds want to know: Who is funding the "science" on what causes obesity, heart disease, or cancer? Is it a transnational corporation that produces sugary sodas? Who conducted this opinion poll? Is it a partisan think tank with an obvious agenda? And what news outlet told you that?

Probing questions must be asked since, as Scripture claims, "The heart is deceitful above all things" (Jer 17:9). But, when taken too far, deconstruction fuels a culture of cynicism and conspiracy theories in which nuance, truth, and trust are casualties of war. Postmodernism thus joins a long line of worldviews (e.g., Marxism) that can exacerbate the very conditions they (ostensibly) seek to diagnose and heal. With our heightened ideological and political divisions, we retreat to silos—listening only to sources that confirm our biases. And across the smoking battlefield of social media, one can trace a flickering line of pixels from Descartes, to Kant, to Nietzsche, to Foucault, and on to the absurdity of our contemporary conspiracy theories. To maim a quote from Nietzsche, "Consensus is dead—and we have killed him!"

Tribalism Is the New Nihilism

But if this is so, why is dogmatism rising? Shouldn't it be the opposite? If certainty has been undermined by that line of thinkers above, why does G. K. Chesterton seem prophetic in his claim that "the special mark of the modern world is not that it is skeptical, but that it is dogmatic without knowing it"?[16] One answer involves the universal tendency to protest most loudly at those moments when our views seem flimsiest, or most threatened. We might call this the heel-digging effect.

By digging in our ideological heels, we argue to win instead of seeking truth. Thus we become like the proverbial preacher who wrote in the margin of the sermon manuscript: "Point is weak; yell louder!"

But heel digging alone cannot account for the contemporary rise in dogmatism. A second factor involves a modification of the insight

---

[16]G. K. Chesterton, *Illustrated London News*, March 15, 1919.

mentioned earlier by Newbigin. In his view, it was precisely the quest for absolute certainty that led to nihilism (the rejection of all moral and religious principles and the belief that life is meaningless). Few of us are either brave or foolish enough to go full Nietzsche—much less full Foucault. Nihilism is a deep burn. So while Newbigin saw the loss of a certainty consensus as producing the abandonment of truth and meaning, it would be more accurate to say that it has contributed to a rise in combative tribalism.

Tribalism is the new nihilism. Or, more accurately, tribalism is a coping mechanism to deal with the confusion of life amidst competing truth claims. Humans are inherently tribal. And that is no bad thing. We need groups with which to identify and form attachments. Tribes can be life giving. Yet as Amy Chua notes, "The tribal instinct is not just an instinct to belong. It is also an instinct to exclude."[17] And in an age of overlapping and conflicting cultures, the ability to form up battle lines by race, religion, class, or political affiliation allows one to be shrewd in deconstructing the ulterior motives of "them," while maintaining an island of unexamined certainty with "us."

The line dividing doubt and dogmatism—like Solzhenitsyn's line dividing good and evil—bisects each heart like an underwater fissure separating continents.[18] Pervasive skepticism (or deconstruction) thus becomes a dogma in itself. And this secular gospel is preached with a zeal that makes it a perfect match for any militant religious propaganda.

Trading Certainty for Obedient Trust

With my brief historical sketch of certitude now finished, it is time to return to what Thiselton calls "psychological certainty"—or what I would speak of as a Spirit-birthed assurance. The Bible extols a firm but humble conviction of God's character and faithfulness. Hebrews states that "faith is confidence in what we hope for and assurance about what we do not

---

[17]Amy Chua, *Political Tribes: Group Instinct and the Fate of Nations* (New York: Penguin, 2018), 1.
[18]Aleksandr Solzhenitsyn, *The Gulag Archipelago: 1918–1956: An Experiment in Literary Investigation*, trans. Thomas P. Whitney and Harry Willets, abridged by Edward E. Ericson Jr. (New York: Harper Perennial, 2007), 75.

see" (Heb 11:1). A paradoxical interplay exists, therefore, between the confidence of Christian hope and the reality that it is pointed toward something we cannot see. So while assurance is not anathema to faith's existence, what Newbigin calls "proper confidence"[19] is hardly the same as the proof-obsessed alternative of absolute certainty.[20] And it is even farther from the land of dogmatism.

Spirit-granted assurance is self-aware enough to recognize that depth of feeling cannot serve as a solid basis for argument with others. Jacobs notes that "we all hold with passionate commitment some beliefs for which we cannot provide strong evidence, in any *public* sense of evidence."[21] This is as it should be. We are whole beings, using emotion, intuition, and gut-level perception to make decisions and articulate beliefs that we cannot always wrap our reason around. We are not mere rational machines. Nor should we want to be. So, although Pascal was right to remark that "the heart has its reasons," it would be foolish to demean others on the basis of a heart-felt experience they have never encountered. Religious dogmatism does that, but so do its secular counterparts.

The humble assurance that comes by the Spirit steers clear of a self-righteous superiority complex that attaches to the dogmatist like an odor: "God," used either as curse word or a prayer, "thank you that I am not like other people—robbers, evildoers, adulterers—or even like this [liberal, conservative, secular, fundamentalist, millennial, Gen-Xer, baby boomer, gay, lesbian, Muslim, snowflake, Social Justice Warrior]" (see Lk 18:11). Depending on one's in-group, the bracketed words will vary, but the commonality resides in a self-righteous certainty that

---

[19] Hence the aforementioned title of Newbigin's book, *Proper Confidence.*

[20] For recent accounts of theological epistemology that distinguish faith from cognitive certitude, see again, Buchak, "Reason and Faith," 56-60. See also, William Alston, "Belief, Acceptance, and Religious Faith," in *Faith, Freedom, and Rationality: Philosophy of Religion Today,* ed. Jeff Jordan and Daniel Howard-Snyder (London: Rowman & Littlefield, 1996), 3-27; Daniel Howard-Snyder, "Propositional Faith: What It Is and What It Is Not," in *American Philosophical Quarterly* 50 (2013): 357-72; and Jonathan L. Kvanvig, "Affective Theism and People of Faith," in *Midwest Studies in Philosophy* 37 (2013): 109-28.

[21] Alan Jacobs, *How to Think: A Survival Guide for a World at Odds* (New York: Currency, 2017), 136 (emphasis original).

lumps others under dismissive labels in a form of tribal virtue signaling.[22]

Biblical scholar Matthew Bates argues that the meaning of *pistis* (often translated as "faith" in the New Testament) is not so much intellectual or psychological certainty but an "allegiance" to Christ and to his kingdom. God's requirement is not that we be absolutely certain of our theological beliefs but that we be "certain enough to yield" in spite of remaining questions. In this way, we sometimes approach Jesus like the father, who cries out, "I do believe; help me overcome my unbelief!" (Mk 9:24). Bates's claim is that *"we must be . . . certain enough that we are willing to give our allegiance (*pistis*) to Jesus as our true king."*[23] In so doing, however, we may find that the Spirit births assurance in us over time so we can say with Paul, "I know whom I have believed, and am convinced that he is able to guard what I have entrusted to him until that day" (2 Tim 1:12).

How is this confidence distinct from what I call "false certainty"? In his own study, Gregory Boyd critiques what he calls the "certainty-seeking" concept of faith. He defines this misconception as the belief that we are "saved by *feeling certain* about particular beliefs"; and he claims that it causes massive harm, not least because it equates doubt with disloyalty and faith with gullibility.[24] In response, Boyd asks why God would "place a premium on one's ability to convince oneself that something is true?"[25] After all, individuals who are best at believing things that fly in the face of evidence are often "either self-delusional or intellectually dull."[26] The claim is that the pursuit of certainty can become an idol because the feeling of certitude replaces God as the source of salvation.

---

[22]The language of "virtue signaling" emerged in academic fields like cultural anthropology and evolutionary biology, but the concept has quickly been popularized as a pejorative that refers to one's showy (but ultimately shallow) display of moral, ethical, or spiritual superiority.

[23]Matthew W. Bates, *Salvation by Allegiance Alone: Rethinking Faith, Works, and the Gospel of Jesus the King* (Grand Rapids, MI: Baker Academic, 2017), 94 (emphasis original).

[24]Boyd, *Benefit of the Doubt*, 15 (emphasis added).

[25]Boyd, *Benefit of the Doubt*, 13.

[26]Boyd, *Benefit of the Doubt*, 13-14.

False Certainty and the Prosperity Gospel

This danger is especially apparent in the theological disaster known as the prosperity gospel. Here the promise is not merely of financial guarantees in exchange for proper prayers and tithing (a kind of Christian Ponzi scheme if there ever was one) but also of guarantees of healing. Suffering Christians are told that physical healing in the here and now is assured by Scripture, though it hinges precariously on our ability—and the ability of those around us—to dispel all doubts that God will do it. The miracle is triggered by our certainty. Such faith is toxic. And I have had enough personal experiences as a pastor to have earned that blunt opinion.

Still, the desperate motives of those harmed by prosperity theology are understandable. After all, who wouldn't want the Bible's miracle cure if it indeed existed? Who wouldn't do anything to save the life of a beloved friend or family member? What frightful bargains might I entertain if it were my child or my spouse? There are even passages in Scripture that have been taken to support the faith-as-certainty formula for answered prayer. "I tell you," says Jesus, "whatever you ask for in prayer, believe that you have received it, and it will be yours" (Mk 11:24). Likewise, James says, "When you ask, you must believe and not doubt, because the one who doubts is like a wave of the sea, blown and tossed by the wind" (Jas 1:6).

I will return to these passages later (chap. 7), but for now it should be noted that the results of a faith-as-certainty theology are both obvious and terrible. Behind the victorious imagery of promised healing in exchange for doubt-free faith, Boyd notes "an image of a cruel, demented deity engaging in psychological torture!"

> Think about it: God is leveraging our friend's life on whether we can successfully engage in what amounts to nothing more than an impossible mental gimmick. If we can muster up enough certainty to get the faith puck far enough up the faith pole, our friend lives; if not, he dies. Is this not sadistic?[27]

---

[27]Boyd, *Benefit of the Doubt*, 37-38.

This is not faith. It is superstitious magic that becomes a harmful dog-matism in its failure to accept critique from other biblical perspectives.[28] The fallout is now witnessed in an entire generation of young adults—the children of the prosperity-gospel generation—who have been driven toward the land of unbelief. Here too doubt and dogmatism are in a re-ciprocal, codependent, and dysfunctional relationship.

Apophasis, Adiaphora, and God's Other Name

Yet prosperity theology is hardly the only way false certainty becomes dogmatism. In the view of the Anglican theologian Sarah Coakley, the Western church has often failed to cultivate an appropriate "apophatic" sensibility in our God-talk.[29] This word describes that tradition that ap-proaches God not by stating confidently what God *is* (cataphasis) but by recognizing what God is *not*. Since the divine nature is beyond human comprehension, apophatic theology reminds us that we must be clear on what we cannot be absolutely clear about.

Like any tradition, this "negative way" (another description of apo-phatic theology) can lead to distortions. In Coakley's case, one rather obvious motive is to challenge some mostly unnamed Christian claims regarding gender and sexuality. Hence, she argues that we must be per-petually open to the fact that the Spirit "blows wherever it pleases" (Jn 3:8) in "a strange subversion of all certainties."[30] To be in a relationship with God is to celebrate "a love affair with a blank."[31] Herein lies danger.[32] In some cases, the enthrallment with "un-knowing" (one of Coakley's

---

[28]Having said this, it would be deeply unfair to equate all elements of the charismatic tradition with the most bizarre and predatory forms of prosperity theology. What's more, to lurch sharply toward a cessationism that rejects the possibility of supernatural healing today (with no biblical support) is to fall into the same tendency toward knee-jerk polarization.

[29]See Sarah Coakley, *God, Sexuality, and the Self: An Essay "On the Trinity"* (Cambridge: Cambridge University Press, 2013).

[30]Coakley, *God, Sexuality, and the Self*, 342.

[31]Coakley, *God, Sexuality, and the Self*, 342. Coakley notes that this phrase comes from Dom Sebastian Moore, "Some Principles for an Adequate Theism," *Downside Review* 95 (1977): 201-13. For additional engagement with this theme, see Sarah Coakley, *Powers and Submissions: Spiritu-ality, Philosophy and Gender* (Malden, MA: Blackwell, 2002), chaps. 2 and 9.

[32]For an appreciative yet critical evaluation of the "apophatic turn" in contemporary theology, see E. Jerome Van Kuiken, "'Ye Worship Ye Know Not What'?: The Apophatic Turn and the Trinity," *International Journal of Systematic Theology* 19, no. 4 (2017): 401-20.

favorite phrases, based partly on the famous anonymous work of medieval mysticism[33]) veers closely to the dedication inscribed on a certain Athenian altar in the book of Acts: "TO AN UNKNOWN GOD." And in response to this form of worship, Paul had criticism: "You are ignorant of the very thing you worship—and this is what I am going to proclaim to you" (Acts 17:23).[34]

Yet the misuse of *un-knowing* does not nullify its proper use.[35] Coakley's insight is needed whenever Christians claim something near omniscience on issues that Scripture itself is unclear about, be that a question of political affiliation or something more theological, like the manner of baptism. Dogmatism fails to recognize the limits of our understanding and to separate issues of orthodoxy from those of adiaphora: matters of "indifference" on which Christians can disagree. The language of *perhaps* is helpful here as well.

A powerful image of both the presence and the hiddenness of divine revelation exists in the brutal western novel by Cormac McCarthy, *Blood Meridian*. Here an ex-priest explains that God's voice is like the sound of horses grazing in the night. We come to notice it most easily only when it stops: "When the horses are grazing and the company is asleep . . . don't nobody hear them." But when they cease, every soul awakes. "No man is give[n] leave of that voice."[36] This manner of divine revelation—both constant and ignorable—gives respect to both the possibility and the mystery involved in hearing God's voice.

Pastors and theologians must reclaim the sacred IDK ("I don't know") on some matters since God's judgments can be "unsearchable"

[33]A. C. Spearing, trans., *The Cloud of Unknowing, and Other Works* (London: Penguin Books, 2001).
[34]Pseudo-Dionysius dealt with this passage by flipping the plain-sense meaning of the text to coincide with his apophatic program. As Charles Stang relates, the Areopagite interprets Acts 17:23 not as Paul *correcting* the Athenian pagans but as Paul *commending* them: "I'm going to proclaim to you a fuller account of the unknowability of the God whom you already rightly worship as unknown." Charles M. Stang, "Dionysius, Paul and the Significance of the Pseudonym," in *Re-thinking Dionysius the Areopagite*, ed. Sarah Coakley and Charles M. Stang (London: Wiley-Blackwell, 2009), 15.
[35]See my prior argument to this effect in Joshua McNall, "Shrinking Pigeon, Brooding Dove: The Holy Spirit in Recent Works by Sarah Coakley and N. T. Wright," *Scottish Journal of Theology* 69, no. 3 (2016): 307.
[36]Cormac McCarthy, *Blood Meridian*, 25th anniv. ed. (1985; repr., New York: Vintage, 2010), 130.

and "his paths beyond tracing out" (Rom 11:33). To claim otherwise is to ignore the voice within the whirlwind, speaking to the shoreline of our human knowing: "This far you may come and no farther; / Here is where your proud waves halt" (Job 38:11). Alongside Faithful, True, and Holy Love—God's other name is "Surprise."[37] And a chastened apophatic sensibility keeps us from taking this name in vain.

There is biblical support for my argument. The Pharisees were certain that it was unlawful for Jesus to forgive sins, the Sadducees were dogmatic in their doubts of resurrection, and the Roman authorities were confident that kings and crosses did not mix. The Judaizers presented prooftexts to confirm the necessity of Gentile circumcision. All were wrong. In each case, false certainty combined with shrillness to become a problem in the land of dogmatism.

Conclusion

My claim in these two chapters is that dogmatism is a matter of tone (chap. 4) and emphasis (chap. 5). It is a posture of combativeness paired with the false assumption that certainty is always possible and virtuous. It is not. Having now surveyed the land of dogmatism, however, it remains for me to support my observations with attention to a particular biblical narrative: a story of three kings (chap. 6).

---

[37]See again Cornelius Plantinga Jr., *Reading for Preaching: The Preacher in Conversation with Storytellers, Biographers, Poets, and Journalists* (Grand Rapids, MI: Eerdmans, 2013), 96. Plantinga credits this observation to a former chaplain of Calvin College, Dale Cooper.

6

We Three Kings

Scripture Contra Dogmatism

Better he kill me than I learn his ways.

<small>GENE EDWARDS, *TALE OF THREE KINGS*</small>

I RETURN NOW TO THE NARRATIVE of Scripture (by way of a fictional depiction) to illustrate how the logic of perhaps is distinct from a harmful and dogmatic certitude. Yet in this case, my imaginative biblical case study comes not from the life of Abraham (chap. 1) but from roughly five centuries later with the advent of human kingship in Israel.

It is a common, though absurd, assumption that theology must come from the hallowed halls of academia. The truth is that many penetrating works of theology exist apart from footnotes and peer review. One such book is *A Tale of Three Kings: A Study in Brokenness*, by Gene Edwards.[1]

A Tale of Three Kings

A Tale of Three Kings is dedicated "to the brokenhearted Christians coming out of authoritarian groups, seeking solace, healing and hope."

---

[1]Gene Edwards, *A Tale of Three Kings: A Study in Brokenness* (Carol Stream, IL: Tyndale House, 1992), 44. To reduce footnotes, I will hereafter cite page numbers parenthetically in the body of my text.

As such, it is a study of submission and authority within God's kingdom. But it also raises relevant points for my discussion of dogmatic certitude.

The book is written as a drama playing out on stage, with a fictitious viewer chiming in occasionally to ask questions of the narrator. The kings are Saul, David, and Absalom. All three sinned grievously. Two were the Lord's anointed, but only one was called a man after God's own heart (1 Sam 13:14). For Gene Edwards, a crucial question for those serving under imperfect leaders is "Who, then, can know who is a David and who is a Saul?" His answer is disconcerting: "God knows. But he won't tell" (44). This point calls for caution in our human judgments—and especially in our desire to lash out. After all, "even Sauls are often the Lord's anointed" (43). And those "who go after the Sauls among us often crucify the Davids" (44). In this last claim, there is a hint toward the Son of David in the New Testament who was scorned as a deceiver.

I will turn to King Saul momentarily, but I begin *in medias res* ("in the middle of the thing")—a phrase that will become important momentarily—with the most famous and least likely of the royals. For David, the upending of dogmatic certitude starts early. He was last-born of his brothers, the eighth pup of the litter, and in a culture that saw seven as the number of completeness.[2]

As Edwards writes, "The youngest son of any family bears two distinctions: He is considered to be both spoiled and uninformed. Usually little is expected of him" (3). While this is not necessarily the case today, it bears noting that Jesse does not bother to retrieve his last-born boy when Samuel comes looking for a future king. He is certain it will not be David, and he is not alone. Samuel makes his certainty explicit. After glimpsing Eliab, the prophet proclaims, "Surely the LORD's anointed stands here" (1 Sam 16:6). But, as I have noted already of Elijah, even prophets can be wrong (1 Kings 19:13), and sometimes when they *feel* quite strongly. "The LORD does not look at the things people look at. People look at the outward appearance, but the LORD looks at the heart" (1 Sam 16:7).

---

[2]Consider the "blessedness" of Job, who had seven sons and three daughters, both before and after his calamity (Job 1:2; 42:13).

Samuel's inner dialogue is not known to us at the instant his certainty dissolved. But we can guess at the confusion. In his prior kingmaking, God seemed to have taken outward appearance into account. Saul was "as handsome a young man as could be found anywhere in Israel" and "a head taller than anyone else" (1 Sam 9:2). Had the Lord changed his policy after a complaint from short and ugly younger brothers? Samuel gets no explanation. After the anointing, "the Spirit of the Lord came powerfully upon David," even as it had departed Saul to be replaced by an "evil spirit from the Lord" (1 Sam 16:13-14). This last line gets no explanation either. And it raises questions that rub against some Christian certainties.

Cohabitating Monarchs

David goes to live with the very unstable king he will later replace. Hence, the Spirit of the Lord resides still in the palace, albeit in the servant's quarters. Here too there is a foreshadowing of things to come (e.g., Is 53; 61). But for the time being David enters "God's sacred school of submission and brokenness" (15). He sings songs to the mad king, fights giants for him, and fosters friendship with the son (Jonathan) who should be his rival. And the mad king, as mad kings often do, responds by throwing spears.

In Saul's violence, we feel not only the danger of dogmatic certainty but also the temptation to fight fire with fire. Edwards asks, "What do you do when someone throws a spear at you?" Whether in the land of ancient Israel or the contemporary realm of social media, the answer is clear: You throw it back! (17).

> In performing this small feat of returning thrown spears, you will prove many things: You are courageous. You stand for the right. You boldly stand against the wrong. You are tough and cannot be pushed around. . . . You are the defender of the faith, keeper of the flame, detector of all heresy. You will not be wronged. All of these attributes then combine to prove that you are also a candidate for kingship. Yes, perhaps *you* are the Lord's anointed.
>
> After the order of King Saul.
>
> There is also a possibility that some twenty years after your coronation, you will be the most incredibly skilled spear thrower in all the realm. And also by then . . . quite mad. (17-18, emphasis original)

David had chances to strike back. And in some cases, retribution might have seemed to carry the serendipitous stamp of divine approval. *Of all the caves of the En Gedi, you had to relieve yourself in mine* (1 Sam 24). But when David finally got hands on Saul's spear, he chose to steal it rather than plunge it through Saul's chest (1 Sam 26).

A clarification is now in order since I have reached a point in Edwards's book that I wish had been different. In highlighting David's respectful posture toward the mad monarch, one must be clear that this is not endorsing the endurance of abuse under the guise that a given authority may still be "the LORD's anointed." This has happened far too frequently within evangelicalism, and in other circles as well. Victims of perverse and abusive leaders should do precisely as David did when he sought safety. All of us must seek justice; and we should shine a light on abuse wherever it exists. Still, there is a difference between the need for justice and the temptation of violent retribution. On that last note, Edwards puts these words in the mouth of young David: "Better he kill me than I learn his ways. Better he kill me than I become as he is. I shall not practice the ways that cause kings to go mad. . . . I will not destroy the Lord's anointed" (36). Dogmatic zealots fail to heed this warning.

It seems obvious to first-time readers that David sinned in ways that appear every bit as egregious—and disqualifying—as the crimes of Saul. Maybe more so. After all, the death verdict on Saul's kingdom comes after his first recorded transgression! And the sin was neither murder nor adultery but an offering to God after Samuel took his sweet time in coming to Israel's quaking and imperiled army (1 Sam 13).[3]

---

[3]The scene shows how seriously God takes proper worship in Israel. Kings are not priests, aside from Melchizedek and the Messiah. There are boundaries to royal power, and especially when it comes to the sanctuary and its sacrifices. That said, David and his men will later be given the consecrated bread to eat (1 Sam 21), which, as Jesus states, "was not lawful for them to do, but only for the priests" (Mt 12:4). David's action was deemed acceptable because of the principle of life preservation ("mercy"; Hos 6:6; Mt 12:7), which is seen to supersede the concern for sanctuary and Sabbath custom.

On these grounds, however, one might argue that Saul's actions should be seen as less egregious. After all, he performs the sacrifice only after waiting on Samuel for seven days, and only to preserve the life of his army, which had "[begun] to scatter" (1 Sam 13:8). The lesson here is not that God was unfair to Saul in 1 Samuel 13 but that what constitutes a "disqualifying action" in the life of the Lord's anointed is not always obvious to us. "The LORD does not look at the things people look at. People look at the outward appearance, but the LORD looks at the heart" (1 Sam 16:7).

Even more offensive to modern sensibilities, the crime that later rips the kingdom from Saul's grasp is his refusal to exterminate the Amalekites in *herem* warfare—that mode of God-ordained conquest by which no creature was to be left alive (1 Sam 15). Not one to shirk from violence, Saul comes close to total slaughter but decides to spare both king and cattle. When confronted for his lack of complete carnage, he offers what must have seemed like genuine repentance, clinging to the prophet's robes and wailing his remorse. David is forgiven for murdering his most loyal officer and bedding the man's wife; Saul's lack of sacred violence (among other things) costs him the crown.

My point is not that God was unjust. A crucial difference between the two kings is that David's repentance was genuine while Saul gave excuses as he sobbed for the crowds and cameras. Indeed, Saul's tear-streaked non-apology could have been choreographed by a modern PR firm. With great emotion, he expressed deep regrets while giving justifications for why his actions were actually driven by praiseworthy motives. The problem is not God's capricious justice but the difficulty that we mortals face as we try to determine who exactly is a Saul and who is a David. This story—like my prior chapters against dogmatism—moves to undermine our sense of certainty as we cast judgments and aspersions.[4]

One of our greatest impediments to understanding stories like this one is that we know how it turns out. Our bird's-eye perspective blinds us to the fog of uncertainty that enveloped those who lived the drama. We live *in medias res*. And this position means that there must be provisionality about our judgments. To flout this caution is to risk becoming an unwitting villain. As Edwards writes, "You who can so wisely discern the presence of an unworthy Saul! Go! Look in yon mirror. That man is *you*! . . . Behold: Absalom the Second!" (50, emphasis original).

Absalom, Absalom!

To pan the camera toward the youngest of the three kings is to reenter the realm of the impressive exterior. "In all Israel there was not a man so

---

[4]Edwards notes that "the Sauls of this world can never see a David; they see only Absalom. The Absaloms of this world can never see a David; they see only Saul" (80).

highly praised for his handsome appearance as Absalom. From the top of his head to the sole of his foot there was no blemish in him" (2 Sam 14:25). Unfortunately, the most dangerous blemishes are found within, in the region only God can see.

Absalom came by his insurrection honestly. David had done next to nothing when Absalom's sister, Tamar, was raped by her half-brother (Amnon). Like many later leaders, David took the coward's way in responding to sexual assault. He was "furious" (2 Sam 13:21); yes, yes, of course . . . ; but he moved to handle the matter "internally." The cover-up left Tamar asking a question that echoes through time: "Where [can] I get rid of my disgrace?" (2 Sam 13:13).

To whom can she turn? Answer: Not to David.

So Tamar goes—as we do still—to David's son.

Although Absalom seems justified in his vengeance against Amnon, his rebellion against his father's rule does not stop there. It rarely does. Once a leader's faults have been revealed (whether they be real or imagined), throwing spears feels justified. There is a muscle memory that makes repetition easy. The initial motivation may be justice, but the eventual drive is vengeful power. Zealous dogmatism results. "There are always problems in any kingdom," Edwards writes, and "to be able to see those problems is a cheap gift, indeed" (84). "Even God had his critics in heaven" (63).

Like Milton's Satan, Absalom rebels in the name of "justice" (2 Sam 15:6). And he accomplishes the coup by leaning on appearances, impressive marketing, and a zealous fanbase. "[He] provided himself with a chariot and horses and with fifty men to run ahead of him. He would get up early and stand by the side of the road leading to the city gate" dispensing justice (2 Sam 15:1-2). His social-media campaign went viral. And just as Amnon stole Tamar's innocence, so Absalom "stole the hearts of the people of Israel" (2 Sam 15:6).

David's response to this rebellion is the most important feature in this whole sad story. For it is this reaction that reveals him as a man after God's own heart. His reply is oddly lacking in violent or dogmatic certitude. It is characterized instead by that strange combination of hope and lamentation (see chap. 4). Rather than imperil the ark of the Lord in a family squabble, he sends it back to the city. "If I find favor in the LORD's eyes," says David, "he will bring me back and let me see it and his dwelling place again. But if he says, 'I am not pleased with you,' then I am ready; let him do to me whatever seems good to him" (2 Sam 15:25-26).

Like Christ, David weeps openly over Jerusalem. *If she only knew the way that leads to peace.* Like Christ, he is cursed without responding.[5] Like Christ, his posture is one of sober hope and steadfast trust amid the swirling questions: "If it is possible, may this cup be taken from me. Yet not as I will, but as you will" (Mt 26:39). Because of these and other connections, Bible scholar Nathan Johnson argues that Matthew's account of Jesus in Gethsemane has been patterned on David's sufferings in the midst of Absalom's revolt (2 Sam 13–18).[6] It is David's "holy maybe" that steers clear of strident dogmatism. "It *may be*," he says, "that the Lord will look upon my misery and restore to me his covenant blessing instead of his curse today" (2 Sam 16:12, emphasis added).

Conclusion

Believing in providence means learning perhaps. And in the imaginative retelling of Edwards, this is precisely the word he uses in a conversation between David and his now departing priest:

> "And now, what will you do, David? In your youth, you spoke no word against an unworthy king. What will you do now with an equally unworthy youth?" . . .
>
> "I will do what I did under Saul. I will leave the destiny of the kingdom in God's hands alone. Perhaps he is finished with me. Perhaps I have sinned too greatly and am no longer worthy to lead. Only God knows if that is true, and it seems he will not tell." (93)

This language stands against dogmatism, but it stands more deeply in abiding hope in Israel's God.

---

[5]Note the shrill dogmatic certainty of the political reactionary, Shimei (2 Sam 16:5-12).
[6]Nathan C. Johnson, "The Passion according to David: Matthew's Arrest Narrative, the Absalom Revolt, and Militant Messianism," *Catholic Biblical Quarterly* 80 (2018): 247-72.

SECESSION

Latitude: 54.6031° N
Longitude: 3.1417° W
GRETA HALL, LAKE DISTRICT, ENGLAND

Summer.

It is worth asking how many of our momentous decisions result not from a weighing of pros and cons, or from a strong desire to do one thing instead of another, but from the simple fact that someone asked us to tag along when we had nothing better to do. Marriages, divorces, hobbies, babies, addictions—all the byproduct of boredom plus an invitation.

By the end of her freshman year, Eliza had settled on a plan of desertion from her Christian college to study abroad. But the problem with deserters—as Robert Graves could have told her—is that people tend to notice. And the problem with studying abroad was *money*.

Eliza's change of major to English literature caused an argument with her father about "useless degrees." And to pair that conversation with a request to spend a semester in England's Lake District reading Coleridge and Wordsworth was the straw—or albatross—that broke the line worker's back.

"Do you think I'm made of money!?" he had shouted in mid-May. The vein in his forehead prodded her to say no.

Eliza worked extra shifts at the Safeway that summer to save money. But she knew England was off the table. She settled for an online class on the Romantic poets, with periodic doses of Coleridge and Wordsworth in the supermarket break room behind the frozen foods. It seemed wrong to read of "raptures" from the "vernal wood" while munching Slim Jims next to an unemptied mop bucket scrawled with a lewd drawing of someone named Becky. The setting proved more conducive to Instagram than to deciphering *The Rime of the Ancient Mariner.*

"What's that?" a girl named Sophie asked when she found Eliza holding the *Norton Anthology of Literature* with her cell phone propped within the fold.

"A poem about opium and a dead bird," Eliza replied.

"I know that neighborhood," Sophie responded wryly.

Eliza smiled. Everyone knew their town had fallen on hard times. These days the local product in the news wasn't Chevy fenders—it was fentanyl. Unemployment was rampant. And the sad reality provided fodder for a pessimistic humor at which Sophie and Eliza excelled.

Sophie was petite, with hazel eyes, tight black jeans, and buzzcut hair. At the moment, the inch-long stubble was dyed pink, but the color was subject to change with barometric pressure. Beneath her Safeway apron, she wore a black T-shirt with a typo on it: "I've half a mind that your a Horcrux." Sophie had designed it herself, but the teenager at the local printshop had proven incapable of a contraction. Sophie was left with two dozen free shirts, one of which she wore daily as an act of grammatical protest.

Eliza couldn't help but like her. The two girls had attended the same high school, and Sophie had a reputation for not caring much what people thought.

In tenth grade, a boy named Brock had started a rumor that Sophie had offered him sex at a weekend party. Rather than deny it, Sophie purchased a pregnancy test, drew a pink line down the middle, and mailed it to Brock's mother. "Your son did this," she wrote. Brock was enrolled in the local Catholic school by next semester.

Sophie also enjoyed mocking Eliza's choice of college education.

"I can't believe you're going back there," she remarked in early June as the girls stocked a shelf with cereal boxes that looked large enough to feed a pack of Weimaraners. "And during an election year."

Eliza barely followed politics. But trying to ignore the subject lately was like trying to overlook the sudden appearance of an extra head while brushing one's teeth in the mirror.

Politics was how Eliza's father had heard of the university. The school's president had appeared on Cable News in a panel of "thought leaders" assembled for gladiatorial combat. He said nothing of education. But he did claim that a certain boorish billionaire running for office was "God's man" to return the country to its Christian heritage.

The rhetoric appealed to Eliza's father. It was a blend of nostalgia, paranoia, and a well-earned sense that people like him had been dismissed and forgotten by the coastal elites. But the appeal of this messaging was not simply because her dad was a no-nonsense guy with little time for pretense (pronounced "BS" in his accent). The other reason was what Eliza's brother had encountered at the state school in Michigan. Jeremy had gone to study engineering: "A solid job." But he had changed his major freshman year and had come home speaking of everything from gender to morality as mere "social constructs."

"Your *paycheck* is a 'social construct,'" her father retorted.

"Yours too," Jeremy shot back.

The ensuing firefight was probably visible from space.

Like Eliza, Sophie had wanted to attend college, to study English and graphic design. But she had taken a gap year to save money. "I can't afford a private school like some people," she said one day in the break room.

"Sure you can," Eliza responded. "Just borrow money from the government like everyone else."

"You have to pay that back," she countered.

"Not if *your guy* gets elected," Eliza quipped with a smile.

Sophie responded with a cry of *"Viva la revolución!"* then jammed her hand into a cereal bag for some purple marshmallows that looked to be providing inspiration for a future hair color.

Eliza paused before uttering the next sentence. She knew it would elicit a strong reaction: "You should come with me. I could use a new roommate."

"Not for all the Lucky Charms in Ireland," Sophie mumbled. "That place is a cult."

"Why do you think I need you?" Eliza remarked, now channeling Coleridge: "It's Kool-Aid, Kool-Aid everywhere, but not a drop to drink. Plus, they give a scholarship for every 'lost sheep' I bring to the fold: extra credit if they have tattoos in something other than Greek or Hebrew."

"Sign me up," Sophie said sarcastically, and a puff of purple dust escaped her mouth, causing both girls to double over with laughter.

Boredom plus an invitation.

By early July, the girls had extended their friendship to the local Starbucks. Sophie helped Eliza get caught up in her summer lit class. They had things in common. Poetry. Wes Anderson movies. An absent parent. Eliza's mom had died of cancer; Sophie's father split when she was two.

Each commonality added energy to the force that moves so much of history: boredom plus an invitation. Friendship as a force of gravity.

Come fall semester, Eliza smiled to recall their "Safeway manifesto." She was helping Sophie hang a Ramones poster above their dorm-room bunk. She also couldn't help but notice how many classmates at the Christian school could trace their collegiate orbits to related forces. It was as if they had been deposited like stranded mariners with little recollection of how they got there.

All hail boredom plus an invitation.

Desertion, as Robert Graves knew well, requires a willingness to leave *alone*. Secession doesn't. Secession needs only a declaration (made initially in secret) that *our* little patch of ground belongs to us—regardless of the ruling regime.

If the end of freshman year found Eliza alone between trenches, then sophomore year brought her a companion and coconspirator. "Open mouth; extract knuckles." Every friendship, someone noted, is a form of secession. And Eliza formalized her private independence with a terse email to her old dormmate, Claire.

"Found a new roommate. Keep the mini fridge. ~E."

Part 3

Against Doubt

Certainty seems bigger than me,
skepticism smaller.
Wonder is just right.

KAREN SWALLOW PRIOR,
BOOKED

7

Descending Santa Scala

How Scripture Counters Doubt
and the Divided Heart

Who knows if it is true?

<small>Martin Luther</small>

As the young monk dragged his aching knees atop the last of the white marble steps, he mouthed the words of the "Our Father." He had longed to make this pilgrimage since youth—even if the holy city had mostly failed to measure up to expectations. There were more brothels than he had imagined. And reports of papal immorality ran rampant. Still, the lure of the stairs had made the journey worth it.

The sacred steps (*santa scala*) were said to have once been part of the Praetorium in old Jerusalem. Hence, Christ himself would have stridden upon them at his trial before Pontius Pilate. For this reason, they were reported to have powerful potential as holy relics. Like Elisha's bones, contact with them could supposedly aid the dead (2 Kings 13:20-21). Constantine's mother was said to have found and shipped the steps to Rome, where they were reassembled at the entrance to the papal palace.

With this history in mind, the monk finished his ascent for an important purpose: his dead grandfather was said to be languishing in purgatory. And tradition held that uttering the Lord's Prayer on each of the twenty-eight slabs of stone could release a loved one's soul to heaven. Yet even as the final "Amen" now left the lips of Martin Luther, he could no longer suppress his doubts. So as he looked out over the teeming city, he spoke aloud, "Who knows if it is true?"[1]

While part two of this book detailed the land of dogmatism, part three surveys the land of doubt. Between these mutually repulsing positions resides what I have dubbed the sacred middle ground of perhaps—a region that involves humility, imagination, and a kind of faith-fueled speculation. But before I venture into the blank space of perhaps in part four, I must first discuss the kind of doubt that stands opposite to dogmatism. And that brings me to Martin Luther.

Should we look down on Luther's question on the sacred steps? Did his honest doubting of the church tradition show an unfortunate weakness in his faith? I think not. But my reasons have nothing to do with being Protestant. In fact, even if I were to accept every one of these potentially dubious medieval traditions—(1) the authenticity of Pilate's steps, (2) the power of ancient relics, (3) the reality of purgatory, and (4) the possibility of springing dead grandfathers by prayer and kneecap punishment—*even then* I would find nothing wrong with Luther's doubt. Because to voice one's honest questions toward the heavens is no bad thing. Doubt is not always the antithesis of dogmatism. And doubt is not always the opposite of faith.

The Wrestling Match of Faith

The Scriptures are quite comfortable with honest questions. The name *Israel* refers to those who "struggle" with Yahweh (Gen 32:28), and this wrestling leads even heroes of the faith to interrogate God's ways. Abraham haggles shamelessly for Sodom and Gomorrah (Gen 18:23-33). Moses asks shrewd questions in an attempt to change God's mind about annihilating Israel (Ex 32:10-14), and he balks against a plan to lead the people to the

---

[1]Cited in Heiko A. Oberman, *Luther: Man Between God and the Devil*, trans. Eileen Walliser-Schwarzbart (New Haven, CT: Yale University Press, 1990), 147.

Promised Land without God's presence (Ex 33:12-16).[2] God does not punish these audacious individuals. All three are answered positively.[3]

Consider the psalmist, who asks openly if Yahweh's promises have failed forever (Ps 77:8). Or to steal a line from the Old Testament, "Consider Job," the most vocal questioner in Scripture. Although Job is often thought to have repented for some ignorant allegations (Job 42:1-6), God nonetheless applauds the honesty of his prayer life. "Unlike his pious-sounding 'friends,' Job's speech was authentic (*kun*, Job 42:7)," writes Gregory Boyd. And "Yahweh clearly appreciates raw honesty more than pious platitudes."[4] Not all these Old Testament passages have to do with doubt per se, but they reveal a relationship with God that allows for honest, even tortured, questions—like that of Luther on the Santa Scala: "Who knows if it is true?"

In one of his notebooks, Fyodor Dostoyevsky proclaimed, "It is not as a boy that I believe in Christ and confess Him, but *my hosanna has passed through a great furnace of doubt*."[5] Similarly, John Calvin wrote that certainty comes mixed with doubt within the believer's mind.[6] And in some cases, these two dispositions seem impossible to separate. Like Luther, we are ambushed by uncertainty. Painful questions stand at the door and knock. And in some cases, we find that opening the latch brings an encounter with a Christ who comes in strange packaging, even cloaked in questions.[7]

Why Speak Against Doubt?

But there is a problem. Although doubt can be helpful, neutral, or unavoidable—it is not always so. Doubt has nuances. And the New

---

[2]It is irrelevant to my current argument whether God actually *does* change his mind in such instances. Unlike Boyd, however, I am not an open theist.

[3]See Gregory A. Boyd, *Crucifixion of the Warrior God: Interpreting the Old Testament's Violent Portraits of God in Light of the Cross* (Minneapolis: Fortress, 2017), 1:10.

[4]Boyd, *Crucifixion of the Warrior God*, 1:11.

[5]Cited in Konstantin Mochulsky, *Dostoevsky: His Life and Work*, trans. Michael A. Minihan (Princeton, NJ: Princeton University Press, 1971), 650 (emphasis original).

[6]John Calvin, *Institutes*, 3.2.18. For Calvin, this is evidence of the believer's continuing sinfulness. Hence, "it never goes so well with us that we are wholly cured of the disease of unbelief." My point is somewhat different. Namely, that not all doubt or questioning *is* sinful.

[7]See especially Rev 3:20 and Mt 25:31-46. The point could be made from many passages since Jesus (like the Old Testament prophets) sought to make his hearers doubt their received certainties when they fell short of God's truth and values.

Testament often speaks against it as something juxtaposed with faith. It is not enough, therefore, to cite the tired adage that "the opposite of faith is not doubt, but certainty."[8] False certainty presents its problems, but so do specific kinds of doubt. Doubt's character depends on its object (the thing being doubted) and the way it is employed. Like a knife, doubt can be a scalpel used to cut away unhelpful dogmatism or an instrument of violence and self-harm.

In reacting against religious dogmatism, some Christians swing the pendulum in the opposite direction—toward a valorization of pervasive, cynical, noncommittal doubt. And this particular continental breakoff from Pangaea is no better than the former one.[9]

This knee-jerk reaction is encapsulated by the great atheist Bertrand Russell. In his view, the biggest problem in our world is that "the stupid are [certain] while the intelligent are full of doubts."[10] Though there is some validity in the statement, it employs a false dichotomy. In Russell's presentation, it must always be either A or B, either pervasive doubt or foolish dogmatism. But what if there are more than two options? Unfortunately, for many who have been exposed to a simplistic and divisive religious fundamentalism, the choice seems easy: Go with Bertrand: "Farewell, Pangaea."

Population density in the land of doubt connects to the upswing of the Nones, and to the small but vocal *ekklesia* of the New Atheism. In light of these groups, it is insufficient to highlight the positive or neutral sides of doubt. We may all be Thomas now, in the winsome phrase of James K. A. Smith, but it matters greatly what we do with the scars and questions that invite our probing.[11] Neither abrasive certainty nor

---

[8]See Anne Lamott, *Plan B: Further Thoughts on Faith* (New York: Riverhead, 2006), 256-57.

[9]Boyd does not valorize *all* doubt, but he does illustrate the tendency to oversimplify the biblical material for pastoral reasons. He rightly reiterates that the Bible "does not view doubt as the antithesis of faith," yet he tends to downplay the way the New Testament frequently juxtaposes faith and doubt, with the latter being spoken of negatively. See Boyd, *Crucifixion of the Warrior God*, 1:9. A similar imbalance exists in Enns.

[10]Bertrand Russell, "The Triumph of Stupidity," in *Mortals and Others: Bertrand Russell's American Essays, 1931-1935*, vol. 2 (New York: Routledge, 2009), 204. I've replaced Russell's word choice of "cocksure" with a more modern equivalent.

[11]James K. A. Smith, *How (Not) to Be Secular: Reading Charles Taylor* (Grand Rapids, MI: Eerdmans, 2014), 4. By *scars* I invoke both the common metaphor of trauma's aftermath and the

pervasive skepticism embodies the life of faith. Now to see what Scripture says on the matter.

The New Testament Against Doubt

"Admittedly," writes Anthony Thiselton, "the actual word 'doubt' occurs more frequently with negative implications than positive ones" within the Bible. Yet even Thiselton's careful study proceeds to all but ignore the negative side of doubt in Scripture. Like Boyd and Enns, he spends most of his chapter reiterating how doubt is unavoidable or even positive.[12] Why? And why specifically does Scripture speak so frequently *against* doubt? To answer, I will explore three famous antidoubt passages from the New Testament while making nods at others along the way:

1. Doubt and mountain-moving prayer (Mk 11:22-24)[13]

2. Doubt and the divided soul (Jas 1:5-7)[14]

3. Doubt after Christ's resurrection (Mt 28:16-20)

I will also relate each passage to the story of Luther on the Santa Scala to differentiate between helpful and unhelpful forms of questioning, uncertainty, and hesitation. My conclusion is that the kind of doubt condemned by Scripture has to do not so much with honest questions but with the divided heart that cultivates ambiguity with regard to one's allegiance to Christ.

Doubt and Mountain-Moving Prayer—Mark 11:22-24

Some of the New Testament's most memorable statements against doubt come in the context of prayer. And a few of these passages might appear to lend credence to the prosperity gospel's claim that Scripture guarantees wish fulfillment in exchange for mental certainty.

---

biblical imagery by which marks from old wounds can serve as conduits of God's convincing grace (e.g., Jn 20:27).

[12]Anthony C. Thiselton, *Doubt, Faith, and Certainty* (Grand Rapids, MI: Eerdmans, 2017), 3.

[13]Cf. Mt 21:21 and Lk 17:6 for parallel passages.

[14]I deviate from canonical order to treat Mark and James in sequence since both authors use the same "doubt" word (*diakrithē*; *diakrinomenos*) and both deal with doubt in relation to believing prayer.

After the cursing of a fig tree, Christ implores his followers to "have faith in God" (Mk 11:22):

> Truly I tell you, if anyone says to this mountain, "Go, throw yourself into the sea," and does not doubt [*mē diakrithē*] in their heart but believes [*pisteuē*] that what they say will happen, it will be done for them. Therefore I tell you, whatever you ask for in prayer, believe that you have received it, and it will be yours. (Mk 11:23-24; cf. Mt 21:21-22; Lk 17:6)

The "whatever you ask" has sparked both hope and frustration for those desperately desiring miracles. But how *should* one interpret Christ's words?

In addressing this question, my goal is not to craft a comprehensive theology of prayer or miracles. Rather, it is to explore why the Scriptures speak negatively of this kind of doubt. For starters, Christ's call to faith (Mk 11:22) is best seen as a demand for trusting allegiance to God rather than as a call for mere belief in God's existence.[15] The "doubt" word that follows is *pisteuē*, which means "to be in conflict with oneself," with one judgment pulling this way while the next pulls in opposition.[16] We have here the first instance of negative doubt referring to a divided heart (*kardia*; Mk 11:23). Yet why is Jesus concerned with conflicting judgments as we pray?

One answer is that Christ desires disciples to trust not only God's greatness (what he *can* do) but also his goodness (what he *wants* to do).[17] After all, "if you, then, though you are evil, know how to give good gifts to your children, how much more will your Father in heaven give good gifts to those who ask him!" (Mt 7:11). From this perspective, the divided heart is not merely an impediment to answered prayer[18] but a roadblock to our delight and trust in God.

If our fervent prayers go unanswered, should we then chalk them up to vestiges of doubt? I think not. Earlier in Mark, Christ answers the prayer of a father who is open about his mixture of belief and unbelief

---

[15]See again Matthew W. Bates, *Salvation by Allegiance Alone: Rethinking Faith, Works, and the Gospel of Jesus the King* (Grand Rapids, MI: Baker Academic, 2017), chaps. 1 and 4.

[16]See R. C. H. Lenski, *The Interpretation of St. Mark's Gospel* (Minneapolis: Augsburg, 2008), 495.

[17]See also these other passages on prayer: Mt 7:7-11; Lk 11:1-13.

[18]See those passages that connect a lack of miracles with a "lack of faith" (Mk 6:5-6; cf. Mt 13:58).

(Mk 9:24). And still later in the prayer in Gethsemane, Christ learns that it is not possible for the cup to pass from him while simultaneously accomplishing the Father's plan (Mt 26:39). Hence, he willingly sets aside his initial prayer request—not because of a divided, doubt-filled heart but because of a singular commitment to the Father's will. Prayer's task is not to conjure mental certainty in exchange for wish fulfillment but to submit one's whole heart (*kardia*) to God's salvific agenda. Jesus demonstrates this perfect submission and perfect allegiance.

There are clues within the mountain-moving text that push against the idea of individual wish fulfillment in exchange for mental certainty. For one, Christ uses plurals when speaking of these requests: "Whatever you [plural] ask for in prayer, . . . it will be yours [plural]" (Mk 11:24). Whether Jesus is speaking primarily to his immediate apostles or to the church universal, the communal nuance is sadly lost in many translations. R. T. France argues on this basis that "prayer is here presented as something which the community of disciples undertakes together, not a private transaction between the individual believer and God."[19]

Finally, there is the meaning of the mountain itself. Numerous scholars note that the focus of the disciples' communal prayer is not so much the "whatever" at the close of the passage but the establishment of God's kingdom on earth, symbolized by the prophetic reference to "this mountain" (Mk 11:23).[20] In Zechariah, the Mount of Olives is divided to make way for "the LORD [to] be king over the whole earth" (Zech 14:9; cf. 4:7). Others see Christ as pointing to the Temple Mount, the destruction of which confirmed his kingdom agenda.[21] Perhaps both notions are in view. In either case, the prayer in question is not a blanket guarantee of personal wish fulfillment but a plea for God

---

[19]R. T. France, *The Gospel of Mark*, NIGTC (Grand Rapids, MI: Eerdmans, 2002), 448.

[20]This fact does not, however, negate the mountain-moving metaphor's proverbial character as pointing to the accomplishment of seemingly impossible realities (like the camel passing through the eye of the needle). See, for instance, France, *Gospel of Mark*, 448. Likewise, Craig S. Keener, *Matthew*, IVP New Testament Commentary 1 (Downers Grove, IL: InterVarsity Press, 1997), 317-18.

[21]N. T. Wright, *Jesus and the Victory of God*, Christian Origins and the Question of God 2 (Minneapolis: Fortress, 1996), 422.

to establish his reign.[22] This is the seemingly impossible reality that the believing community must collectively pray for with an undivided heart; it is the promise of "your kingdom come, . . . on earth as it is in heaven" (Mt 6:10).

Moving back to Santa Scala, compare Christ's words against doubt (Mk 11:22-24) with Luther's anguished question. Should the young monk have gone away berating himself for having stranded his dead grandfather in purgatory because he dared to ask, "Who knows if it is true?" Not at all. Like the biblical father who brought his child to Christ in spite of uncertainty (Mk 9:24), Luther lays the fate of his grandfather before Jesus, in spite of questions.

Like Christ in Gethsemane, Luther's prayer is limited by what is "possible" (Mt 26:39). If the traditions regarding (1) Pilate's steps, (2) the power of relics, and (3) the reality of purgatory are false, then it makes no difference if Luther feels certain as he kneels there. Regardless of the value of these medieval traditions,[23] Luther's attitude is one of obedience. The question does not lead him to depart for a weeklong bender in the Roman brothels. Nor does it correspond directly to a repudiation of church tradition.[24] This shift would come later through his outrage at indulgences, and by reading Paul. At the moment, Luther simply walks down the stairs. He descends the Santa Scala—because a willingness to walk and wait and pray is the best response to doubt.

Doubt and the Divided Soul in James

The book of James brings our next antidoubt passage. I address this text now because both Mark and James use the same "doubt" word (*diakrithē; diakrinomenos*), and both deal with doubt in relation to prayer.

---

[22]See William L. Lane, *The Gospel of Mark*, NICNT (Grand Rapids, MI: Eerdmans, 1974), 410.

[23]Chapter 12 will bring me back to the speculative status of purgatory through an analysis of C. S. Lewis's *The Great Divorce: A Dream* (1946; repr., New York: Harper, 2001).

[24]As Oberman notes, "We know nothing of a 'breakthrough experience' in Rome from Luther's writings." Oberman, *Luther*, 149-50. A much later account from Luther's son Paul accords great significance to the Santa Scala incident, yet Oberman judges the recollection to be "untenable" (150).

If any of you lacks wisdom, you should ask God, who gives generously to all without finding fault, and it will be given to you. But when you ask, you must believe [*pistei*] and not doubt [*diakrinomenos*], because the one who doubts [*diakrinomenos*] is like a wave of the sea, blown and tossed by the wind. That person should not expect to receive anything from the Lord. Such a person is double-minded [*dipsykos*] and unstable in all they do. (Jas 1:5-8)[25]

This text has also been used to endorse the faith-as-certainty mentality. So allow me to make three observations that challenge that reading.

First, James clearly places "faith" (*pistei*) and "doubt" in opposition. Hence, one should again be wary of an overcorrection that attempts to harmonize the two concepts completely. As in Mark 11, the "doubt" word (*diakrinomenos*) carries the sense of one who lacks decisiveness or is at odds within the self—judging now in one way and a moment later in another.[26] Likewise, *dipsychos* refers literally to the "two-souled" person, as hinted by the NIV's translation of "double-minded."[27] The emphasis in both cases is not on a person with honest questions but on the inner war of one who has chosen to leave a foot in both camps, with one part of the self trusting God and another distrusting him.[28] This problematic form of Christian doubt has to do with a divided heart.[29]

Second, note specifically what is asked for with conflicting loyalties. The thing requested is not some mass of earthly possessions but "wisdom" that comes in the context of suffering: "trials of many kinds" (Jas 1:2). Given James's Jewish roots, the link between wisdom and suffering is unsurprising. Books like Job and Psalms reveal God's pattern of bringing

---

[25]In Jas 4:7-8, the critique of "double-mindedness" continues: "Submit yourselves, then, to God. Resist the devil, and he will flee from you. Come near to God and he will come near to you. Wash your hands, you sinners, and purify your hearts, you double-minded [*dipsychos*]."
[26]See, for instance, R. C. H. Lenski, *The Interpretation of the Epistle to the Hebrews and the Epistle of James* (Minneapolis: Augsburg, 2008), 530.
[27]Scot McKnight, *The Letter of James*, NICNT (Grand Rapids, MI: Eerdmans, 2011), 89-90.
[28]McGrath argues that for the Christian this sinful attitude involves "keeping [certain] options open long after we ought to have closed them." Alister McGrath, *Doubting: Growing Through the Uncertainties of Faith* (Downers Grove, IL: InterVarsity Press, 2006), 52.
[29]I say "Christian doubt" because James is writing to Christ-followers who are part of "the twelve tribes scattered among the nations" (Jas 1:1).

forth wisdom from the crucible of earthly trials. In many cases, this wisdom is the fruit of faithful, if uncensored, prayers.

Third, James's focus is always on what faith (*pistis*) *does* when it goes public (see esp. Jas 2:14-26) rather than on the internal requirement to gin up certitude for wish fulfillment.[30] The problem James confronts is not, therefore, having questions in the midst of prayer, but the toleration of a divided soul (*dipsychos*, "double-minded"; Jas 1:8; 4:8) so that one's allegiance to the Messiah falters in the inner civil war.[31] For this unstable individual, wisdom cannot follow because the person is perpetually "tossed by the wind" (Jas 1:5-6) of a divided loyalty.

A fitting picture of James's two-souled person is the "Mr. Facing-both-ways" of John Bunyan's *Pilgrim's Progress*.[32] This man attempts to hold contradictory views for the purpose of hedging bets and remaining non-committal. Now contrast this version of doubt with Luther on the Santa Scala. While Mr. Facing-both-ways willfully cultivates a divided heart by leaving options of allegiance open, Luther's face is set like flint toward heaven. Heiko Oberman writes that "[Luther's] flash of doubt is certainly not indicative of the emergence of a 'new skepticism' and the onset of the Enlightenment; his kind of skepticism rather arose from the conviction that God would not allow himself to be pinned down in this way."[33] In other words, some questions emerge precisely *from* allegiance to God, as God is revealed in Christ and Scripture.

---

[30]Proof of this point comes in James 3 and 4, where "demonic" false "'wisdom'" is connected with "envy and selfish ambition" (Jas 3:15, 16), and with the desire to "spend what you get on your pleasures" (Jas 4:3).

[31]See J. H. Ropes, *A Critical and Exegetical Commentary on the Epistle of St. James* (Edinburgh, 1916), as cited in McKnight, *Letter of James*, 73. Here, the *diakrinomenos* is described as the man "whose allegiance wavers." See also Peter H. Davids, *The Epistle of James*, NIGTC (Grand Rapids, MI: Eerdmans, 1982), 75-76.

[32]The connection is noted by both Ropes and McKnight in their aforementioned commentaries on James.

[33]Oberman, *Luther*, 147.

Doubt After the Resurrection—Matthew 28:16-20

Matthew 28 is my final antidoubt passage. After Jesus' resurrection appearance to two women named Mary (Mt 28:1), the text turns to the counternarrative being circulated: the claim that the disciples stole Christ's body "while [the guards] were asleep'" (Mt 28:13). It is against this backdrop of conflicting narratives that Matthew gives his only account of Christ appearing to the male disciples: "Then the eleven disciples went to Galilee, to the mountain where Jesus had told them to go. When they saw him, they worshiped him; but some doubted" (Mt 28:16-17).

The "doubt" word is *distazō*. It carries the sense of "holding back, hesitation, or wavering between two minds."[34] Herein lies a crucial point. In the discussion of pervasive modern doubt, one cannot simply conduct an English word search for *doubt* and then note whether the reference is negative or neutral. Context and linguistic nuance matter. In Matthew 28, they cause us to reconsider what is being hesitated over. One possibility is that some disciples were wavering over whether they should worship Jesus, and not over whether he was standing there alive. After all, the text says clearly that "they saw him" (Mt 28:17).[35]

The disciples were good Jews. And although resurrection proved that Jesus was special, it need not be taken as a carte-blanche call to break the first commandment! Only some risky reimagining of Jewish monotheism (the ability to say "perhaps . . .") could overcome this hesitation. Maybe this is why the risen Jesus does not scold their doubt[36] with a dogmatic outburst; instead, he moves lovingly against it:

---

[34]See McGrath, *Doubting*, 49; similarly, Thiselton, *Doubt, Faith, and Certainty*, 2.

[35]Another possibility is that the risen Christ was some distance away when the eleven "saw him" (Mt 28:17); hence, the *distazō* might involve whether the distant figure was indeed Christ. This possibility may be supported by the next verse, which states, "Then Jesus came to them . . ." (Mt 28:18).

[36]A related usage of *distazō* appears in the story of Peter leaving the boat to walk upon the water (Mt 14:22-36). After grasping Peter, Christ says, "You of little faith . . . why did you doubt?" (Mt 14:31). Then, as in Mt 28, Jesus works *against* the *distazō* (doubt) of his disciple by word and deed (calming the storm) so that those in the boat end up "worship[ing] him" (Mt 14:32). In all of this, the two passages (Mt 14 and 28) are similar.

1. He proclaims that all authority in heaven and on earth belongs to him (Mt 28:18).

2. He includes himself within a threefold proclamation of the divine "name" (Mt 28:19).

3. He promises to be with them "always, to the very end of the age" (Mt 28:20).

4. He ascends, though it is not mentioned in Matthew, to the single throne of heaven (Lk 24:51-52; Acts 1:9).

Some overarching observations are now in order, in response to this more nuanced reading of the passage. First, it is not always clear that the English word *doubt* (with all its modern connotations) is the best way to speak of biblical moments of uncertainty or hesitation before Christ. Second, while the *distazō* of the disciples is not praised, it is also understandable. Hence, Jesus acts against it not by dogmatic rebuke but by nudging them onward by actions, words, and (eventually) his poured-out Spirit. Third, the cure for honest hesitation in one's faith journey is often time under the Spirit's influence, enmeshment in a worshiping community,[37] and the courage to say perhaps.

On the aforementioned question of worshiping Jesus, the later doctrine of Christ's two natures—fully human and fully divine—is itself a remarkable example of how to say perhaps. This doctrine was formalized at Chalcedon (AD 451), and in the words of James K. A. Smith:

> A [less imaginative] approach might have simply said: "Look, based on our current philosophical knowledge, it's impossible to affirm that someone is both human and divine. So you have to resolve this tension in one direction or the other: *either* Jesus is human *or* he is divine. But he can't be both." Feeling the tension and the challenge, the Council of Chalcedon exhibited remarkable theological imagination and generated what is now one part of the heritage of the church.[38]

---

[37]There may also be an example of some beneficial peer pressure in Matthew 28. We learn to worship, after all, by seeing and hearing those around us worshiping—just as a child learns to speak.

[38]James K. A. Smith, "Our Chalcedonian Moment: Christological Imagination for Scientific Challenges," in *Christ and the Created Order: Perspectives from Theology, Philosophy, and Science,*

Examples like this show why more nuanced approaches are needed than simply the valorization or demonization of religious doubt.[39] In some cases, prolonged hesitation is a sign of a divided heart. Thus Scripture still contrasts it with believing allegiance.

Take, for instance, Doubting Thomas. On the one hand, his brand of ancient empiricism seems warranted in light of the extraordinary claim of resurrection. Nonetheless, the risen Christ still juxtaposes it with faith: "Stop doubting and believe" (Jn 20:27). The words "doubting" and "believing" are the same word in the Greek: *pistos,* with the negative (*a-pistos*) meaning "faithlessness." In this juxtaposition, we see again the glaring problem in the cliché that "the opposite of faith is not doubt, but certainty."[40] For Thomas, as with the disciples in Matthew 28, the opposition of the two concepts is quite obvious, even as we must remember that faith has more to do with trust and allegiance than with intellectual certitude.[41] The problem with the cliché is not, therefore, that it is entirely wrong but that, like Bertrand Russell, it presents only two choices when we need something like a spectrum. We need a sacred middle space.

Back on Santa Scala, we see that not all "hesitation" (*distazō*) is created equal. To fence sit eternally, after Christ reveals himself, is to enter a realm of culpable "doubting" (*a-pistos*; faithlessness) that is sinful. It demonstrates the disloyalty of a divided heart. But in Luther's case we do not see a sinful hesitation. He is faithfully engaged in the act of prayerful devotion as uncertainty assails him. He came to the "mountain" as commanded, he worshiped, and he left with questions. Far from being sinful, however, his question may be viewed as the first faint whisper of the Spirit calling him to say perhaps while others remained content with business as usual.

---

ed. Andrew B. Torrance and Thomas H. McCall (Grand Rapids, MI: Zondervan Academic, 2018), 2:182-83 (emphasis original).

[39]At a more popular level, A. J. Swoboda is excellent on this point. *After Doubt: How to Question Your Faith Without Losing It* (Grand Rapids, MI: Brazos, 2021), xii.

[40]See again Lamott, *Plan B*, 256-57.

[41]See again Bates, *Salvation by Allegiance Alone*, 94.

Conclusion

My claim in this chapter has been that it matters greatly what one means by *doubt* within the Christian life. Doubt's character depends on its object (the thing being doubted) and the way it is employed (how we wrestle with our questions). The kind of doubt Scripture works most strongly against involves a divided heart that both tolerates and cultivates an ambiguity with regard to one's allegiance. Hence, not all questions and hesitations are created equal.

Importantly, even when a form of Christian doubt seems understandable (e.g., Mt 28:16-20; Jn 20:27), Christ acts consistently against it without resorting to a form of angry browbeating that confuses faith with mental certitude. There are different forms of doubt, just as there are both secular and religious varieties of dogmatism.

8

Cogito, ergo None?

A Snapshot of Conversion

Now that I have become a man,
I have put away childish things.

EDWARD THE ATHEIST,
MARILYNNE ROBINSON, *GILEAD*

THE REGION OF PERHAPS sits uncomfortably between the popular extremes of doubt and dogmatism. Yet in mapping the geography of doubt, it is time now to transition from the biblical world to the contemporary one. It is often noted that the fastest growing religious affiliation in the United States is "None"—a reality that has led some pundits to rejoice, others to weep, and still more to monetize the moment with a spate of diagnoses, cures, and existential ointments.

Rather than ruminate on the origins of modern skepticism or the biblical passages that relate to doubt, I aim now to listen to the real-life deconversion story from a Christian who suddenly found himself adrift and cut off from the evangelical Pangaea that he once called home. In response, my move will not be a dismissive takedown but an attempt to understand some lessons that deserve attention. These include

- What Charles Taylor calls the "cross-pressures" of a secular age.[1]
- The triggers for unbridled doubt, especially trauma.
- The importance of what I will call "team shaming" and "fringe revulsion."

A recurring reference point will be the work of the Canadian philosopher Charles Taylor as he sought to describe what it means to live in *A Secular Age*. For Taylor, the secular is not centered on the absence of belief; nor is it a neutral space between religiosity and godlessness. It is rather a haunted and contested realm, built on the rubble of Christendom from its discarded materials. In this space, believers are assailed by doubt, and unbelievers long for transcendence.[2] But since Taylor deals with the macro picture of a slide toward secularity, my chapter sketches a micro image of the forces he describes by focusing on one story in particular.

Listening to Science Mike

One of the more compelling (de)conversion accounts I've read recently comes from the author, speaker, and podcaster Mike McHargue. Known as Science Mike for his ability to unpack scientific principles for nonspecialists, McHargue's story of losing and regaining a version of Christian faith was recounted in the popular *Liturgists* podcast[3] and in his first book: *Finding God in the Waves: How I Lost My Faith and Found It Again Through Science.*[4]

---

[1]Charles Taylor, *A Secular Age* (Cambridge, MA: Belknap Press of Harvard University Press, 2007), chap. 16.

[2]For an accessible overview of Taylor on these points, see James K. A. Smith, *How (Not) to Be Secular: Reading Charles Taylor* (Grand Rapids, MI: Eerdmans, 2014).

[3]See especially the episodes titled "Lost and Found" (parts 1 and 2): Michael Gungor and Science Mike, "Lost and Found," *The Liturgists*, October 14 and 27, 2014, https://theliturgists.com/podcast/2014/10/14/episode-6-lost-and-found-part-1; https://theliturgists.com/podcast/2014/10/27/episode7-lost-and-found-part-2. After leaving *The Liturgists* in 2019, McHargue now hosts *The Cozy Robot show*, which explores a variety of topics with what he dubs "empathy and skepticism," https://cozyrobots.com.

[4]Mike McHargue, *Finding God in the Waves: How I Lost My Faith and Found It Again Through Science* (New York: Convergent, 2016). Subsequent references will be noted in parentheses in the body of the text. Since McHargue's listeners know him best as Science Mike, I will often follow that format in what follows. McHargue has now published a second book, *You're a Miracle (And a Pain in the Ass): Embracing the Emotions, Habits, and Mystery that Make You You* (New York: Convergent, 2020). Although he still identifies as a Christian, this second publication is less theological in nature, focusing instead on the science and psychology of self-understanding.

I choose Mike's story because it gained attention within Christian and atheist subcultures, and especially among the spiritually homeless. I also choose it because I like Mike personally, despite never having met him, and despite having very different theological commitments. I find his story compelling not because it mirrors that of every None who drifts from Christianity but because it illustrates some hunches I have on how doubt often functions in the mind of the afflicted.

Raised Southern Baptist, Mike became a Christian at age seven (25). He was a lonely child, intelligent but frequently bullied for his weight and social awkwardness. Due to a learning disability, his grades were poor, but he would not discover until adulthood that he is a person with autism. Mike battled depression and occasional thoughts of suicide. His closest relationships were with his parents and with God. "When I felt lonely hiding in the woods to escape bullies, I would talk to Jesus . . . about feeling fat, slow, and stupid." But these talks were not all sadness: "We'd [also] talk about how the world worked and all the things in nature that amazed me" (14).

After discovering computers and the bass guitar in young adulthood, Mike found his niche. He married a Christian girl named Jenny, they had two children, and he became a deacon in a Southern Baptist congregation at the age of twenty-five. Mike was a self-professed "science nerd"; he believed in evolution but had little trouble reconciling it with an inerrant Bible and a personal God. Then came the trauma that would be a tipping point: his parents divorced.

Mike's father, whom he idolized, announced that he was having an affair and that he was ending his marriage. The situation did not compute for Mike. His father was a professing Christian; he had no "biblical grounds" for divorce. Yet in spite of daily attempts to change his father's mind, Mike was getting nowhere. To remedy the problem, Mike began to pray fervently, and he embarked on a "binge reading" of the Bible— completing the canon four times in a year (36)! Far from helping, however, the Bible reading made things worse. Where Mike had once found solace in Scripture, he now saw contradictions, senseless violence, and injustice. Problems were everywhere: the days of creation, Noah's flood, the Canaanite conquest. "Forget inerrant—this book seemed downright immoral" (42).

In a past attempt to convert an atheist friend online, Mike had agreed to a book exchange whereby the atheist would read a Christian text and Mike would read *The God Delusion* by Richard Dawkins. While most of the book was unexceptional, one portion struck a blow to his faltering faith. Prayer had been the footing of Mike's Christianity, and with his confidence in Scripture failing, talking to God sustained him (49). Dawkins eroded this foundation with a volley of statistics purporting to show prayer's ineffectiveness. Then he issued a challenge: instead of praying to God each day, direct your requests to a jug of milk on the breakfast table, and compare results. Mike asked his milk jug for a raise at work and got one. The experience led him to binge read other atheist literature.

The final straw for Mike's Christianity came from a book by the American astronomer and astrophysicist Carl Sagan: *Pale Blue Dot.* The title alludes to the photograph for which Sagan was responsible when he convinced operators of the *Voyager 1* spacecraft to turn its camera back to Earth, which was 3.7 billion miles away. The image is iconic. Our planet appears in it as a "tiny blue speck, incredibly small and insignif- icant" (66). From this vantage point, Sagan waxed poetic:

> Look again at that dot. That's here. That's home. That's us. On it everyone you love, everyone you know, everyone you have ever heard of, every human being who ever was, lived out their lives. The aggregate of our joy and suffering, thousands of confident religions, ideologies, and economic doctrines . . . every saint and sinner in the history of our species lived there—on a mote of dust suspended in a sunbeam.[5]

The words shook Mike. Yet the assault on his faith came in the next chapter, written by Sagan's widow, Ann Druyan. Her challenge was to "stare at the dot for any length of time, and then try to convince yourself that God created the whole universe for one of the 10 million or so species of life that inhabit that speck of dust" (66-67).

---

[5]Carl Sagan, *Pale Blue Dot: A Vision of the Human Future in Space* (New York: Ballantine Books, 1994), 6.

Mike closed the book and found himself on the cusp of atheism. "God was no longer merely distant. He seemed implausible. A myth concocted by frightened apes in a dangerous world." For some reason, Sagan's book had lodged in Mike's mind far deeper than other atheist manifestos. The image of the pale blue speck had "shifted the frame and revealed the notion of a God who cares for our Earth as being silly in a cosmos whose scale dwarfs our imagination" (68).

Yet what is a lifelong Southern Baptist to do in order to convert to atheism? Mike's answer was to pray: "God, I don't know why I'm praying. You aren't even real." What happened next is both poignant and painful:

> The feeling I associated with the presence of God left me, like morning mist. . . . I felt as if a trapdoor opened beneath me and I fell through it.
>
> A series of dark insights entered my mind with terrifying speed. I realized that all the people I had loved and who had died before me were gone. Forever. . . .
>
> I felt a profound grief, an inky-black darkness, as I realized there was neither mission nor redemption for humanity. The universe was indifferent to us. We were all just an accident of the self-organizing principles of physics—mere quirks of gravity, electromagnetism, and chemistry. This was it. This was the end of my search.
>
> "God, I don't know why I'm praying. You aren't even real."
>
> In the time it took to say those 11 words, I'd become an existential nihilist.
>
> And my parents got divorced anyway. (69-70)

Farewell, Pangaea.

I pause here not because Mike's story is finished but because his plunge into atheism affords an opportunity to embark on the second movement in this chapter. I want to explore facets of Mike's secular conversion in the way a sociologist might walk into a sawdust-floor revival. Despite the obvious fallibility of my observations, the basic question follows: What should we notice about the way doubt evolves into full-fledged unbelief?

Mike Beneath the Microscope

My first observation is that Mike's movement into atheism hardly felt like a joyous liberation from religion's superstitious shackles. It felt like a death. Like the former pastor John Suk, Mike sensed that "all my life I have romanced a woman—faith—whom I cannot have."[6] The feeling of loss corresponds to the secularism described by Charles Taylor. Taylor notes that many postreligious persons experience their journey toward unbelief with a sense of painful "cross-pressure" whereby "faith is pretty much unthinkable but abandonment to the abyss is even more so."[7] To use Taylor's language, the modern soul feels caught between the malaise of "immanence" and memory of "transcendence." The agnostic author Julian Barnes writes the following words as the opening line of his memoir: "I don't believe in God, but I miss him."[8]

The pains of cross-pressures are often ignored by the noisy zealots that suck up all the oxygen in the God debate: religious dogmatists and their "Ditchkens" doppelgängers.[9] James K. A. Smith puts the point astutely:

> If our only guides were new atheists or religious fundamentalists, we would never know that this vast, contested terrain even existed, even though most of us live in this space every day. . . . While stark fundamentalisms—either religious or secular—get all the press, what should interest us are these fugitive expressions of doubt *and* longing, faith *and* questioning. These lived expressions of "cross-pressure" are at the heart of the secular.[10]

This fragility was at the heart of McHargue's post-Christian story. He describes a "transcendence withdrawal" (88) that he experienced largely alone since he had hidden his unbelief from those closest to him.

---

[6]John Suk, *Not Sure: A Pastor's Journey from Faith to Doubt* (Grand Rapids, MI: Eerdmans, 2011), 5.

[7]These words are those of James K. A. Smith, in summary of Taylor's argument. Smith, *How (Not) to Be Secular*, x.

[8]Julian Barnes, *Nothing to Be Frightened Of* (New York: Knopf, 2008), 1. I first encountered this line in Smith, *How (Not) to Be Secular*, 66.

[9]*Ditchkens* is the pithy label Terry Eagleton attaches to the noisy minority of New Atheists that buy their "rejection of religion on the cheap . . . as though one were to dismiss feminism on the basis of Clint Eastwood's opinions of it." Terry Eagleton, *Reason, Faith, and Revolution: Reflections on the God Debate* (New Haven, CT: Yale University Press, 2009), xi.

[10]Smith, *How (Not) to Be Secular*, 4, 14 (emphasis original).

Mike even admits to having led his eldest daughter to Christ during his years as an undercover atheist, weeping as he baptized her (74). He had a hard time breaking his daily prayer habit (79). And on dark days he admits to doubting his doubts (80). So while others delightedly dismantled the faith of naive Christians, Mike never had that zeal: "It broke my heart to see good people lose God" (85). Such is the state of spiritual cross-pressure.

My second observation from Mike's story involves a trigger for unbridled doubt. His plunge began with the shock of his parents' divorce, and the realization that Bible verses failed to restore his father to marital fidelity. This led to a furious rereading of the Scriptures with the deconstructive aid of the New Atheists. A lesson here is that deconversions are often sparked more by emotional trauma than by a string of rational objections to Christianity. Mike had surely seen Christian couples get divorced in his lifetime. And he must have been aware that "machine-gunning" Bible verses (his phrase) might not automatically restore the union. But things were different when it was his family. So it is with many of us.

Mike admits that trauma contributed to his new reading of the Scriptures: "My deconstruction of faith hadn't been the rational and clinical pursuit I believed it to be. When I opened Genesis, I wasn't just looking for answers: I had a bone to pick" (106). "This God whom I'd loved and worshiped . . . had sat by and done jackshit while my parents' marriage fell apart" (105).

In these uncensored observations, one meets the modern equivalent of the psalmist's wails and shouts over God's refusal to intervene for Israel (e.g., Ps 77:8). And one senses that a simplistic and hyperrational apologetic of evidence demanding a verdict will do little to help. Since the deconversion wasn't primarily about uncovering a rational "defeater" to Christianity, supplying a rational counterargument is unlikely to undo it.[11]

Finally, the poetic words from *Pale Blue Dot* reveal how unbelief is often triggered more by emotion and aesthetic pathos than by careful

---

[11]See Myron Bradley Penner, *The End of Apologetics: Christian Witness in a Postmodern Context* (Grand Rapids, MI: Baker Academic, 2013), 7.

argument. After all, the mere fact that Earth is extremely small in comparison to the universe hardly has any bearing on whether the Christian God exists. This assumption is like saying that Shakespeare cannot have authored *Macbeth* because, after all, the Library of Congress is very large. The reasoning is terrible even if the atheist turned out to be correct about God's nonexistence. In this case, it would be like claiming that Shakespeare cannot have authored *War and Peace* based on the library's square footage. Whether Druyan is right or wrong about God's existence, her argument is very poor.

As far back as Psalm 8, humans have felt the existential vertigo of smallness. Yet this might just as easily lead to reverential awe as to disbelief. Like many arguments of the New Atheism, this onramp to unbelief becomes convincing only after it succeeds in fashioning what Herbert McCabe calls "the idolatrous notion of God as a very large and powerful creature."[12] *Behold Andromeda! What spirit-animal could have possibly made that!?* The critique of Christianity sees Scripture as basically a botched attempt to explain both literally and scientifically how the physical world works. The Bible is assumed to be a shoddy first draft of Newton's *Principia Mathematica*. And this, in Terry Eagleton's words, is "like seeing ballet as a botched attempt to run for a bus."[13]

One should not hear in my critique a denial that any atheistic arguments have force. Some are downright difficult. But here and elsewhere, both Ditchkens and certain religious fundamentalists often display a similar approach to Scripture. In fact, one is tempted to suggest that Ken Ham and Richard Dawkins might coauthor a hermeneutics book without serious disagreement as to method. They would clash fiercely on the Bible's truth. But they would stand in surprising alignment as to the kind of thing the text is trying to do and how one may approach it while ignoring ancient contexts and the varied history of interpretation.

Beyond the construal of God as a superintelligent extraterrestrial, Sagan's "pale blue dot" assertion has still less to do with the possibility that a particular deity might bestow his image upon a frail creature

---

[12]Herbert McCabe, *Faith Within Reason* (London: Continuum, 2007), 76.
[13]Eagleton, *Reason, Faith, and Revolution*, 50.

known as *human*. And especially if this God were rumored to delight in using weak and foolish things (1 Cor 1:27). The power in Sagan's passage—and it is powerful in its own way—resides not in rational argument but in the evocation of desolate emotion by way of cold poetic beauty. Mike's story bears witness to the fearful rush of loneliness that lies dormant in the modern soul, like a bit of malware embedded in our operating system: *Do you feel your isolation, earthling? You are stranded on this mote of dust.*

My point is not to ridicule anyone for finding the words of *Pale Blue Dot* compelling. I too feel their tug. A key part of my own argument is that we *need* wonder, emotion, and story-laden links to the God who unites beauty, truth, and goodness in himself. My aim here is not to dismiss affective drivers for faith or doubt. It is merely to highlight them—and then to say quite clearly (in the case of Druyan's claim as it comes cloaked in the disguise of reason and science) that not all of them are worth their salt.

To acknowledge the importance of transrational forces is not necessarily to become a full-fledged postmodern-relativist-Romantic-fideist-*i*gnostic-woo-woo hippy. Careful reasoning matters as we evaluate the coherence of belief, and especially as we separate defeaters from mere rhetoric. Yet such cognitive deliberations may not be the primary triggers for doubt and deconversion that either apologists or New Atheists suppose. This is how we humans function: a great many of our doubts, beliefs, and intellectual conclusions are affected more by the aesthetic, the embodied, the traumatic, and the emotive than by the rational, the cerebral, and the scientific.[14] In the words of Alan Noble, "A bad breakup in sixth grade, the death of your father, your favorite band, and your experience as a prematurely bald man will have deep effects on you, just as will your parents' conservative politics and your school's teachings on origins, maybe even more so."[15] For Christians to assume otherwise when

---

[14]Consider advertising: whether it is a dish soap that all but promises a hunky man to the buyer or a can of soda that promises a carefree, dancing-through-the-streets existence, no one rationally expects these products to deliver on their promises, but their aesthetic appeals still lead us to choose them over competitors that make lesser claims. See this point in Alan Noble, *Disruptive Witness: Speaking Truth in a Distracted Age* (Downers Grove, IL: InterVarsity Press, 2018), 76.

[15]Noble, *Disruptive Witness*, 52.

dealing with doubt is like trying to treat anxiety by machine-gunning passages from a psychiatric manual like the DSM-5. The apologetic cure may only exacerbate the ailment.[16]

Charles Taylor suggests that it is rarely science that has done the heavy lifting in "scientific" deconversions from religious faith. Rather, it is the form of science as a narrative of firmness, maturity, and expertise. The scientific story has a refreshing concreteness that can rarely be attained in spiritual matters. And in times of pain and trauma, that sense of firmness and order is needed. Martin Luther, for instance, was said to have found solace after the death of his beloved daughter only by immersing himself in the regularity of Greek grammar: nominatives and genitives.[17] Similarly, the ordered world of science can be "a mighty fortress" in life's storms. But as Luther would likely point out, it is not a "bulwark never failing."

For those struggling with spiritual uncertainty, there can be an aura of maturity and expertise that hovers around the patron saints of science like a halo. Thus, even when the sacred pontiffs of science overstep their bounds to speak *ex cathedra* in the realm of theology (e.g., Druyan: *The universe is really big, so, no God*), the individual already captured by the firmness of their material claims may go along with the subsequent leap of logic on the grounds of something like papal infallibility and a sense of maturity that comes with the conclusion.

This tendency of creeping expertise (the assumption that mastery in one field automatically transfers to all others) is evident in McHargue's narrative when he notes that "some of the most brilliant scientists of the modern era" (Dawkins and Sam Harris) conclude that "religion actually harms us" (154). I do not doubt that many atheistic scientists are smart, but the better question is as follows: Why should scientists be considered the unquestioned authorities on topics like ethics, religion, psychology, political theory, and personal wellness? Is this not like trusting a good

---

[16]See Penner, *End of Apologetics*. As he writes, "Defending Christian belief is not an unqualified good; it may actually be counterproductive to faith." Unfortunately, Penner's failure is to radicalize this conclusion so all apologetic endeavors are seen to be "a curse" (9).

[17]This story was relayed to me via the retirement address of my former professor, Scott Hafemann, esteemed Greek teacher at the University of St. Andrews.

mechanic to order your diet and romantic habits? The reason this move seems justified has to do with the firmness and feeling of grown-upness that attends the material claims of scientists so that their expertise is assumed to creep into the realm of the divine.

A fictional example of the scientific creepiness is found in Marilynne Robinson's Pulitzer Prize–winning novel, *Gilead*. Near the beginning, we learn that the narrator's brother, Edward, had gone to Germany to study ministry in the early 1900s. Graciously, Edward's home church in Iowa took up a collection to support him. He came back "Herr Doktor"—an atheist—having written a monograph on Feuerbach. Upon Edward's return to the family dinner table, his pastor-father asks him to pray, to which he refuses. When pressed to show respect for family custom, Edward's reply is an icy quote from Scripture: "When I was a child, I thought as a child. Now that I have become a man, I have put away childish things."

The insinuation is that atheism is merely the objective result of a rational maturity. Yet Edward's brother tells the backstory: "There were two sisters and a brother between us, all carried off by diphtheria in less than two months. He knew them, and I, of course, did not."[18]

We have been told that scientific conversions amount, quite simply, to *Cogito, ergo* None, but this narrative is itself a simplistic take on a more complex reality. Hence, one is tempted to respond to the Herr Doktors of scientism with a mangled line from yet another Scripture: "Physician *feel* thyself." Feel the extent to which even atheistic conversions are moved by aesthetic, affective, and emotional forces that rival those of sawdust-floored revivals. In the words of Taylor, "The appeal of scientific materialism is not so much the cogency of its detailed findings . . . as the stance of maturity, of courage, of manliness, over against childish fears and sentimentality."[19]

To be fair to the critics of Christianity, the sense of childish faith is not always an illusion. James K. A. Smith draws on the work of Taylor to note the "immature" and "Sunday-schoolish" belief that renders one ripe for

---

[18]Marilynne Robinson, *Gilead: A Novel* (New York: Picador, 2004), 26.
[19]Taylor, *Secular Age*, 365.

deconversion.[20] Science Mike suggests that this was true of him. The literalistic fundamentalism of his home church left him with the impression that on one side stood a great crowd of learned witnesses (Dawkins, Harris, Sagan) while on the other stood a clan of well-meaning bumpkins.

Team Shaming and Fringe Revulsion

This explains why concepts of "team shaming" and "fringe revulsion" are important. They are my words, not Taylor's, but they describe occurrences that have been highlighted already. In an age of polarization and dogmatic shrillness, an effective conversionary move can be to shame others by connecting them to a team that appears embarrassing, uninformed, or harmful. In some cases, team shaming backfires, causing the maligned group to dig in their heels and embrace the dogmatic stereotypes. But in other cases, shaming speeds defection.

In an age of social media, team shaming can become a career, with algorithms that prioritize and amplify outrageous behavior. Twitter followers, a branded podcast, and the Cable News circuit may await if you play your cards right. Unfortunately, while this outrage-based approach boosts clicks and ad revenue, it also drives traffic to the lands of doubt and dogmatism. The spiritual cost is high.

Mike's story evidences this feeling of team shaming as fringe elements of evangelicalism repulse thoughtful people (hence, fringe revulsion). And when certain team members get loud or large enough, we may be tempted to throw up our hands and defect from faith entirely. I have certainly felt this temptation. *I don't want to be on team evangelical! Look at our self-appointed captains!*

For this reason, the New Atheism relies on ridicule. Shame can be a powerful emotion, and it works on us without us knowing it.[21] For his own part, Mike is careful not to describe the conservative congregants

---

[20]Smith, *How (Not) to be Secular*, 77.

[21]One of the ironies I've witnessed is the extent to which ex-vangelicals preach incessantly against shame as a tool used by fundamentalists while shaming mercilessly those who hold to historic orthodoxy. For a look at how shame functions in the Scriptures, see Te-Li Lau, *Defending Shame: Its Formative Power in Paul's Letters* (Grand Rapids, MI: Baker Academic, 2020).

of his former church as backwoods bigots. Yet even in moments of apparent kindness, embarrassment shines through. "I go to a church of loving, sweet Fundamentalists," he tells a room of progressive Christians. "They're like, 'We love gay people. We're going to change them, but we love them'" (114).

In talking to my own students and conversing with post-Christian friends and family members, it is apparent how large team shame and fringe revulsion bulk in the migration to the land of None. These concepts join with others to help us grasp the ways that pervasive doubt begins to germinate and grow within us.

Conclusion

Mike's deconversion story reminds us that a view of the human person as primarily a "thinking thing" (*res cogitans*) is a fairy tale concocted to support a narrative of rational maturity within the land of modern doubt. "*Cogito, ergo* None," we say, with a sense of mournful superiority. Yet alongside that intellectual "I think" (if not in place of it) are other words—not all in the first person singular!—involving trauma, intuition, fear, desire, worship, habit, love, bitterness, and suffering. Thankfully, Mike's deconversion story does not end there.

9

Split Brains or Divided Hearts?

A Snapshot Continued

*The two hemispheres of my mind
were in the sharpest contrast.*

C. S. Lewis, *Surprised by Joy*

WHAT HAPPENS WHEN JESUS shows up to ruin your deconversion story? The present chapter continues to explore the land of doubt that stands opposite religious dogmatism. But as the title of Mike McHargue's book, *Finding God in the Waves*,[1] suggests, *unbelief* is not the last word to describe his spiritual journey. Nor does his narrative end with an atheistic prayer while holding Carl Sagan's *Pale Blue Dot* like a secular Bible.

Unlike the prior chapter on the slide toward unbelief, the focus here will be on ways in which doubt is problematized by lived experience, a desire for transcendence, and a God who seeks lost sheep that no longer

---

[1]See again Mike McHargue, *Finding God in the Waves: How I Lost My Faith and Found It Again Through Science* (New York: Convergent, 2016). Again, page numbers will be cited parenthetically in the body of the text.

believe in the "social construct" of a Shepherd. To note such cross-pressures, however, is not necessarily to craft a simplistic reconversion story whereby one leaves uncertainty to live blissfully with Jesus. Some doubts may remain in the brain even after Christ moves powerfully to reclaim the heart. Thus, my snapshot concludes by noting the importance of the following forces:

- Suprarational experiences that defy reductionistic explanation

- Embodied habits that shape our brains as well as our divided hearts

- Relational connectedness that counters loneliness and virtual community

Now back to Mike's story.

God in the Waves

Nearly two years after his *Pale Blue Dot* conversion, Mike agreed to attend a conference in Southern California with the well-known and controversial "ex-vangelical" teacher, Rob Bell. The event was on creativity, and Mike was there for work, to set up a portion of the meeting's website. Upon arrival, he was intrigued by the scientifically literate gathering of spiritual leaders, though he remained frustrated that so many clung to a version of Christianity (112). Eventually, Mike couldn't take it anymore. During one session, his hand shot up, and he released a torrent of questions and critiques. These criticisms were aimed not merely at fundamentalist Christianity but at progressive versions as well. He ended with a question: "How can anyone who understands how the universe works believe in God?" (115).

The group's reaction was unexpected.

They just accepted me. And they even thanked me for caring.

When I look back at that moment in that room with fifty strangers, I imagine what would've happened if someone had rebuked me, told me that the devil was after me, or that I was in rebellion against God. . . . My path back to God was paved with grace by those who received my doubt in love. (118-19)

In short, the best response to honest doubt is never dogmatism.

But Mike's atheism remained unfazed. Then came the end of the conference when participants were invited to receive Communion. The message involved the ordinariness of bread and wine—just simple protons, neutrons, and electrons—that become sacred as they are set aside for special use. Bell's point was that humanity too has been set aside for a purpose: to be "broken and poured out for others" (121-22). Mike found this idea appealing (minus the religious bits) so he decided to go along. He prayed; he stood to take Communion. Then came the part that he admits sounds crazy (122). After having second thoughts on the way to the front, Mike decided to leave: "But just when I was about to turn, I heard a voice say, 'I was here when you were eight, and I'm here now'" (124). In shock and confusion, he took the bread and ran crying from the room (125).

What had happened? Mike didn't know. After scouring the scientific literature, the closest explanation he could find was a hallucination aided by a highly suggestive state and pent-up emotion (125). Yet, on that particular night, he found himself alone on the beach, praying. He poured out complaints about the problem of evil, miracles, religious exclusivity, and a Bible that sometimes seemed "archaic and brutal" (126). But his long and rambling prayer concluded with a frank acknowledgement: "I met Jesus tonight" (127).

Upon saying "Jesus," a wave crashed in front of Mike and water soaked his legs. He was startled since he remembers being well beyond the point that any prior wave had reached. At that moment he recalled that Christ's final service to his followers before the cross was to wash their feet. In response to this saltwater footwashing, Mike prayed again: "'Is that you, God? Is this really happening?' And the whole world fell away, like the veil lifted from the face of a bride on her wedding day" (127). The experience did not stop there. But in Mike's view, it would be impossible to capture it with words. "Mystical experiences transpire outside the realm of thought and language." Thus the mystics choose simply to sit "with the experience and let it change them" (129).[2]

---

[2]For the most robust defense of Christian mystical experience from the field of analytic philosophy, see William P. Alston, *Perceiving God: The Epistemology of Religious Experience* (Ithaca, NY: Cornell University Press, 1991).

I pause here to ask an important question: What place should unverifiable firsthand accounts have within our exploration of Christian faith between doubt and dogmatism? For some, Mike's experience may serve as proof of God's power and love, even if it transpired through the ministry of someone who has been dubbed a heretic. But mystical experiences do not last forever. And for skeptics they prove nothing. The world is filled with individuals who swear by absurd experiences. Why believe this one? Mike admits that this was precisely his question. The experience did not quell his doubts. In his words, "I had become an emotional and experiential Christian who [was still] an intellectual atheist" (129). What does that mean?

Doubt and the Split Brain

This chapter can now stitch together content from the two previous ones. In chapter five I argued that many biblical statements against doubt are critiques not of honest questions but of contrary allegiances that create a double-minded and unstable person. In chapter six I noted how this instability is heightened by emotional, philosophical, and traumatic cross-pressures. Although we prefer to ground our deconversion stories in the claims of reason and science, the reality is usually more complicated.

My question here is different: How does the double-mindedness of biblical doubt connect with ongoing uncertainty even after returning to some form of Christian faith? Does this persistent doubt reveal the divided heart that Scripture denounces? Thankfully, there is an entire section in Mike's book on the scientific relevance of "split brain" experiments for understanding the conflict between faith and doubt. And though Mike does not make the connection between the split brain of science and the double-mind of Scripture (e.g., Jas 1:8), the comparison is worth exploring.

In one sense everyone is double-minded because the human brain is divided into two hemispheres: left and right. These apparently identical halves communicate with each other across a thick channel of nerves called the corpus callosum (130). Still, the conversation and cooperation across the corpus callosum does not mean that brain hemispheres are always in agreement. Like Earth's two hemispheres, there is the potential for continental drift.

This neurological condition was revealed when scientists severed the corpus callosum in certain patients, to relieve them of maladies like epileptic seizures. Many of these patients appeared unchanged. But over time an unsettling reality known as "alien hand syndrome" (AHS) emerged. In one instance, a man reached out to hug his wife with one arm only to be horrified as he punched her with the other. In another case, a woman selected a business-appropriate dress for work from her closet, only to watch in dismay as her other hand grabbed a much louder print. In a final episode, a patient was terrified to sleep because of fear that his alien hand might strangle him in the night (132).

Moving past the horror-movie quality of these stories, the emerging hypothesis involved the same metaphor I have used to describe the world of post-Pangaea evangelicalism: "The two hemispheres of the brain [had begun] to 'drift'" (132). The patients had become, if not double-minded, at least double-brained.[3]

To test the hypothesis, scientists devised a method to communicate with each half of the brain in isolation. They asked questions of either hemisphere and then compared results. One young man was asked what job he planned to pursue after completing his education. His left brain responded with the sensible career of a draftsman; his right brain spelled out "automobile racer." In Mike's words, the two hemispheres had very different aims and agendas, despite inhabiting the same cranium (133).[4]

Another individual was asked about God. His right brain responded that he was a believer; his left brain claimed he was an atheist. In one head, there apparently resided opposite opinions on God's existence. For Mike, these split-brain experiments helped him reconcile something about himself.

---

[3]For the most famous work on the scientific, psychological, and cultural results of hemispheric brain functions, see Iain McGilchrist, *The Master and His Emissary: The Divided Brain and the Making of the Western World* (New Haven, CT: Yale University Press, 2009).

[4]McGilchrist argues that "there is no such thing as the brain, only the brain according to the right hemisphere and the brain according to the left hemisphere." McGilchrist, *Master and His Emissary*, 175.

For all its bizarreness, the phenomenon of split-brain patients gives me strange comfort. Suddenly, I don't feel so weird for identifying with both skeptical and spiritual people. There is an atheist in my brain who remains wholly incredulous about the idea of a divine being who once dwelt among us. . . . There is a Christian in my brain who is indescribably and enduringly comforted by the idea and love of a supernatural Savior. I've stopped trying to deny, starve, or otherwise do away with either of them. (134)

Since his mystical experience came along a shoreline, Mike makes a connection to the call of Christ to Peter and his fellow fishermen. These men followed Jesus despite a less-than-perfect understanding of who he was, and in spite of questions. In the same way, McHargue concludes that Christian Mike should "drop his nets" and follow Jesus while allowing Atheist Mike to tag along for the ride (134). Is it okay for Christ-followers to make peace with this kind of dual citizenship? Before answering, we should note that the struggle is not unique to Mike McHargue.

The Mariner and Narnia's Magician

During his own tortured period of a conflict between faith and doubt, the poet Samuel Taylor Coleridge (1772–1834)—most famous for authoring "The Rime of the Ancient Mariner"—wrote that he "had too much Vanity to be altogether a Christian" but "too much tenderness of Nature to be utterly an Infidel." As a modern man, Coleridge could derive pleasure from reading the skepticism of Voltaire. But he also acknowledged that "my Heart forced me to admire the beauty of Holiness in the Gospel [and] forced me to *love* the Jesus, whom my Reason . . . would not permit me to worship."[5]

Coleridge sought shelter, as did Science Mike, in the mystical tradition, calling it "a pillar of fire" during his wandering so he never

---

[5]Samuel Taylor Coleridge, "To George Coleridge (30 March 1794)" (letter 44), in *The Collected Letters of Samuel Taylor Coleridge*, ed. Earl Leslie Griggs (Oxford: Clarendon, 1956), 1:78. Cited in Malcolm Guite, *Mariner: A Theological Voyage with Samuel Taylor Coleridge* (Downers Grove, IL: IVP Academic, 2018), 43 (emphasis original to Coleridge).

perished in "the sandy deserts of utter unbelief."[6] Eventually, he returned to a more robust Christian faith. While Coleridge did not think faith was entirely voluntary or involuntary, he did believe we can "cultivate such habits of thinking and acting, as will give force and effective Energy to the arguments on either side."[7] I will return to the theme of cultivated habits momentarily.

C. S. Lewis describes a similar experience. Describing his brief but tortured time between faith and unbelief, he writes, "The two hemispheres of my mind were in the sharpest contrast. On the one side a many-sided sea of poetry and myth; on the other a glib and shallow 'rationalism.' Nearly all that I loved I believed to be imaginary; nearly all that I believed to be real I thought grim and meaningless."[8] For both Lewis and Coleridge, the road back to faith came not primarily by a suprarational experience but by God's use of beauty, poetry, and literature to kindle the imagination for something more than a lonely, God-stripped universe. Art became an ark in which to weather stormy seas between the lands of doubt and dogmatism

Science Mike seems somewhat different from Lewis and Coleridge. By his own account, his mind remains more unmended.[9] And this point raises an important question toward which I have been building: How does the split brain relate to the divided heart or double-mind of biblical doubt? Are they the same?

Separating Split Brains from Divided Hearts

I do not think these two concepts are identical. There is a difference between the soul/heart/mind of Scripture and the brain of modern neuroscience. In the Bible, the first cluster of concepts has primarily to do with trusting allegiance (*pistis*) in spite of fluctuations in emotion

---

[6]Samuel Taylor Coleridge, *Biographia Literaria*, ed. James Engell and W. Jackson Bate (Princeton, NJ: Princeton University Press, 1984), 152. Cited in Guite, *Mariner*, 253.

[7]Coleridge, "To George Coleridge" (letter 44), 1:78. Cited in Guite, *Mariner*, 43.

[8]C. S. Lewis, *Surprised by Joy: The Shape of My Early Life* (New York: Harcourt, 1955), 170.

[9]Lewis himself acknowledged that his more common temptation was to believe "too much" (with regard to spiritualism) rather than "too little" and return to atheistic unbelief. See Alan Jacobs, *The Narnian: The Life and Imagination of C. S. Lewis* (New York: HarperOne, 2005), 38, 130, 292.

and evidence evaluation. Something like this point was made previously by the New Testament scholar Matthew Bates when he argued that God's requirement is not that we be absolutely certain of our theological beliefs but that we be "certain enough to yield" in spite of our remaining questions.[10]

A similar point is made by the philosopher Jonathan Kvanvig. In *Faith and Humility*, Kvanvig's claim is that faith is not an act of cognitive gymnastics whereby we generate untroubled belief in a given proposition, perhaps in ways that run contrary to the evidence.[11] *Pistis* is not therefore what Mark Twain mocked by saying, "Faith is believin' what you know ain't so."[12] Kvanvig views faith as a commitment to a cause; it is a "disposition in service of an ideal."[13] And in Christianity that ideal happens also to be a person: Jesus, the saving King.[14] This functional account of faith must be balanced by humility since the absence of this self-effacing virtue results in "arrogance that generates zealots of the most despicable sort" (in other words, dogmatism).[15] In the end, neither Bates nor Kvanvig denies that we should know or believe important propositional truths,[16] but they are distinguishing faith as embodied commitment from faith as mental certainty.[17]

This distinction may be applied by returning to the young man whose brain was split between the occupations of draftsman and racecar driver. Biblically speaking, the important question is not whether the two hemispheres continue to have differing inclinations but rather, What will he

---

[10]See Matthew W. Bates, *Salvation by Allegiance Alone: Rethinking Faith, Works, and the Gospel of Jesus the King* (Grand Rapids, MI: Baker Academic, 2017), 94.

[11]Jonathan L. Kvanvig, *Faith and Humility* (Oxford: Oxford University Press, 2018). Thanks to an anonymous reviewer of my manuscript who alerted me to Kvanvig's work.

[12]Mark Twain, *Following the Equator: A Journey Around the World* (Hartford, CT: American Publishing, 1897), 67.

[13]Kvanvig, *Faith and Humility*, viii.

[14]See Matthew W. Bates, *Gospel Allegiance: What Faith in Jesus Misses for Salvation in Christ* (Grand Rapids, MI: Brazos, 2019).

[15]Kvanvig, *Faith and Humility*, 153.

[16]For a related argument, see Dru Johnson, *Biblical Knowing: A Scriptural Epistemology of Error* (Eugene, OR: Cascade, 2013).

[17]For other views of faith that are less predicated on untroubled cognitive beliefs, see Lara Buchak, "Reason and Faith," in *The Oxford Handbook of the Epistemology of Theology*, ed. William J. Abraham and Frederick D. Aquino (Oxford: Oxford University Press, 2017), 46-63.

do about it? Questions of vocation (and even more, questions of allegiance) require a choice and whole-hearted devotion. Without that commitment, the likely result is instability, unhappiness, and failure—like the tortured college student who ends up deep in debt because he has changed his major every semester.

Fulfillment and eternal fence-sitting don't mix.

This truth is illustrated by Yann Martel in the novel *Life of Pi*. As one character notes, doubt may be appropriate for a season, but "to choose doubt as a philosophy of life is akin to choosing immobility as a means of transportation."[18] For this reason, the words of Joshua and Jesus come to us not as cruel ultimatums but as merciful prompts to nudge us off the fence: "Choose for yourselves this day whom you will serve" (Josh 24:15). "No one can serve two masters. Either you will hate the one and love the other, or you will be devoted to the one and despise the other" (Lk 16:13).

You can reject the divided heart of contrary allegiance even if you wrestle mightily with the split brain of conflicting questions and emotions. The two concepts (heart and brain) are different. Thus, whatever his faults, Kierkegaard's emphasis on a "leap" toward God is helpful.[19] We see also the importance of Coleridge's prior line about the cultivation of certain habits that allow God to renew not just our "mind" (Rom 12:2) but our split brain as well.

How Habit Shapes Desire, Belief, and Brain

In a winsomely titled chapter, "Teach us, neuroscience, to pray," McHargue tells how he returned to a vibrant prayer life, post-milk jug. To get past feelings of silliness and superstition, he formed an axiom that described prayer as "at least a form of meditation that encourages the development of healthy brain tissue" (177).

He acknowledges that the axiom falls woefully short of a traditional Christianity. But Mike's claim is that it helped him keep praying during moments of doubt so that the practice (or, rather, the Spirit) could work upon his brain (178). This habit-based approach builds on an

---

[18]Yann Martel, *Life of Pi* (New York: Harcourt, 2001), 28.
[19]See again chap. 1.

understanding of the brain's plasticity—ability to be rewired in response to repeated praxes and sensory inputs.[20] So although the practice of prayer may not provide a rational argument for God's presence, "it may help you encounter God" (181).

James K. A. Smith makes a related point in his Cultural Liturgies project.[21] Smith follows Augustine's conviction that we are guided by our loves in ways that affect both belief and behavior. But "the way our love or desire gets aimed in specific directions is through practices that shape, mold, and direct [it]."[22] Routines and rituals are crucial because they often work on us at subconscious levels.[23] Take, for instance, the avid churchgoer who listens to one sermon per week and then commutes "for three hours each day . . . all the while listening to inflammatory talk radio."[24] Which "gospel" (or shall we say, which apocalypse) is likely to be more formative? And how exactly will the "radio liturgy" shape one's desires, beliefs, and attitudes?

Admittedly, not all habits are as "thick" as others. Few would suspect that my routine of showering twice a day has much to do with my creeping tendencies toward doubt or dogmatism. But Smith's contention is that the line between "thick" and "thin" practices—the sacred and mundane—gets blurry. Some habits that we take to be relatively nonformative—say, meeting weekly for a breakfast with friends, praying before a meal, or listening regularly to a podcast that paints all Christians as brainwashed fundamentalists—may be thicker than we think. The

---

[20]John Suk's book on doubt also cites recent studies on the subject of brain plasticity. Suk, *Not Sure: A Pastor's Journey from Faith to Doubt* (Grand Rapids, MI: Eerdmans, 2011), 42n17. See, for instance, Norman Doidge, *The Brain That Changes Itself: Stories of Personal Triumph from the Frontiers of Brain Science* (New York: Penguin, 2007); Steven Johnson, *Mind Wide Open: Your Brain and the Neuroscience of Everyday Life* (New York: Scribner, 2004); and Richard Restak, *The New Brain: How the Modern Age Is Rewiring Your Mind* (New York: Rodale Press, 2004).

[21]This trilogy from Baker Academic includes (1) James K. A. Smith, *Desiring the Kingdom: Worship, Worldview, and Cultural Formation* (2009); (2) Smith, *Imagining the Kingdom: How Worship Works* (2013); and (3) Smith, *Awaiting the King: Reforming Public Theology* (2017). A popular-level distillation is available as Smith, *You Are What You Love: The Spiritual Power of Habit* (Grand Rapids, MI: Brazos, 2016).

[22]Smith, *Desiring the Kingdom*, 80.

[23]See also Dru Johnson, *Human Rites: The Power of Rituals, Habits, and Sacraments* (Grand Rapids, MI: Eerdmans, 2019).

[24]Smith, *Desiring the Kingdom*, 82.

overarching point, backed by a variety of research and artistic examples, is that our way of intuiting reality is "not so much learned as absorbed."[25] And the most formative absorption takes place at a communal level.[26]

Faith and Doubt as Communal Contagions

Communal traditions mark us, and never more than when we rebel against them.[27] We tend to borrow not just our ideas but our loves from those around us. Corroboration comes from the French literary critic and anthropologist René Girard (1923–2015). Girard's project builds upon a novel notion of human longing called *mimesis*: the idea that we want what we see others wanting.[28] As a parent of small children, I watch this process daily. If my two young sons are playing in the same room, nothing will make the elder brother want a discarded toy like the sight of his younger sibling appearing to take interest in it, or merely walking near it.

In Girard's theory, the contagiousness of our loves often leads to violence, just as it sometimes does with my two sons. Thus the Ten Commandments warn of coveting (Ex 20:17; Deut 5:21). Yet Girard also argues that mimesis is not inherently evil. It opens the self to others since it is through the other that desires are ignited.[29] And it enables a unique connection to God as the Spirit prods us to imitate the desires of Jesus through discipleship and what Girard calls the "mimesis of love."[30] Paul therefore calls Christians to "follow my example, as I follow the example of Christ" (1 Cor 11:1).[31]

---

[25]Smith, *Desiring the Kingdom*, 120.
[26]For a related argument, see the work of William P. Alston on how "doxastic practices" actually shape our beliefs. "A 'Doxastic Practice' Approach to Epistemology," in *Knowledge and Skepticism*, ed. Marjorie Clay and Keith Lehrer (Boulder, CO: Westview Press, 1989), 1-29.
[27]As evidence, I have argued elsewhere that even Descartes's seminal insight of *cogito, ergo sum* was drawn almost verbatim from church tradition, and specifically from Augustine. See Joshua McNall, *A Free Corrector: Colin Gunton and the Legacy of Augustine* (Minneapolis: Fortress, 2015), chap. 8.
[28]René Girard, *I See Satan Fall like Lightning*, trans. James G. Williams (Maryknoll, NY: Orbis, 2001), 15.
[29]See René Girard, *The Girard Reader*, ed. James G. Williams (New York: Herder, 1996), 64.
[30]Girard, *Girard Reader*, 63.
[31]For a fuller and more critical view of Girard's project, see Joshua M. McNall, *The Mosaic of Atonement: An Integrated Approach to Christ's Work* (Grand Rapids, MI: Zondervan Academic, 2019), chap. 12.

This contagious view of human desire informs the wrestling match with doubt. Since desire and belief are shaped by both habit and community, it matters greatly what type of community, and what authorities surround us.[32] In Science Mike's case, two points stand out. First, an aching loneliness, and, second, the less-than-helpful guides to whom he often turned. Because of the rigid nature of his church context, he felt unable to share his questions. And his online and published sources came largely from the ranks of simplistic apologetics or New Atheism.

The loneliness of Mike's deconversion was captured by a friend who noted that trying to find deep community based on atheism is like "trying to form a league of people who don't play golf" (78). In the end, both faith and doubt are shaped not only by evidence and experience but by community as well. On this final point, I am reminded of a story told by a former professor of mine when he confided in the theologian Stanley Hauerwas concerning his struggles in ministry. "You know what your problem is?" Hauerwas asked in his inimitable Texan bluntness: "You're too damn lonely." Indeed.

In Mike's case, this shared struggle was encountered in unexpected places. The book is partly dedicated to his since departed grandfather, who Mike notes was the first to hear its words. After listening, he told Mike about his own doubts; then he paused for a moment and said, "Don't tell your grandma."

Those of us in church leadership must cultivate communities in which the Science Mikes (including pastors) are driven neither underground nor away by the blind guides of religious or secular dogmatism. As the Gospels reveal, Jesus is often most present in other people. He comes cloaked in the "least of these," who serve as incognito incarnations of his presence (Mt 25:45), or with "a cup of cold water" given and received along the way (Mt 10:40-42). Not all of us will get a mystical encounter like Mike's, but we may encounter Christ in other humans who are conduits of his presence, and filled with his Spirit.

---

[32]See Johnson, *Biblical Knowing*, 209.

These guides may also include the saints and scholars of the past since one cure for superficial contemporary Christianity is to plunge into the great tradition. Where the living fail us, the dead may be our guides.[33] In a variety of ways, relational connections (in the flesh and across the centuries) can join together with inexplicable experiences and embodied habits so that we sojourn well through the wilderness of doubt.

Conclusion

Mike's brand of liberal-mystical Christianity remains very different from my theological zip code. By his own admission, his beliefs reside "far outside" of Christian orthodoxy (191). And at some points, his conclusions seem driven by a "fringe revulsion" against positions that are not expressly theological. Much of his recent work can be boiled down not to science but to the verbatim opinions of progressive American politics.

Although I sympathize with Mike's reaction to evangelical partisanship, a danger of a knee-jerk response is that we simply trade one set of partisan talking points for another. *Our enemies tend to rub off on us.* And this furthers the false sense that our only options are red or blue. On this point, A. J. Swoboda laments that one often hears little from progressive Christians that is not a basic repetition of CNN; just as one sometimes hears little from conservative evangelicals that is not a "retweet of Fox News."[34]

The gospel offers something better.

I am grateful that Christ showed up to ruin Mike's deconversion story, but I also wonder if there is a path forward that does not result in a designer Christianity that discards those elements of orthodoxy that bump against a postmodern Zeitgeist. What would this alternative look like? Having now surveyed the lands of dogmatism and doubt, the final portion of the book will flesh out the theological implications of the sacred imagination as it learns how to say perhaps. It's time to head toward those blank spaces.

---

[33]Thanks to Jerome Van Kuiken for this insight.

[34]A. J. Swoboda, *After Doubt: How to Question Your Faith Without Losing It* (Grand Rapids, MI: Brazos, 2021), 166.

WILBUR

Latitude: 32° 22′ 0.52″ N
Longitude: -86° 17′ 59.89″ W

Bus Stop, Montgomery, Alabama

Sophomore year.

Converting ordinances come in a variety of forms. For John Wesley, it was bread and wine offered to those without assurance of salvation, in hopes that the Lord's Table would be a means by which they said yes to Christ in faith. For Sophie Castinakis it was a seven-hundred-pound Galápagos tortoise, free access to a washer and dryer, and a refrigerator stocked with smoky sweet-potato hummus. "All things are yours," remarked the apostle. But we are getting ahead of ourselves.

In her first week at "Fundamentalist U" (her description), Sophie tagged along with Eliza to the annual expo in the noisy confines of the campus gymnasium. The space was filled with booths for local businesses and churches—all designed to connect students with jobs and services. And since neither Sophie nor Eliza could survive without employment, they went.

Between stands for the College Republicans and the local Humane Society, Sophie stumbled upon Ethel Mercer. Literally.

The short, gray-haired woman appeared to be in a wrestling match with a folding table that looked (if possible) older, heavier, and more arthritic than she was. After nearly tripping over her, Sophie knelt across from Ethel to extend a rusty table leg so the two of them could flip the whole thing upright.

"Oh! Thank you, young ma- ," the old woman exclaimed. But she stopped short as Sophie's soft features looked up from beneath the buzzcut head that formerly hid her face.

"No problem," Sophie responded. Then she spotted the homemade sign.

FREE LAUNDRY AND HOME COOKING (LADIES ONLY)

Sophie's interest piqued. First, because the dormitory laundry room smelled like a wet Labrador rolled in sports bras and Febreze. And second, because the campus cafeteria seemed to be exploring a fall theme titled "twenty-seven variations on a carbohydrate." Not even her love of Lucky Charms had emerged unscathed.

"Are you hiring?" Sophie asked.

"Not officially," Ethel remarked. "I'm a retired professor: biology. It's just me and my husband, and I need someone to look in on Wilbur when I'm gone."

"Is Wilbur your husband?"

"Oh, no," Ethel cackled. "Wilbur is a *Chelonoidis nigra*." Her voice went up as if she was imitating the Queen of England as she said it. "A Galápagos tortoise. He weighs seven hundred pounds and is almost ninety years old. My husband, Frank, is only eighty-two and considerably lighter since they revoked my faculty card in the cafeteria." She cackled again, clearly pleased with herself.

Sophie cracked a smile. She helped Ethel unpack the remaining contents of the crate and made small talk about the grammatical error on her Horcrux t-shirt. Then she did something that would have seemed absurd five minutes prior. She entered Ethel's information in her cellphone.

Boredom plus an invitation, plus a seven-hundred-pound tortoise.

Just then Eliza walked up holding two free chicken sandwiches from a neighboring booth and the encounter was over. Sophie waved goodbye, and the two girls walked out of the gymnasium to purchase books for the semester.

One of the required books was a novel by Evelyn Waugh, *Brideshead Revisited*. Neither girl had heard of it, but they took satisfaction in assuming that they would be reading at least one female author.

The story was of college life, religion, doubt, and the spiral of addiction. It seemed apropos. On page 120, Eliza later read how "it was normal to spend one's second year shaking off the friends of one's first." Indeed.

Eliza hadn't seen her old roommate, Claire, since last semester. But she was growing perplexed at how well her new roommate (Sophie) was adapting to some aspects of the Christian school.

Despite the unflattering description of "Fundamentalist U," Sophie commented that the classes weren't all bad. The professors, by and large, were better than the ones she'd encountered in community college. And it soon became apparent that the private secession that she and Eliza had agreed upon was not limited to them.

There were, it seemed, two universities. First, the public and political one that attracted Eliza's father while filling the girls with a nauseous bewilderment. And second, there was the private, educational one in which students lived, professors taught, and athletes trained. The two landmasses collided occasionally—as when politicians (always from the same party) spoke in chapel services—but they soon drifted back apart, as if driven by a subterranean force.

Eliza and Sophie noted how heavy-handed efforts to indoctrinate their peers were more likely to be met with eye rolls than assent. "If you want to make them brush their teeth," their history professor observed of Prohibition, "make it illegal."

Secession was a pact the girls made that summer in isolation, but they arrived to find a population that had long ago drafted its Declaration of Independence.

In October, Sophie and Eliza finally visited the squat, ranch-style home of Frank and Ethel Mercer, two blocks south of campus. Eliza went under duress.

"I can't believe we're going to see an old lady you've known for, like, five minutes!" she grumbled as the girls cut across the lawn behind their dormitory. "What's gotten into you?" But before there was time to answer, Ethel's hunched figure appeared behind the screen door.

"Now where's your laundry!?" she said without a hello to greet them. "Don't tell me I made Frank move his dirty underwear for nothing!"

Somehow, the absence of social nicety ("Hello"; "Glad to meet you"; "Do come in . . .") had the effect of making Sophie feel at home. It did the opposite to Eliza. The smell of pot roast engulfed them as they stepped inside.

Passing through the entryway, the girls caught a glimpse of Frank in the kitchen: a slender, balding, Black man. He was chopping garlic and sweet potatoes. Being hard of hearing, Frank missed the joke about his underwear, but Eliza and Sophie soon sensed that it would not have fazed him. Sixty years of marriage, pastoring three small congregations, and four boys had conditioned him to "just keep chopping." Finally, Ethel shouted to get his attention so he could welcome their guests.

"We limit the invitation to ladies," Frank said over dinner. "We always wanted a daughter."

Scanning the mantel, Eliza saw pictures of other girls (though, sadly, no photo of the rumored tortoise). She also spotted pictures showing older versions of the women, some holding children. *What did we sign up for?* was her reaction. More disconcertingly, Sophie seemed to love it.

Through the evening, conversation ranged between the unlikely points of Frank and Ethel's shared experience—animal biology, Jesus, and the civil rights movement of the 1960s. Eventually, Sophie's blend of bluntness and curiosity couldn't take it.

"Excuse my question," she interjected between mouthfuls of pot roast, "but how the hell did you end up together? I mean . . . scientist and preacher? White and Black? It seems like an unlikely marriage!"

Eliza choked on a carrot. Sophie seemed impervious to the awkwardness of the question. And the tightness in Eliza's chest compelled her to break the tension. "Uh . . . ," she spluttered with her mouth still full, "I heard you have a giant turtle."

Ethel cackled. Then to Eliza's dismay, Frank returned to Sophie's question. Wilbur, the much-anticipated tortoise, was forgotten like a promised perk at the end of an ever-lengthening tour of time shares.

Thus began a long and winding tale that would—over months and years—enfold both girls. *Boredom plus an invitation.*

The evening proved to be a converting ordinance of sorts—softening and hardening the two young women, respectively. And it would drive a wedge between them. "Not peace but a sword," Eliza remembered reading in her Bible homework.

By midsemester, Sophie (of all people!) mentioned that she was meeting Ethel for prayer and Bible study with a couple of other women.

The practice grew out of a private tutoring session that began when Sophie earned a C on her first exam in physical science.

In one of these meetings, Sophie heard the full story of how Frank and Ethel came together. A public transit boycott: Montgomery, Alabama. An upstart feminist biologist. A handsome young Black man who happened to walk beside her as they marched past bus stops, fielding dirty looks. A scandalous dinner date, several three-hour church services, and four sons eventually followed.

Stories are converting ordinances too. And Sophie sat entranced— lured by laundry, food, and *Chelonoidis nigra*. "All things are yours," remarked the apostle. But we are getting ahead of ourselves.

Part 4

Practicing Perhaps

*"And this also," said Marlow suddenly,
"has been one of the dark places on the earth."*

JOSEPH CONRAD,
HEART OF DARKNESS

10

Dead Animals

Creation, Science, and Prehuman Sacrifice

The earth that's nature's mother is her tomb;
What is her burying grave, that is her womb.

Shakespeare, Romeo and Juliet

ONE OF THE QUESTIONS that haunted Charles Darwin's soul pertained to "the sufferings of millions of the lower animals throughout almost endless time."[1] While sailing on the *Beagle*, the biologist remembered being mocked for his belief in Scripture as a moral authority. And he entertained the idea that human suffering might serve God's goal of "moral improvement." But the number of humans seemed like nothing compared to all the other creatures that suffer terribly without any moral gain. His question was simple: Why would an all-powerful and all-loving God permit so many animals to languish in the countless centuries prior to human beings?[2]

Over time, Darwin gave "free scope to [his] imagination"—a phrase I will return to later—and the worry over animal suffering contributed to

---

[1]Parts of this chapter were published previously in a series on my blog, *joshuamcnall.com*, in particular, Joshua McNall, "Red in Tooth and Claw (pt. 1)," March 21, 2019, https://joshuamcnall .com/2019/03/21/red-in-tooth-and-claw-pt-1.

[2]Charles Darwin, *The Autobiography of Charles Darwin: 1809–1882*, ed. Nora Barlow (New York: Norton, 1958), 85-90.

him abandoning the Christian faith. As he concluded, "What a book a devil's chaplain might write on the clumsy, wasteful, blundering low and horridly cruel works of nature!"[3] Farewell, Pangaea.

Beyond the Montagues and Capulets

Part four of this book highlights three case studies on topics that demand a fruitful use of the Christian imagination between doubt and dogmatism. This first one asks what sacred speculation might say regarding Darwin's dilemma on the supposed suffering of creatures that predate humanity. This discussion has sadly (d)evolved in modern times into the tired debates between the Montagues and Capulets of Genesis interpretation: the house of science and the house of faith. The blood feud has provided certain partisans with a source of income.[4] But it has also spawned "a plague [on] both . . . houses,"[5] in the form of fierce polemics, and a false sense that Christians must choose simplistically between science and the Scriptures.[6]

I will approach the debate with reference to one of Shakespeare's most famous plays: *Romeo and Juliet*. I do so not because it is the Bard's best work but because it is viewed as a tragedy that results in a surprising reconciliation between warring houses by way of an apparently wasteful sacrifice. All these themes figure prominently in my chapter as I ask how some theological imagination might have helped Darwin avoid both crippling doubt and narrow dogmatism. Now to the carcasses.

---

[3]Charles Darwin, letter to Hooker, July 13, 1856, in *More Letters of Charles Darwin*, ed. Francis Darwin and A. C. Seward (London: Murray, 1903), 1:94. See also Richard Dawkins, *A Devil's Chaplain: Reflections on Hope, Lies, Science, and Love* (Boston: Houghton Mifflin, 2003).

[4]Recent works have sought to subvert this trend. See especially a pair of helpful volumes edited by Andrew B. Torrance and Thomas H. McCall, *Knowing Creation: Perspectives from Theology, Philosophy, and Science*, vol. 1, and *Christ and the Created Order: Perspectives from Theology, Philosophy, and Science*, vol. 2 (Grand Rapids, MI: Zondervan Academic, 2018).

[5]William Shakespeare, *Romeo and Juliet*, 3.1.88.

[6]Happily, the narrow scope of my chapter allows me to sidestep certain debates. I will not directly consider the merits of evolution, "young" versus "old-earth" creationism, intelligent design, or even the best ways to parse out the literality of Genesis 1–3. My conviction (as noted in chap. 3) is that "all Scripture is God-breathed" (2 Tim 3:16), but this does not mean Christians should approach all texts with a wooden literalism. To assume otherwise is to baptize a bit of Capulet fake news and call it gospel.

Responding to Darwin's Dilemma

What are the basic options in response to Darwin's worry about animal suffering in long ages past? A first possibility, set forth by some Christians, has been to deny that animals suffer at all. René Descartes, for instance, viewed nonhuman creatures as soulless biological machines, devoid of emotion, higher thought, and suffering. This belief led him to perform terrible experiments, including the torture and vivisection of live dogs.[7] Given our experiences with animals, this view may rightly seem barbaric.[8] Still, Descartes claimed that animal suffering is not a problem for theology because animal suffering does not exist.[9]

A second alternative comes from young-earth creationists. The idea here is that while creaturely suffering may be unfortunate, it did not actually occur before the fall of Adam and Eve. Animal suffering is a result of human sin; it does not precede it. Despite scientific objections, this view clings to Paul's claim that "death" entered the world because of "sin" (Rom 5:12), just as the "wages of sin is death" (Rom 6:23; cf. Jas 1:15). From this perspective, animal suffering is an outcome of human rebellion, which would mean that Darwin's assumptions (not to mention his science) are profoundly flawed.

This perspective may seem to absolve God for the cruelty of animal suffering in ages past,[10] but it is also seen as falling afoul of both science

---

[7]See A. C. Grayling, *Descartes: The Life and Times of a Genius* (New York: Walker & Co., 2005), 30, 134-35. Nicolas de Malebranche, one of Descartes's disciples, was said to have violently kicked a pregnant dog in the stomach to demonstrate to friends how lifelike these "machines" can be. See Richard A. Watson, *Cogito, ergo sum: The Life of René Descartes* (Boston: David R. Godine, 2002), 11.

[8]For a criticism of various denials of animal suffering, see Trent Dougherty, *The Problem of Animal Pain: A Theodicy for All Creatures Great and Small* (New York: Palgrave Macmillan, 2014), 56-95.

[9]Michael Murray suggests that Descartes's later view is more complex. In a letter from 1646, Descartes claims that animals do experience "sensation" even while they do not suffer or experience self-reflection. See Michael J. Murray, *Nature Red in Tooth and Claw* (Oxford: Oxford University Press, 2008), 50-52. For the contrast between his earlier and later views, see René Descartes, *The Philosophical Writings of Descartes*, vol. 3, *The Correspondence*, trans. John Cottingham, Robert Stoothoff, Dugald Murdoch, and Anthony Kenny (Cambridge: Cambridge University Press, 1991), 148, 366.

[10]Ronald Osborn argues that this young-earth perspective does not remove the theological problem of animal suffering because it sees God as responding to human sin by unjustly punishing animals. He likens this cruel decision to that of a parent who chooses to teach children about

and the Scriptures. "You will certainly die" (Gen 2:17) is a line spoken to humans, not to animals.[11] Thus, even Thomas Aquinas deemed it "quite unreasonable" to think animals did not die before the fall.[12] Furthermore, some evangelicals believe the sin-wrought death of which Paul speaks is either (1) of an exclusively human variety or (2) of a spiritual kind that points to our separation from God's life apart from grace. After all, Adam and Eve do not physically die upon consuming the fruit, despite the warning that "in the day that you eat of it you shall surely die" (Gen 2:17 ESV). Perhaps the death spoken of in Genesis 2 is spiritual in nature.[13] If this reading is correct, then animal mortality before the fall of Genesis would not necessarily contradict biblical theology.[14]

Another problem for the denial of animal death before the fall is that animal predation (the preying of one animal upon another) is sometimes depicted in Scripture as part of creation's God-given glory. When God speaks to Job from the whirlwind, there is no hint of carnivores being an unfortunate byproduct of sin. The Creator himself gives meat to the ravens (Job 38:41), he commands the eagle to "build its nest on high" to "feast on blood" (Job 39:29-30), and he provides prey for the lions (Job 38:39-41). In response to this awe-inspiring tour of creaturely life and death, Ronald

---

the dangers of fire by placing the family cat upon the stove. Ronald E. Osborn, *Death Before the Fall: Biblical Literalism and the Problem of Animal Suffering* (Downers Grove, IL: InterVarsity Press, 2014), 138. Osborn seems to ignore the obvious fact, however, that in Scripture sin's consequences often affect more than just the transgressor. In other words, human transgression almost always brings collateral damage.

[11]See Thomas H. McCall, *Against God and Nature: The Doctrine of Sin* (Wheaton, IL: Crossway, 2019), 316.

[12]Thomas Aquinas, *Summa Theologiae* I, q. 86.1.

[13]See the claim of T. Desmond Alexander that "'death' in this context need not necessarily imply the end of life; rather, it indicates spiritual separation from the one who is the source of all life." Alexander, *From Paradise to the Promised Land: An Introduction to the Pentateuch*, 3rd ed. (Grand Rapids, MI: Baker Academic, 2012), 128. Likewise, Victor P. Hamilton, *Handbook on the Pentateuch*, 2nd ed. (Grand Rapids, MI: Baker Academic, 2005), 30.

[14]Long before Darwin, Martin Luther conceded that animals might have died before (or apart from) Adam's fall: "Animals do not die because God is angry at them. On the contrary, for them death is . . . a sort of temporal causality, ordained indeed by God but not regarded by Him as punishment. Animals die because for some other reason it seemed good to God that they should die." Martin Luther, *Luther's Works*, vol. 13, *Selected Psalms II*, ed. Jaroslav Pelikan (Saint Louis: Concordia, 1956), 94. For a contemporary evangelical example of this argument, see John H. Walton, *The Lost World of Adam and Eve: Genesis 2–3 and the Human Origins Debate* (Downers Grove, IL: InterVarsity Press, 2015), 159.

Osborn claims that Job's "Creator takes full responsibility for animal predation, and there is no hint that it is anything other than *very good*."[15]

Others take a moderate approach. Perhaps animal predation was an allowance in a pre-fall world that was "good" (*tob*) but not yet perfect.[16] The Bible never teaches that the original creation was entirely idyllic. Genesis 1–2 states a need for image-bearers to bring cultivated order, dominion, and perhaps even a form of redemption to the world. Creation's not-yet-perfect status is reflected not merely in the serpent but in the command to "subdue" (*kabash*) the earth[17] and "guard" (*shamar*) it (Gen 2:15). Some theologians therefore see Eden as a beachhead of shalom that God carved out within a broader world that had long experienced the force of bloodshed and mortality in the animal realm.[18]

If the world beyond Eden was even less idyllic than the uncultivated garden,[19] then animal suffering and death might be attributed either to a prior rebellion of Satan and other spiritual powers[20] or to the fact that non-human predation simply does not carry the evil weight that violent grasping does among God's image-bearers. In this last suggestion, the human fall is seen as a catastrophic movement backward, not merely to the non-order that existed prior to human sin (Gen 1:2) but to culpable disorder (Gen 3) since God's vice-regents brought human sin into existence by rejecting their calling to steward creation to its intended goal.[21] As a result, the whole creation is now "groaning as in the pains of childbirth" (Rom 8:22).

---

[15]Osborn, *Death Before the Fall*, 153-54. Osborn's own view on animal death before the fall is more complex; hence, he is here only summarizing Job's perspective.

[16]See, for instance, James K. A. Smith, "What Stands on the Fall?: A Philosophical Exploration," in *Evolution and the Fall*, ed. William T. Cavanaugh and James K. A. Smith (Grand Rapids, MI: Eerdmans, 2017), 61-62.

[17]Deborah and Loren Haarsma argue that this word elsewhere denotes "real struggle against real opposition." Haarsma and Haarsma, "Christ and the Cosmos: Christian Perspectives on Astronomical Discoveries," in Torrance and McCall, *Christ and the Created Order*, 2:233.

[18]See J. Richard Middleton, "Reading Genesis 3 Attentive to Human Evolution: Beyond Concordism and Non-Overlapping Magisteria," in Cavanaugh and Smith, *Evolution and the Fall*, 77.

[19]See, for instance, Stephen H. Webb, *The Dome of Eden: A New Solution to the Problem of Creation and Evolution* (Eugene, OR: Cascade, 2010).

[20]C. S. Lewis entertained this view: "It may have been one of man's functions to restore peace to the animal world, and if he had not joined the enemy he might have succeeded in doing so to an extent now hardly imaginable." Lewis, *The Problem of Pain* (New York: Harper, 1996), 140.

[21]See Brian Brock, "Jesus Christ the Divine Animal?: The Human Distinctive Reconsidered," in Torrance and McCall, *Christ and the Created Order*, 2:70. This view was anticipated, long ago, by

A Simplified Schema of "Whodunit?"

"WHODUNIT?"	VARIANTS
I. NOBODY	A. Because there is no God or gods.[22] B. Because the universe is eternal.[23]
II. HUMANS	A. Because human fall occurred before material creation.[24] B. Because human fall occurred at the beginning of the material creation.[25]
III. GOD	A. But God is beyond good and evil.[26] B. But animal predation (at least in some forms) is not evil.[27] C. But God is united with the process, suffering in and with it.[28] D. But predation is the only way to bring about some greater good(s).[29] E. But God designed it with a foreknown human fall in view.[30]

Alexander Balmain Bruce, *Apologetics; or, Christianity Defensively Stated*, 2nd ed. (Edinburgh: T&T Clark, 1893), 62-63. See also Walton, *Lost World of Adam and Eve*, propositions 14-15.

[22]See Richard Dawkins: "The universe that we observe has precisely the properties we should expect if there is, at bottom, no design, no purpose, no evil, no good, nothing but pitiless indifference." Dawkins, *River out of Eden: A Darwinian View of Life* (New York: Basic Books, 1995), 132.

[23]Process theology takes this line in rejecting creation *ex nihilo.*

[24]Origen of Alexandria believed that the archetypal human creature "fell" into time and matter. See Origen of Alexandria, *On First Principles,* trans. G. W. Butterworth (Notre Dame, IN: Ave Maria Press, 2013), 2.9.

[25]This view persists especially among young-earth creationists. See, for instance, Henry Morris, who claimed that a God who used predation and death over billions of years must be evil. Henry M. Morris, "The Day-Age Theory," in *And God Created,* ed. Kelly L. Segraves (San Diego: Creation-Science Research Center, 1973), 72-73.

[26]See B. Jill Carroll, *The Savage Side: Reclaiming Violent Models of God* (Lanham, MD: Rowman & Littlefield, 2001); and to a lesser extent, John R. Schneider, "Recent Genetic Science and Christian Theology on Human Origins: An 'Aesthetic Supralapsarianism,'" *Perspectives on Science and Christian Faith* 62, no. 3 (September 2010): 196-212.

[27]See William Edgar, "Adam, History, and Theodicy," in *Adam, the Fall, and Original Sin: Theological, Biblical, and Scientific Perspectives,* ed. Hans Madueme and Michael Reeves (Grand Rapids, MI: Baker Academic, 2014), 316, 320. See also Lewis, *Problem of Pain,* 132-33.

[28]See Holmes Rolston III, *Science and Religion: A Critical Survey* (1987; repr., Philadelphia: Templeton Foundation Press, 2006), 144-45; and Jürgen Moltmann, *The Way of Jesus Christ: Christology in Messianic Dimensions,* trans. Margaret Kohl (London: SCM Press, 1990), 291-305.

[29]See Christopher Southgate, *The Groaning of Creation: God, Evolution, and the Problem of Evil* (Louisville, KY: Westminster John Knox, 2008), 16; and Austin Farrer, *Love Almighty and Ills Unlimited: An Essay on Providence and Evil, Containing the Nathaniel Taylor Lectures for 1961* (London: Collins, 1962), 51.

[30]See Emil Brunner, *The Christian Doctrine of Creation and Redemption,* trans. Olive Wyon (Philadelphia: Westminster, 1950), 131.

"WHODUNIT?"	VARIANTS
IV. EVIL SPIRIT(S)	A. The Gnostic claim that the material realm was the work of a lesser deity, the demiurge. B. Satan and his minions are responsible.[31]
V. ANIMALS	A. Because moral evil and creaturely freedom (which lead to suffering) may have emerged first in animals, along a spectrum of culpability.[32]
VI. DON'T ANSWER	A. Such speculation is unfruitful or unholy.[33]

Figure 2. Answers to "Whodunit?"

To sum up, figure 2 presents a simplified account of various answers to the question of Whodunit? when it comes to animal predation and suffering. To put matters simply, the choices are (I) nobody did it; (II) humans did it; (III) God did it; (IV) evil spirit(s) did it; (V) animals did it. Or, speaking now to those who opt to avoid speculation entirely by refusing to answer the question, (VI) "Don't do it!"

Not all these responses remain within the realm of Christian orthodoxy while some others represent paths that I would personally reject. My goal, however, is not to evaluate each individual proposal, much less to "bite my thumb at them"[34]—especially when the stage is filled with zealous Montagues and Capulets now wielding Twitter followings. My aim is to explore an imaginative suggestion that exists as a possible non-contrastive approach. This suggestion involves the idea of sacrifice.

---

[31]After Darwin, this view includes the so-called gap theory of Thomas Chalmers, *The Evidence and Authority of the Christian Revelation* (Hartford, CT: Sheldon and Goodrich, 1816). See also, Gregory A. Boyd, *Satan and the Problem of Evil: Constructing a Trinitarian Warfare Theodicy* (Downers Grove, IL: InterVarsity Press, 2001), 293-318.

[32]See Joshua M. Moritz, "Animal Suffering, Evolution, and the Origins of Evil: Toward a 'Free Creatures' Defense," *Zygon* 49, no. 2 (2014): 348-80.

[33]See, e.g., Job 38–41; Isa 55:8. See also John Webster's refusal to react with speculation to the problem of evil in Webster, *God Without Measure: Working Papers in Christian Theology*, vol. 1, *God and the Works of God* (London: Bloomsbury T&T Clark, 2016), 127-29. Under the heading of unfruitful speculation, see the so-called inscrutability response (i.e., the claim that the existence or nonexistence of animal suffering cannot be known). This view is outlined and critiqued by Bethany N. Sollereder, *God, Evolution, and Animal Suffering: Theodicy Without a Fall* (New York: Routledge, 2019), 46-47.

[34]Shakespeare, *Romeo and Juliet*, 1.1.40.

Into the Wild

But first, a brief diversion. To understand the nature of creaturely predation, one must leave the stuffy confines of the classroom to behold the grandeur and the groaning of the wild. This move is required if we are to avoid two unhelpful extremes:

1. **Sentimental Bambi-ization**: ascribing human emotion and suffering to animals[35]

2. **Callous Cartesianism**: reducing animals to unfeeling machines

Consider first the grizzly bear. I listened recently as a hunter described an encounter between a male and female bear, and the female's cubs. The male bear brutally attacked the cubs and killed them despite the mother's desperate efforts to protect them. He then left the cubs to rot since his only instinctual aim was to send the female into heat so he could implant his own DNA within her. The mother bear, now having fought ferociously to protect her young, proceeded to eat the cubs lest available calories go to waste. This is a harsh reality of the animal world, far removed from the "Bambi-izing" tendency that would endow these creatures with human traits. How many talking-bear cartoons (from Yogi to *The Jungle Book*) depict this scene?

Consider crocodiles. Having been a missionary kid in Africa, Ronald Osborn raises the possibility that the "Behemoth" of Job 40 may actually be a crocodile, described as "chief of God's works" as it "devours cattle as if they were grass" (Job 40:19, 15 NEB).[36] Osborn then asks how God's apparent endorsement of this carnage matches up with his own experience: "I have seen crocodiles on the riverbanks of Masai Mara in Kenya, near the end of the wildebeest migrations, their bellies distended from feasting. It is said they continue to kill even after they are engorged, without any interest in eating their prey." In the face of seemingly purposeless bloodshed—in which creatures *prey* without ceasing—Osborn

---

[35]"Bambi theology" is a delightful phrase that is coined by Southgate, *Groaning of Creation*, 6.

[36]This translation, from the New English Bible, is far from certain. Most translations, like the NRSV, take a vegetarian approach: "Look at Behemoth . . . ; it eats *grass* like an ox" (Job 40:15; emphasis added). See Osborn, *Death Before the Fall*, 153.

concludes that "these are the realities we must add our 'Amen' to if we grant the God of the whirlwind who glories in the Behemoth and the Leviathan the final word."[37]

Lastly, consider the pelican. The mother bird of this species lays two eggs. If the first egg hatches safely, then the second chick (the so-called insurance pelican) is simply shoved over the edge of the nest by its mother to die.[38] This seems very different from Christ's likening of himself to the sacrificial hen who shelters her chicks (plural) under her wings at great cost to herself (Mt 23:37).[39] In this contrast, between the mother hen and the mother pelican, there are questions raised of the Creator—and with those questions now in view we are finally prepared to bridge the gap between the apparently un-Christlike behavior of the strong kill the weak and the idea of animal (self-) sacrifice.

Of Suffering and Sacrifice

In some continuity with Darwin, the New Testament has always claimed that life comes from a death of incalculable proportions. We call this the doctrine of atonement.[40] Similarly, some argue that the metaphor of sacrifice can help us think theologically about animal suffering in long ages past. The pastor-theologian Daniel Harrell asks, "What if the apparent wastefulness" of creaturely death before the fall was "understood as *sacrifice*?" The final word is italicized for emphasis, but Harrell never explains his meaning beyond the claim that "the universe and humanity come about at immense cost, a cost that ascribes to them immense value (cf. Jn 3:16)."[41]

---

[37]Osborn, *Death Before the Fall*, 157.

[38]This example comes from Rolston, *Science and Religion*, 137-39.

[39]N. T. Wright claims that Christ draws on the common occurrence of a farmyard fire in which a hen would gather chicks beneath her so that, though she would be scorched to death, the young birds might survive beneath her charred remains. N. T. Wright, *Jesus and the Victory of God*, Christian Origins and the Question of God 2 (Minneapolis: Fortress, 1996), 570-71.

[40]See my prior treatment of atonement and the historical Adam in Joshua M. McNall, *The Mosaic of Atonement: An Integrated Approach to Christ's Work* (Grand Rapids, MI: Zondervan Academic, 2019), chap. 2.

[41]Daniel Harrell, afterword to *Adam and the Genome: Reading Scripture After Genetic Science*, by Dennis R. Venema and Scot McKnight (Grand Rapids, MI: Brazos, 2017), 195. Harrell became editor in chief of *Christianity Today* in 2020.

A second thinker urging the use of sacrificial language is Holmes Rolston III.[42] Rolston claims that animal death and predation were actually necessary to produce later goods. "The cougar's fang has carved the limbs of the fleet-footed deer, and vice versa."[43] Life would not have developed in so many extraordinary ways, says Rolston, without the survival of the fittest and the sacrificial (life-improving) deaths of countless less-fit creatures. To cite Shakespeare, the cougar's fang is God's "happy dagger," and the cobra's venom is God's "true apothecary," both of which bring forth the present world.[44]

Rolston seeks to lessen the problem of animal suffering by finding God within the process, suffering in and with his creatures.[45] His theology is thus a version of panentheism—the idea that creation exists within the divine life, although God is not exhausted by the physical world.[46] Sacrifice comes into play here because, just like at Golgotha, nature sacrifices the individual for the sake of the whole. Animal victims therefore "speak for God" even as they "participate in the divine pathos."[47] Long before the arrival of humanity, "the way of nature was already a *via dolorosa*"—a signpost pointing to the cross.[48] I will respond to this poetic proposal momentarily.

Finally, Sarah Coakley is a third theologian who presses the theme of sacrifice to speak of creaturely death in primal history. Her 2012 Gifford Lectures were titled "Sacrifice Regained: Evolution, Cooperation and God."[49] She builds her argument on evolutionary game theory, which emphasizes not merely the selfishness that fuels creaturely development

---

[42]See esp., Rolston, *Science and Religion*.

[43]Rolston, *Science and Religion*, 134.

[44]Shakespeare, *Romeo and Juliet*, 5.3.169 and 5.3.119, respectively.

[45]Note the combination of III.C with III.D from fig 2. See Rolston, *Science and Religion*, 144-46.

[46]Rolston, *Science and Religion*, 144 (emphasis original).

[47]Rolston, *Science and Religion*, 145.

[48]Holmes Rolston III, "Kenosis and Nature," in *The Work of Love: Creation as Kenosis*, ed. John Polkinghorne (Grand Rapids, MI: Eerdmans, 2001), 60.

[49]These (still unpublished) lectures can be viewed online: Sarah Coakley, "Sacrifice Regained: Evolution, Cooperation and God," *The 2012 Gifford Lectures*, April 17, 2012, www.youtube.com /watch?v=M6xiYZeclwE. A condensed form of the argument can be found in Sarah Coakley, *Sacrifice Regained: Reconsidering the Rationality of Religious Belief* (Cambridge: Cambridge University Press, 2012). See also Martin Nowak and Sarah Coakley, eds., *Evolution, Games, and God: The Principle of Cooperation* (Cambridge, MA: Harvard University Press, 2013).

(i.e., the strong eat the weak) but the place of creaturely cooperation. Some animals pass on their DNA by being willing to endure a loss, including death, to give life to others—usually their young or other members of their species. If this is true, then the same body (or rather, bodies) of evidence that Darwin saw as signs against God's holy character might be interpreted in the opposite way: as shadows of the cross.

Coakley is clear that animal cooperation and self-sacrifice fall far short of the more radical sacrifice displayed by Christ or Christian martyrs. Like Jesus, these human disciples go far beyond the kind of in-group love displayed by creatures for members of their herd or species. Some animals might well sacrifice to see their own young survive, but this is quite different from dying for one's enemies, and being willing to leave no descendants (e.g., Acts 8:33; Is 53:8).[50] "If you [only] love those who love you," Jesus might be heard to remark, "what good is that!? Even orcas, hens, and grizzly bears do that!" (Lk 6:32).

In this gap between animal cooperation and the seemingly irrational Christian sacrifice for enemies, Coakley finds an evolutionary argument for the truth and beauty of Christianity.[51] She frames it as a question, and a cautious case of speculation: Can the radical, inspiring, and sacrificial selflessness displayed by Jesus and his martyred followers set forth the most winsome argument for the Christian faith?[52] Indeed, parts of the tradition have long held that we are drawn to God by the example of those whose depth of love and devotion seem to make no earthly sense.[53] This argument connects to the famous claim by Joseph Cardinal Ratzinger (later Pope Benedict XVI) that the most effective defense of Christianity involves "the saints the Church has produced and the art which has grown in her womb."[54] I will return to art momentarily, but in this inscrutable loss that is a gain, Coakley sees a signpost pointing to the Savior.

---

[50]Southgate does note, however, rare cases in which "maladaptive" (read: sacrificial) behavior does take place, as in the lioness who showed motherly love to some young oryxes, a species that lions normally devour. Southgate, *Groaning of Creation*, 67.

[51]Coakley, *Sacrifice Regained*, 26.

[52]See Coakley, *Sacrifice Regained*, 27.

[53]Coakley points especially to Gregory of Nyssa's work, *On Virginity*.

[54]Joseph Cardinal Ratzinger with Vittorio Messori, *The Ratzinger Report: An Exclusive Interview on the State of the Church* (San Francisco: Ignatius Press, 1985), 129.

Coakley organizes her entire argument around three colors that paint the backdrop to her study:

1. Red for *violence*

2. Blue for cool, analytic *rationality*

3. Purple for Christ's *passion*, mixed appropriately out of red and blue

Creaturely cooperation, including the willingness to die so another might live, is what Coakley calls the "thin purple line" woven through the animal kingdom, leading to the concept of sacrifice.[55] As humans, Coakley believes we retain the choice to disown and discredit it.[56] Nonetheless, this purple line of creaturely self-sacrifice represents God's "subtle pressure" woven into our biology "without which we would not be here at all." And in Coakley's estimation, it is the practice of this sacrificial lifestyle (Rom 12:1-2) that "the world now urgently needs."[57]

Evaluating Three Sacrificial Suggestions

Having presented these sacrificial views, it is time to submit them to a "priestly" inspection. First, Daniel Harrell hinted that we may reframe the apparent waste of animal death before the fall as a kind of sacrifice that helps us see the costly value of the present world. This is a version of theodicy (an attempt to sort through the problem of evil) that reveals a "greater good" that results from creaturely mortality (see option III.D in fig. 2). The payoff is a lesson whereby humans may gain gratitude for the price paid by animals to get us here.

The weakness of this proposal lies, first, in its lack of development. It is just a snippet within a book by two other authors.[58] And it is unclear why this teachable moment on creation's value should require so much bloodshed to make humans grateful. Indeed, Harrell's claim (by itself) seems rather like a cattle rancher who decides to teach his children to be thankful for their warm beds by allowing his herd to perish in a blizzard,

---

[55]Coakley, *Sacrifice Regained*, 23.
[56]A charge Coakley would likely level at Dawkins.
[57]Coakley, *Sacrifice Regained*, 28.
[58]The suggestion comes in Harrell's afterword to Venema and McKnight, *Adam and the Genome*.

and then shuttering the local Humane Society for good measure. Even if the cruel scenario did make his children grateful, it is hardly obvious why this lesson might be the only way to produce gratitude. Is it not an example of excessive force? At this point, we feel the angst of the novelist Cormac McCarthy, when he has a character within *All the Pretty Horses* reflect that the world's heart seems to "beat at some terrible cost," as if "the blood of multitudes" has been "exacted for the vision of a single flower."[59]

Second, Holmes Rolston III combined the only-way-to-greater-good defense (option III.D in fig. 2) with the idea of God's co-suffering in creation (option III.C). From this panentheistic perspective, sacrifice is not just a metaphor to teach us to be grateful (Harrell) but a reality in which suffering is inherently redemptive since it results in the "perfecting" of future life.

While Rolston should be commended for desiring to see the world through the lens of Christ and his cross, his way of doing so unfortunately "baptizes" the way of the Dragon (the strong kill the weak) and confuses it with the way of the Lamb. If he is correct, then the cross is not a singular event that upends the world's wisdom and power but a principle that sanctifies all violent grasping in a frightful case of the ends justifying the means.[60] If this is so, then certain feminist and liberationist opponents of atonement doctrine were right all along: what happened on Golgotha is not just "divine child abuse"[61] but a plenary indulgence in the face of all abusive power plays and animal cruelty. This disaster cannot be overcome by locating God within the process.[62]

Now for Sarah Coakley. While Coakley's work is intriguing, it is unclear how it helps with Darwin's doubt-inducing dilemma and how it fits

---

[59]Cormac McCarthy, *All the Pretty Horses* (New York: Vintage, 1992), 282.

[60]Denis Edwards critiques Rolston by stating that the cross "is not to be seen as some kind of necessary outcome of creation, or as a principle behind creation." Rather, it is "God bringing life out of what was in itself a sinful and destructive act." Denis Edwards, "Every Sparrow That Falls to the Ground: The Cost of Evolution and the Christ-Event," *Ecotheology* 11, no. 1 (2006): 108.

[61]See Joanne Carlson Brown, "Divine Child Abuse," *Daughters of Sarah* 18, no. 3 (Summer 1992): 28.

[62]Southgate likewise critiques Rolston's misuse of sacrifice language and his tendency to forget that, while Christ *chose* to suffer for the good of others, the victims in evolutionary sacrifice normally do not have a choice. See Southgate, *Groaning of Creation*, 50.

with my prior of schema "Whodunit?" (Who ultimately is responsible for animal predation and suffering: options I-VI in fig. 2?). With reference to her "thin purple line"—the self-sacrificing impulse—implanted within creatures, she appears to be saying that "God did it"[63] while she acknowledges the dangers of both cooperation and competition.[64] Coakley also attempts to highlight a kind of teachable moment in animal death that is both an apologetic tool and a signpost pointing to Golgotha—the ultimate sacrifice. Still, she remains free of the reductionism of claiming that humans are *entirely* responsible for animal suffering, of straightforward pan(en)theism, and of the terrible idea that God is evil's author.

What is absent from Coakley's argument, perhaps because it clashes with her rationalistic "blue," is any reference to the role of Satan or evil spiritual powers in animal predation (option IV).[65] This is unsurprising for at least two reasons. First, Scripture is unclear about what part, if any, fallen spirits played in this process. And second, Satan often strikes the modern mind as an embarrassment. The devil remains, in the words of Walter Wink, "a scandal, a stone of stumbling, a bone in the throat of modernity."[66] Nonetheless, my own eulogy on the carcasses will consider whether they are not merely "the poor sacrifices of our enmity" (to steal a line from Juliet's father) but the sacrifices of the enmity of some other spirit.[67] It's time to say perhaps in the face of Darwin's tortured question.

---

[63]This reading is confirmed in Sarah Coakley, "Evolution, Cooperation, and Divine Providence," in Nowak and Coakley, *Evolution, Games, and God*, 377. Though she might be open to some aspect of option V; see Moritz, "Animal Suffering."

[64]"Even dictators can at times be splendid cooperators for their own nefarious ends." Coakley, "Evolution, Cooperation, and Divine Providence," 380.

[65]The publication of Coakley's Gifford Lectures and the furtherance of her *théologie totale* may shed more light on this aspect of her theology. There is no mention of Satan, demons, or the devil in the index of Sarah Coakley, *God, Sexuality, and the Self: An Essay "On the Trinity"* (Cambridge: Cambridge University Press, 2013). Nor do these concepts appear in the index of a work that might be thought to reference them, Coakley, *Powers and Submissions: Spirituality, Philosophy and Gender* (Malden, MA: Blackwell, 2002).

[66]Walter Wink, *Unmasking the Powers: The Invisible Forces That Determine Human Existence* (Philadelphia: Fortress, 1986), 9 and 6, respectively.

[67]Shakespeare, *Romeo and Juliet*, 5.3.304.

Extending the Purple Line

Let's recap. I began by noting how Darwin's journey to unbelief was sped by a concern over the suffering of millions of animals in primal history. Then I noted various options to address Darwin's dilemma (options I-VI, fig. 2). Finally, I concluded with three speculative proposals (Harrell, Rolston, Coakley) that suggest we view these dead animals through the lens of sacrifice in order to take both science and Christianity seriously.

My goal now is to say perhaps in a way that will allow me to borrow from the best of these perspectives without falling victim to their biggest weaknesses. My inspiration (from *Romeo and Juliet*) is Friar Lawrence, that accidental "devil's chaplain,"[68] who says this of nature's dual nature:

> For naught so vile that on the earth doth live
> But to the earth some special good doth give;
> Nor aught so good but, strained from that fair use,
> Revolts from true birth, stumbling on abuse. . . .
> Within the infant rind of this weak flower
> Poison hath residence, and medicine power.[69]

His point is that even seemingly "vile" aspects of creation can perform "some special good"—although no created thing (perhaps angels and animals included!) is immune from corruption.[70] All things work together for the good of those who love God (Rom 8:28). But that does not mean all things are good.

Keeping in mind the speculative guardrails (chap. 3), here is my proposal. Perhaps we may view the long blood-trail of dead animals as a kind of prehuman sacrifice that functions analogously to sacrifices of the Old Testament. These are neither actual atonements for sin (Heb 10:4) nor intrinsic goods by themselves but signposts pointing forward to the greater good of

---

[68]I say accidental because the friar suggested the sleeping potion that unwittingly resulted in the deaths of the young lovers.

[69]Shakespeare, *Romeo and Juliet*, 2.3.17-24.

[70]The flood narrative of Genesis 6:11-14 states that "all flesh [*kol basar*] had corrupted its ways upon the earth" by violence, so God "determined to make and end of all flesh" (NRSV).

1. Christ's one true sacrifice on the cross, and

2. The new creation, which may transform even the animal kingdom.

"Now these things occurred"—we might say of the lives and deaths of prehuman creatures—for us (1 Cor 10:6) as the instrumental means to bring about God's goal: to create image-bearers who will reflect Christ in our stewardship of creation and the subversion of our violent, grasping impulses.

Despite the instrumental good of some creaturely predation, one wonders if the current sacrificial shadow will be one day replaced by the perfect things to come (Heb 10:1), a world in which the wolf lies down with the lamb "and a little child will lead them" (Is 11:6). What this verse means remains unclear, but allow me to combine some aspects of my prior schema (options II-V, fig. 2) in an imaginative way that may speak to Darwin's doubt.

The "End" of Creaturely Predation

Suppose modern science is correct in claiming that animal predation precedes humans by a vast period of time. This need not mean that the human fall had no adverse consequences for the animal realm (option II, fig. 2). Could it be that there were no cannibalizing, cub-eating grizzlies before the human fall but that salmon-eaters were declared "good" (Gen 1)? "Of these things we cannot speak in detail now" (Heb 9:5 ESV), and it is best not to be dogmatic.[71] Scripture is clear, however, that both "things on earth" and "things in heaven" stood in need of a "peace" made possible by Christ's blood shed on the cross (Col 1:19).

Acceptance of at least some creaturely predation as part of God's good creation need not imply that the Creator is simply beyond good and evil, so that God wills all manner of horrors (option III.A, fig. 2). One need not go all the way with Descartes to contend that animal predation is not as problematic as suffering experienced by divine image-bearers

---

[71]See again guardrail #1 in chap. 3: be clear about the unclear. It is uncontroversial, however, to say that humans have brought major consequences upon certain species (e.g., domestication and extinction).

(option III.B).[72] We do not know what it is like to be an animal. And another form of "Bambi theology" comes from Richard Dawkins when he describes the creaturely realm as primarily a torture show of whimpering, slashing, devouring, starving, and raping—all "during the minute that it takes me to compose this sentence."[73] While nature is bloody, Dawkins is dishonest in depicting only the groaning (minus the glory and cooperation[74]) with sensationalized language that implies an almost-human level of torment. It is not difficult to see what agenda lies behind this double fault.

Perhaps it is right to say that God allowed a form of animal predation in order to accomplish a greater good that would not have otherwise occurred (option III.D, fig. 2). Perhaps some higher animals even exercise something approximating a kind of freedom and moral choice though we shouldn't build elaborate theories of "animal sin" at this point either (option V).[75] Perhaps the greater good that flows forth from this creation was "the dignity of causality" that results from creatures that can act upon one another in such a way as to move toward greater levels of complexity and relationship.[76] Perhaps it was the good of courage and creational grandeur that results from the interplay of cooperation and competition. This is the suggestion of Richard Swinburne, that the world is made "richer" by the complex struggle of the animal kingdoms so that "the redness of nature . . . is the red badge of courage."[77]

---

[72]Michael Murray has a helpful survey of what he sees as the still-flawed "Neo-Cartesian" options (i.e., the claim that while animals experience pain, they lack the higher order mental and psychological states that make human suffering uniquely terrible). Murray, *Nature Red in Tooth and Claw*, chap. 2.

[73]Dawkins, *River out of Eden*, 132-33.

[74]See again Sarah Coakley and Martin A. Nowak, "Introduction: Why Cooperation Makes a Difference," in Nowak and Coakley, *Evolution, Games, and God*, 1-34.

[75]Despite the thought-provoking value in his study, Moritz goes too far out on the speculative limb in suggesting that Scripture teaches "animal sin" on the mere basis that the serpent was a creature (Gen 3:1), and a couple of other prooftexts (e.g., Gen 6:11-14). See Moritz, "Animal Suffering."

[76]Building on an insight from Aquinas, this is the suggestion of Michael Rota, in the volume co-edited by Coakley: Rota, "The Problem of Evil and Cooperation," in Nowak and Coakley, *Evolution, Games, and God*, 365-66.

[77]Richard Swinburne, *Providence and the Problem of Evil* (Oxford: Clarendon, 1998), 173. I find this argument poetically pleasing but philosophically weak. As with Dawkins's argument, it tends toward "Bambi theology" in its anthropomorphism, and as such it is an example of an analytic philosopher given over to "non-decorative metaphor." On the "non-decorative metaphors," see

The Colors of the King's Disguise

Or perhaps—in a suggestion that is most compelling to me—the goodness to be seen amidst animal predation is that of a strange providence: the partial divine hiddenness that must exist to bring about what God desires, relationships that require faith in place of certainty.

This type of world would need to point to the existence of a Creator—in its grandeur, its complexity, and its "purple thread" of sacrifice—while not testifying in such a heavy-handed way so as to destroy our creaturely freedom and our need to trust in things unseen (Heb 11:1). To be in real relationship with God this side of the eschaton, perhaps we need the capacity to "suppress the truth" (Rom 1:18) as we do when we see only the red (violence) or blue (rationality) but not the purple (sacrificial love). In the argument of Michael Rota

> If God had created the various species directly and immediately, humans would very probably [have] come into possession of an almost unassailable theistic argument from biological design. And perhaps this would be more evidence of his existence than God wishes us to have, or evidence of the wrong sort.[78]

The claim here is not that God deceived us by ordaining this kind of world but that his partial hiddenness enables the kind of authentic relationship God desires.[79]

The ambiguity of the animal kingdom—both grand and groaning, both beautiful and bloody—bears an analogy to the famous parable of Kierkegaard: the king who disguises his identity, not because he hates the humble maiden that he seeks to wed but because he wants to preserve the authenticity of her choice, and of their love relationship.[80] Are red

---

Thomas H. McCall, *An Invitation to Analytic Christian Theology* (Downers Grove, IL: InterVarsity Press, 2015), 16-21.

[78]Rota, "Problem of Evil and Cooperation," 369.

[79]This view relates to what Murray calls the instrumental good of a universe endowed with "nomic regularity." See Murray, *Nature Red in Tooth and Claw*, chap. 5.

[80]Søren Kierkegaard, *Philosophical Fragments*, ed. and trans. Howard V. Hong and Edna H. Hong (Princeton, NJ: Princeton University Press, 1985), 29. The analogy between divine hiddenness in nature and Kierkegaard's parable is noted by Rota, "Problem of Evil and Cooperation," 365-66.

and blue the colors of the king's disguise? Might they one day bleed together so that only a regal purple remains?

My speculative proposal (III.D, fig. 2) need not imply that God smiles on every aspect of animal instinct. Nor should it infer that other approaches (options II, IV, V, and VI) have nothing to utter above the carcasses. Red is also associated with the devil, whom John calls "a murderer from the beginning" (Jn 8:44). Might we suppose that the violent impulse of "that ancient serpent" (Rev 12:9) predates even our beginning? It would seem strange if it did not. Don't serial killers always start with the neighbor's dog? One advantage in acknowledging a dark spiritual presence at work within the world prior to humanity is that it allows Christians to say something that scientists have long said: the universe has a backstory that may be longer, darker, and more complex than even some creationists would like to admit.

When it comes to precisely how human or demonic rebellion changed creaturely predation (option II and IV, fig. 2), one encounters, again, the value of option VI ("Don't answer!"). We should be clear about what remains unclear (see chap. 3) even if John Webster goes too far in denouncing all speculative approaches to the problem of evil as "vicious."[81] It is entirely consistent with Scripture to suppose that human sin genuinely affected the created order in adverse ways, just as Scripture also implies that a dark power was at work within the world before we got here. This is enough to keep options II and IV in the mix even while it need not result in ridiculous theories that picture Satan, in a red jumpsuit, sprinkling carbon-fabricated T-Rex bones across the plains of Texas. There are limits to holy curiosity, and I have now reached those. But, finally, Shakespeare.

---

[81]With a near total lack of argumentation, Webster claims that "curiosity" is the corruption of "studiousness," which displays the "wickedness of intelligence" that "pridefully" seeks "to know as God knows." John Webster, *The Domain of the Word: Scripture and Theological Reason* (London: T&T Clark, 2012), 193-96. In this way, *curiosity* becomes a liquid term that can be applied to anyone with whom one disagrees (cf. *fundamentalist, liberal,* etc.).

Conclusion

For Charles Darwin, the problem of animal suffering in long ages past drove him toward the land of doubt. In response, I have argued for a cautious, noncontrastive form of perhapsing (options II-VI, fig. 2) that includes the metaphor of sacrifice to see the greater good produced by our groaning world. This issue matters because the supposed war between religion and science involves not just animals on the literal Pangaea but people (and especially college students) who have been told that they must choose between science and faith. We must move past the doubt of Darwin and the dogmatism of religious hardliners.

Am I so foolish as to think my proposal will bring a pax upon the feuding Montagues and Capulets? No. But it is worth remembering that Shakespeare's most famous tragedy ends with reconciliation ("a glooming peace") between two warring houses. As in my study, this peace is achieved by reflection on seemingly senseless deaths: the corpses that are, as father Capulet proclaims, the "sacrifices of our enmity."[82]

For the Christian, however, this temporal truce is not enough. While agreeing not to kill each other may seem like an improvement in our current cultural climate, it is far less than the ending promised in Scripture. The divine comedy, unlike Shakespeare's tragedy, ends not with a "glooming peace" by which "heaven finds means to kill your joys with love"[83] but with resurrection and renewed creation that mock the reign of "love-devouring death."[84] For this reason, our hope is that we may say, not just of Christ's body (in both ecclesial and incarnate forms) but perhaps of certain animals as well, "Thou art not conquered . . . / And death's pale flag is not advanced there."[85]

---

[82]Shakespeare, *Romeo and Juliet*, 5.3.316.
[83]Shakespeare, *Romeo and Juliet*, 5.3.317, 304.
[84]Shakespeare, *Romeo and Juliet*, 2.6.7.
[85]Shakespeare, *Romeo and Juliet*, 5.3.94-96. I will return to creaturely resurrection in chap. 12.

11

What If God?

Rethinking Vessels of Wrath

Timshel

JOHN STEINBECK,
EAST OF EDEN

"IT SAYS GOD MADE SOME PEOPLE TO BE TRASHCANS." That
was the blunt description offered by my lifelong friend for why he had
discarded Romans 9 and the apostle Paul with it. My response, as we
stood by the dumbbells in the local fitness center, was something scholarly
along the lines of "Huh?" (*What is the Greek cognate for "trashcan"?*) He
was referring to a pair of questions in Romans 9:22-23: "What if God,
desiring to show his wrath and to make known his power, has endured
with much patience vessels of wrath prepared for destruction, in order to
make known the riches of his glory for vessels of mercy, which he has
prepared beforehand for glory . . . ?" (ESV).

In my friend's colorful description, a "vessel" whose sole purpose is
destruction could be described as a kind of dumpster made to transport
souls to the incinerator of divine wrath.[1] If Paul says God made certain

---

[1] Admittedly, my friend's analogy is a bit muddled since it fails to clarify if the "vessel" is the
conveyer to the location of destruction, the *object* consumed, or the *place* where destruction

people for that purpose, then this God was unworthy of worship. The New Testament scholar C. H. Dodd concurred: "The trouble is that man is not a pot"; thus the passage was deemed "the weakest point in the whole epistle."[2]

To hear my friend tell it, Romans 9:22-23 sped his defection to the continent of doubt. He had been a ministry student from a conservative Christian university, and he had gone on to be a pastor before a series of events caused him to leave the church. There were, of course, other factors in this post-Pangaea breakup. But Paul's question, "What if God . . . ?" unsettled him—and he would drift for years to come. All this makes Romans 9 my second case study in the Christian imagination, sitting between the polarized extremes of doubt and dogmatism.

Volition, East of Eden

Once again, I have a literary conversation partner. In this case, it is John Steinbeck's California midrash on family, freedom, and the fall: *East of Eden*.[3] The saga spans generations as it chronicles two frontier clans—the Trasks and the Hamiltons—who put down roots in Salinas Valley, California. It is a eulogy to the promised land of the American West, stretching from the Civil War till the early 1900s. But it is also a retelling of several scenes from Genesis.

"Two stories have haunted us . . . from our beginning," says Samuel Hamilton, the Irish immigrant and beloved patriarch of his clan, "the story of original sin and the story of Cain and Abel." [4] With regard to the latter, Steinbeck's question is as follows: Why did God delight in Abel's offering while despising Cain's (Gen 4:3-5)? Does the Creator simply choose to love some children and hate others (cf. Rom 9:13)? Within the

---

happens. Still, lest one object that this reading is a caricature, John Piper's book-length treatment of Romans 9 uses virtually the same language to describe God's sovereign predestination: "We should picture," writes Piper, "a vessel placed outside the house and used, say, as an incinerator." Piper, *The Justification of God: An Exegetical and Theological Study of Romans 9:1-23*, 2nd ed. (Grand Rapids, MI: Baker Academic, 1993), 201.

[2] C. H. Dodd, *The Epistle of Paul to the Romans* (London: Dodder & Stoughton, 1932), 159.

[3] John Steinbeck, *East of Eden*, Steinbeck Centennial Edition (1952; repr., New York: Penguin, 2002).

[4] Steinbeck, *East of Eden*, 264.

novel reside questions that are asked of Romans 9. Were some humans predestined for destruction? And if so, "then why does God still blame us? For who is able to resist his will?" (Rom 9:19).

These worries hang especially over twin brothers in Steinbeck's *East of Eden*. Aaron and Cal (Caleb) Trask are, in various ways, Jacob and Esau, Abel and Cain, Isaac and Ishmael. Their mother was a murderer whose soul seemed bent from birth. She conceived the twins by seducing her husband's brother and then abandoning the family. Later, young Cal wonders if his mother's blood (or divine predestination) has warped him too. Had "an angry and disgusted God poured molten fire from a crucible to destroy or to purify his little handiwork of mud"?[5] The imagery alludes to the metaphor of the biblical potter and his clay (Is 29:16; 45:9). "Does not the potter have the right to make out of the same lump of clay some pottery for special purposes and some for common use?" (Rom 9:21).

Perhaps God has that right. Yet divine prerogative does not address the deeper question of God's character if he made some people for the express purpose of destruction. Steinbeck's own thoughts on the matter provide not just a Californian version of the Torah (like an American Moses coming down from Cedars-Sinai) but a glimmering testament to the rugged freedom of the human will:

> The free, exploring mind of the individual human is the most valuable thing in the world. And this I would fight for: the freedom of the mind to take any direction it wishes, undirected. And this I must fight against: any idea, religion, or government which limits or destroys the individual . . . the one thing that separates us from the beasts. If the glory can be killed, we are lost.[6]

How would the apostle Paul respond to this ode to American individualism?

---

[5]Steinbeck, *East of Eden*, 598. These lines are spoken by Lee, a Chinese servant and surrogate father to the Trask twins. Still, they are meant to describe Caleb's sense that his irreparable faults were determined long before birth.
[6]Steinbeck, *East of Eden*, 131.

What Hath Rome to Do with California?

Thankfully, my treatment of Romans 9–11 will not be a mere replay of the tired fights between Wesleyan-Arminians and their Reformed counterparts. In the words of Michael Bird, "Paul is not writing this to people who have John Calvin's *Institutes* in one hand and a copy of Jacob Arminius's *Works* in the other."[7] But Paul's words are important to those later debates. Broadly speaking, the crucial parts of Romans 9 have been read in two different ways: either through the lens of individual predestination to salvation (and damnation)[8] or via a redemptive-historical approach that focuses on God's freedom to elect groups and individuals to play roles in history, yet not in a way that predetermines their eternal destinies.[9] Two questions are in play:

1. Does the text deal with individuals or groups?

2. Does it deal with predestination to salvation and damnation or to roles in history?

How might a refired imagination offer a fresh take on this old battleground of biblical interpretation, especially as we consider the role of "perhaps" and "what if" styles of questioning? Romans 9:22-23 employs two "what if" questions at a crucial point in Paul's argument (at least in many English translations). And although the text has been picked over by countless interpreters—some "red in tooth and claw"—it is surprising how scant coverage has been of the fact that Paul frames his most

---

[7]Michael F. Bird, *Romans*, Story of God Bible Commentary (Grand Rapids, MI: Zondervan, 2016), 335.

[8]Modern representatives of the Augustinian-Calvinist reading include Thomas R. Schreiner, *Romans*, BECNT (Grand Rapids, MI: Baker Academic, 1998); Douglas J. Moo, *The Epistle to the Romans*, NICNT (Grand Rapids, MI: Eerdmans, 1996); John Murray, *The Epistle to the Romans*, 2 vols. (Grand Rapids, MI: Eerdmans, 1959–1965); and Piper, *Justification of God.*

[9]Modern representatives of the redemptive-historical approach include the likes of C. E. B. Cranfield, *Epistle to the Romans*, 2 vols., ICC (Edinburgh: T&T Clark, 1975–1979); Leon Morris, *The Epistle to the Romans* (Grand Rapids, MI: Eerdmans, 1988); Joseph A. Fitzmeyer, *Romans*, AB (New York: Doubleday, 1993); William Sanday and Arthur C. Headlam, *A Critical and Exegetical Commentary on the Epistle to the Romans*, 5th ed., ICC (Edinburgh: T&T Clark, 1902); Leander E. Keck, *Romans*, ANTC (Nashville: Abingdon, 2005); and Ben Witherington III with Darlene Hyatt, *Paul's Letter to the Romans: A Socio-Rhetorical Commentary* (Grand Rapids, MI: Eerdmans, 2004).

controversial vessel-of-wrath suggestion as a seemingly unanswered question: "What if God . . . ?"[10]

Is this portion of Romans 9 itself a case of imaginative perhapsing? My answer will be a qualified yes—though that puts me in a somewhat strange position between traditional battle lines. But to understand the purpose of Paul's "what if," we will have to dive into the nuts and bolts not just of his Greek grammar but of Romans as a whole. More context is needed.

Reframing Romans 9–11

In the United States, 9/11 has become synonymous with religious extremism, an aftermath of war, and partisan bickering. So too with Romans 9–11. I recall watching on television as the Twin Towers collapsed in a hail of fire, steel, and broken bodies. The event is seared in my memory. But when I recently asked my own university students the familiar question—"Where were you on 9/11?"—I received a shocking answer: they weren't alive yet. Thus the original context is somewhat foreign to them. The same could be said for this portion of Paul's letter.

Rather than attempting to address Reformed and non-Reformed views of salvation and divine sovereignty, Paul's concern was to rebut a question that had arisen in the fractious Roman house churches, divided largely along ethnic lines. Though Rome's church had been founded by Jews, it was now numerically dominated by Gentiles in a city with a long history of anti-Judaism. The shift occasioned painful questions: Had God rejected Israel? Did Paul's gospel imply that the divine word (the covenant) had foundered on the crags of Israel's hardened hearts? Some Gentiles undoubtedly thought so.[11] And some Jews would agree that Paul's preaching on food and circumcision implied a failure of God's

---

[10]Grammatically, Paul begins a conditional sentence with the protasis ("But if . . .") without ever supplying an explicit apodosis ("then . . ."). For this reason, most English translations supply a question mark to indicate the incompleteness. For various interpretive options, see Moo, *Epistle to the Romans*, 604-5.

[11]See N. T. Wright's point that "Gentile 'boasting' against unbelieving Jews" is one of Paul's key concerns in Romans 9–11. Wright, *Romans*, NIB 10 (Nashville: Abingdon, 2002), 636.

Israel operation.[12] How else could it be that the Jewish Messiah was being rejected by most of Abraham's bloodline?

In this painful paradox lies the context of Romans. It is not Paul's attempt at a systematic theology for individuals of any era. It is a letter to (perhaps) five different house churches, each with different backgrounds and grievances.[13] Paul's task is daunting: against Jewish claims that his gospel implied God's unrighteousness, he must assert that the Torah requirements were both necessary and now fulfilled in Christ. And against Gentile boasting, he must claim that both the covenantal past and the eschatological future involve Israel being saved (e.g., Rom 11:26)—even if it is an Israel that now strangely includes the Messiah's uncircumcised followers. Oh yes, and on top of all that, he needs to raise money for a Spanish mission trip (Rom 15:23-28)!

Paul claims that far from showing God's infidelity to the covenant, the gospel reveals God's righteousness since it was always the Creator's purpose to form a Jew-plus-Gentile family defined by *pistis* alone (Rom 1:16-17). This word, as we have seen already, encompasses not just "faith" or "trust" but also "fidelity" and something like "believing-allegiance" to Jesus as Lord.[14] The construction of this new humanity—carved out by the Spirit from the Messiah's crucified and resurrected body—reveals God's power since the gospel "brings salvation to everyone who believes: first to the Jew, then to the Gentile" (Rom 1:16). This multiethnic family goes into the Roman world as living sacrifices (Rom 12:1-2) through whom the God of peace will soon crush Satan as he ushers in a new creation (Rom 16:20).

---

[12]See Douglas A. Campbell, for a recent commentator who sees Romans 9–11 as a response to a Jewish "Teacher." Campbell, *The Deliverance of God: An Apocalyptic Rereading of Justification in Paul* (Grand Rapids, MI: Eerdmans, 2009), esp. 774-77.

[13]See Reta Halteman Finger, *Roman House Churches for Today: A Practical Guide for Small Groups,* 2nd ed. (Grand Rapids, MI: Eerdmans, 2007). Finger's study builds on the work of Peter Lampe and Robert Jewett.

[14]See again Matthew W. Bates, *Salvation by Allegiance Alone: Rethinking Faith, Works, and the Gospel of Jesus the King* (Grand Rapids, MI: Baker Academic, 2017).

Salvation via Hardening Mercy and Judgment

What I left out in this whirlwind tour of Romans—aside from almost everything!—is the peculiar tendency of Israel's God to bring forth salvation not in spite of wrath and judgment but precisely through it. This happened, of course, with Noah, but the prime example to which Paul turns is the exodus. In this story, it is God's radical mercy and patience that produce hardened hearts.[15] So too in the Messiah. Yet in this case, Christ is both the Son who dies and the one who leads the true exodus. As with Noah, it is "salvation by catastrophe"[16] and deliverance via judgment. In both cases, Paul notes a gracious deliverance that comes through the hardening of rebellious hearts against God's mercy.

The pattern continues in the early church. Here, the breaking off of some Jewish branches because of unbelief (*apistis*) coincides with the ingrafting of wild ones (Rom 11:15). But this is no cause for arrogance! Paul commands the Gentile Christians to remember, "You do not support the root, but the root supports you" (Rom 11:18). Branches broken off by unbelief may be grafted back in through faith in Christ, just as prideful wild shoots will fall if they apostatize and turn away from *pistis* (Rom 11:20-21).

The possibility of both apostasy and reattachment of amputated limbs calls into question (1) a rigid predeterminism and (2) a later Augustinian commitment to the "perseverance of the saints."[17] Incredibly, Paul places Israel in a role played previously by the Messiah[18]—the one who endures a loss that is a gain for others: because "if . . . their loss means

---

[15]This is true in the Gospels too. It is God's *mercy* to the undeserving that causes hardening in others. The welcome of the younger brother fills the elder son with rage (Lk 15:11-31); kindness shown to workers hired later fills the early laborers with resentment (Mt 20:1-16); the elevation of Hebrew slaves infuriates Pharaoh (Ex 5–14); and the welcome of former pagans by Israel's God occasions the painful issues Paul must tackle in the Roman (and Galatian) churches. Hardening is the result, not of capriciousness but of divine mercy.

[16]Philip G. Ziegler, *Militant Grace: The Apocalyptic Turn and the Future of Christian Theology* (Grand Rapids, MI: Baker Academic, 2018), 9.

[17]On the latter, see John M. G. Barclay, *Paul and the Gift* (Grand Rapids, MI: Eerdmans, 2015), 557; on the former, see Glen Shellrude, "The Freedom of God in Mercy and Judgment: A Libertarian Reading of Romans 9:6-29," *Evangelical Quarterly* 81, no. 4 (2009): 315-17.

[18]"The mystery of Israel is seen," says N. T. Wright, in the "Christ-shaped, cross-shaped" nature of her role within God's plan. It involves "being cast away that the world might be redeemed." Wright, *Romans*, 635.

riches for the Gentiles, how much greater riches will their full inclusion bring!" (Rom 11:12). In the hope of reattachment of the severed branches, the Roman Christians are to live lives of sacrificial love (Rom 12), practicing voluntary submission (Rom 13), and bearing with the weak who have different views on food and drink and sacred days (Rom 14–15). This practice of sacrificial love is what Paul refers to as "the obedience that comes from faith"; hence it is this exhortation that bookends the epistle (Rom 1:5; 16:26).

A Walk Through Romans 9

Having sketched the big picture for Romans 9–11, it is now time to return to Romans 9 with an eye toward my friend's initial question: Does the passage really teach that God makes some people to be trashcans?

After voicing anguish over unbelieving Jews—and even wishing that he could be damned in their place (Rom 9:3)—Paul utters a crucial sentence: "It is not as though God's word had failed [literally: 'fallen']. For not all who are descended from Israel are Israel" (Rom 9:6). The focus is relentlessly God-centered.[19] God has proven faithful to his covenant; therefore, God is righteous. This reality is proven by the fact that not all of Abraham's biological descendants were ever members of the covenant people.[20] So too, not all offspring of the patriarchs were members of the line that led to Christ. The Lord did not choose Jacob from the womb because he was more righteous than Esau; for neither had done anything good or bad at the time (Rom 9:12). Nor had God simply foreseen that Jacob would be more deserving later since a quick survey of his youthful scheming casts him in at least as a bad a light as his hungry, hairy brother. Nevertheless, "Jacob I loved, but Esau I hated" (Rom 9:13).

---

[19]John Piper is therefore right to say that "what is at stake *ultimately* in these chapters is not the fate of Israel; that is penultimate. Ultimately, *God's own* trustworthiness is at stake." Piper, *Justification of God*, 19 (emphasis original).

[20]I follow N. T. Wright (and others) in arguing that Paul contrasts a merely ethnic Israel with the true Israel. But this is not, as it is sometimes slurred, a "replacement theology" for the simple reason that nothing is being replaced. It is a theology of expansion and inclusion, pruning and ingrafting. The faithful remnant within ethnic Israel has been *expanded* to *include* Gentiles who have given believing allegiance (*pistis*) to Israel's Messiah. This strange reversal likewise gives Paul hope for those branches that are currently cut off. See Wright, *Romans*, 636.

Does this make God unjust? After all, a fetus-hating favoritism would seem to impugn the perfect character of God, at least to modern readers. In *East of Eden*, a connection appears in the story of two other sons (Adam and Charles Trask) who bless their harsh father (the Colonel) with different gifts. Charles works for weeks to buy a pocketknife that is promptly ignored by his dad. Adam, on the other hand, gives his father a mongrel pup that becomes the old man's prized possession.[21] "He liked everything you brought him," Charles states. "He didn't like me."[22] The judgment is harsh but true, for as the aging Colonel once admitted to his younger son, "I love you better. I always have."[23]

Is God this sort of Father? In response to "Jacob I loved, but Esau I hated," one approach (especially in my own Wesleyan tradition) is to note that Paul's quotation is from Malachi, not Genesis. The text (Mal 1:2-3) is said to speak not of Esau the individual but of his Edomite descendants whose sin deserved God's "wrath" (Mal 1:4). The real Esau, though passed over as a member of the line of promise, shows no signs of being either damned or despised by God, despite a willingness to value some red stew above his birthright. The historical Esau ends up reconciled to his once-conniving twin, blessed by Yahweh, and with his face likened to the forgiving gaze of God himself (Gen 33:10).

In Paul's passage, however, Esau the individual does seem to be in view—even if the discussion pertains to something other than salvation or damnation. By Paul's lack of explanation, we see that he intends the quote from Malachi to fall like a bombshell on the playground of the ethnic or cultural boasters.[24] Esau's intended individuality is then proven by the ensuing question (Rom 9:14): "Is God unjust?" No reader of Israel's Scriptures would ever ask this of the judgment brought against the

---

[21]The story mimics that of Cain and Abel, not merely in the first letters of the boys' names (Charles and Adam) but in the nature of their gifts. A pocketknife is used to cut things that grow from soil while a pup is a creature of flesh and blood (cf. Gen 4:3-4).

[22]Steinbeck, *East of Eden*, 63.

[23]Steinbeck, *East of Eden*, 27.

[24]A critique of human boasting pervades the letter (Rom 2:17-20, 27; 4:2; 11:25; 12:3, 16). Barclay argues that Paul intends to conclude this portion of his argument with what sounds like a "brutal statement" accompanied by "no explanation, no rationale, nothing to indicate why one and not the other." Barclay, *Paul and the Gift*, 534.

Edomites. The question gains force only when its focus is a fetus. Still, Paul's answer is emphatic: "Not at all! For [God] says to Moses, 'I will have mercy on whom I have mercy, and I will have compassion on whom I have compassion'" (Rom 9:1-15, quoting Ex 33:19). The formula is as an *idem per idem* construction, and its point is to highlight the subject's freedom to perform an action however he or she desires.[25] God's freedom is then confirmed by the ensuing example of Pharaoh:

> It does not, therefore, depend on human desire or effort, but on God's mercy. For Scripture says to Pharaoh: "I raised you up for this very purpose, that I might display my power in you and that my name might be proclaimed in all the earth" [Ex 9:16]. Therefore God has mercy on whom he wants to have mercy, and he hardens whom he wants to harden. (Rom 9:16-18)

Once more, non-Reformed commentators turn to the Old Testament to note that Pharaoh hardened his own heart before the explicit references to God hardening him. True enough. Yet Paul focuses also on God's act of raising up the murderous ruler (Rom 9:17) for the express purpose of displaying divine power through the exodus. "There is no authority except that which God has established" (Rom 13:1). Thus even the most hardened and cynical of earthly rulers would not have any power if it had not been granted to them "from above" (Jn 19:11). Once more, the paradoxical pattern emerges: redemption via hardening mercy and divine judgment.

At long last, we are prepared for the specific Pauline questions toward which I have been building. "One of you will say to me: 'Then why does God still blame us? For who is able to resist his will?'" (Rom 9:19). This is precisely the question posed to deterministic views of divine sovereignty. For in the words of James D. G. Dunn, "Anyone knows that if blame attaches to a puppet's actions it is the puppeteer who should be blamed, not the puppet!"[26]

---

[25]See Piper, *Justification of God*, 82. Likewise, Childs notes that the tautology testifies "to the freedom of God" in a way that is "closely akin" to the divine name in Ex 3:14: "I AM WHO I AM" or "I will be who I will be." See Brevard S. Childs, *The Book of Exodus, A Critical Theological Commentary* (Philadelphia: Westminster, 1974), 596.

[26]James D. G. Dunn, *Romans 9–16*, WBC 38B (Dallas, TX: Word Books, 1988), 564.

A survey of Jewish literature from around Paul's time reveals that discussions of free will versus God's all-determining sovereignty began long before Augustine, Calvin, Arminius, and Steinbeck. Books like the Psalms of Solomon (ca. first century AD), 4 Esdras (ca. AD 100), and the Wisdom of Solomon (ca. 200 BC–AD 50) affirmed more robust views of human freedom. The opposite view was held in Qumran and (perhaps) in Sirach, where all things were attributed to Yahweh's fore-ordination.[27] This view is often called divine determinism since God is seen as actively causing all earthly occurrences apart from human free will. Finally, Josephus detailed a middle way that he associated with the Pharisees, who purportedly emphasized a "cooperation" between the human will and those things "brought about by destiny" (*Antiquities* 18.1-3).[28] In short, one cannot know Paul's view simply by inquiring after *the* Jewish perspective.

The trashcan question must be settled by Paul's statements on the matter, if indeed he does address it. And Paul's own words sound rather harsh.

> But who are you, a human being, to talk back to God? Shall what is formed say to the one who formed it, "Why did you make me like this?" [Is 29:16; 45:9]. Does not the potter have the right to make out of the same lump of clay some pottery for special purposes and some for common use?
>
> What if God, although choosing to show his wrath and make his power known, bore with great patience the objects of his wrath—prepared for destruction? What if he did this to make the riches of his glory known to the objects of his mercy, whom he prepared in advance for glory—even us, whom he also called, not only from the Jews but also from the Gentiles? (Rom 9:20-24)

In response to a question of divine determinism ("Why does God still blame us? For who is able to resist his will?" [Rom 9:19]), Paul's move is

---

[27]See 1QS III, 15–IV, 26; XI, 10-11; Sir 33:7-13. Sirach 33 is especially relevant since it likens humans to clay in the hands of a potter (Sir 33:13) who "appointed their different ways" (Sir 33:11). Piper (*Justification of God*, 197) sees this passage as a clear example of individual determinism, though I am not so sure since Sir 15:11-20 may be taken to imply that God's predestination is based on foreknowledge of our genuine human choices.

[28]See Witherington, *Paul's Letter to the Romans*, 246-49.

not to clarify that humans still exercise free will but to sternly shush his questioner and reassert the freedom of God to do what he wants with his creations.[29]

A similar shushing takes place in *East of Eden*. The severe and devout wife of Samuel Hamilton, Liza, chides her inquisitive husband for always "picking at" and "questioning" the meaning of the New Testament: "You turn it over the way a 'coon turns over a wet rock," she states, "and it angers me." Samuel responds that he is merely "trying to understand it." To which Liza snaps, "Who wants you to understand it? If the Lord God wanted you to understand it He'd have given you to understand or He'd have set it down different."[30]

Is this Paul's tactic? "Who are you to ask the obvious question!? So what if God created some people to be trashcans!?" In answer, the scholarly argument turns to Greek grammar, and the question of the (1) causal or (2) concessive sense of the divine will (Rom 9:22):

1. Causal: "But (what) if God, *because* he wished to show his wrath and make his power known, bore with great patience . . ."

2. Concessive: "But (what) if God, *although* he wished to show his wrath and make his power known, bore with great patience . . ."[31]

Either reading technically allows for the trashcan interpretation. Yet the concessive rendering places the accent on God's patience toward wrath-deserving vessels. For this reason, it is both friendlier to non-Reformed interpretations and more in keeping with the biblical emphasis on a God who is longsuffering, allowing every possibility for repentance (Rom 2:4; 1 Tim 2:3-4). Divine patience is what stands out both in biblical history and thereafter. In 2 Peter, we read, "The Lord . . . is patient with you, not wanting *anyone* to perish, but *everyone* to come to repentance" (2 Pet 3:9, emphasis added).

Against the trashcan interpretation, commentators highlight the contrast between the vessels "prepared in advance [*katērtismena*] for

---

[29]See Wright (*Romans*, 641): "Paul again refuses to take the easy way out, to assure his readers that humans are free to do what they want."

[30]Steinbeck, *East of Eden*, 255.

[31]Translations by Moo, *Epistle to the Romans*, 605.

glory" (Rom 9:23) and those merely "fitted" (*proētoimasen*) for destruction (Rom 9:22). Paul does not say that God crafted the latter "in advance" to be vessels of wrath, and the distinction opens the possibility that their current position is the result of their own lack of *pistis* in the face of God's self-revelation (cf. Rom 1:20)[32] rather than a predetermined outcome of damnation, shall we say, "by fate alone."

Importantly, Paul rejects the notion that one's status as a vessel of wrath or mercy is necessarily a permanent condition (cf. Jer 18). Just as Yahweh was patient with Israel after the incident of the golden calf, so he has—in the words of Michael Bird—"prepared 'objects of wrath' who may yet become 'objects of mercy' because of his forbearance ([Rom] 9:22-23; 11:32)."[33] Other passages (Eph 2:3-5; 2 Tim 2:20-21) reveal that one may begin as a vessel of wrath and be transformed into a child of God. Indeed, Romans itself says the same about both Gentiles (who start out under wrath in Rom 1 only to be grafted into the Israel tree by faith in Rom 10–11) and Jews (who may be regrafted to the olive tree in Rom 11). "The issue," argues Witherington, "is where one is in the story of a particular vessel, not some act of divine predetermination of some to wrath."[34]

All these considerations raise objections to the trashcan interpretation, although Romans 9:22-23 remains a thorn in the flesh of non-Reformed interpreters—a messenger, if not of Satan, then of Augustine, Calvin, and Edwards—sent to torment us. And plead as we might, it will not be taken away. Now it is time to voice my own proposal.

Between a Rock and a Reformed Place

My conclusions on these verses place me in an odd position between battle lines. On the one hand, I sense that some Reformed and Augustinian readings downplay both the catastrophic implications for God's

---

[32]"The former are 'fitted for destruction,' leaving it at least ambiguous whether they have simply done this to themselves or whether God has somehow been involved in the process. The latter, though, have been 'prepared for glory' by God himself." Wright, *Romans*, 642; see also Shellrude, "Freedom of God," 315.

[33]Bird, *Romans*, 338.

[34]See Witherington, *Paul's Letter to the Romans*, 259.

character and the clash with other Scriptures, including Pauline ones. A particularly honest, if egregious, example exists in the work of the pastor-theologian John Piper. In his book-length treatment of Romans 9, Piper follows Jonathan Edwards in admitting that God's will is "arbitrary" in its utter predetermination of salvation or damnation. God's will is driven only by his "righteous" desire to magnify his own glory by saving some and damning others.[35] On Romans 9:22-23, Piper's interpretation mirrors the dumpster interpretation of my friend, despite differing over whether God should be praised for such behavior. "We should picture," writes Piper, "a vessel placed outside the house and used, say, as an incinerator ('where the worm does not die, and the fire is not quenched,' Mk 9:48)."[36]

When pressed on how this divine action could be praiseworthy, Piper responds that God's greatness is his complete freedom to do whatever he pleases to magnify his glory. Indeed, God "must" act in this way for two reasons: (1) to remain free and (2) to allow the full range of his glory to be externalized.[37] This result can only happen, says Piper, by outpouring wrath on those people created specifically for eternal torment.

One objection to this interpretation is that it makes God into a monster who bears striking similarities to the pagan deities Paul's audience knew well. This deity seems like little more than an extension of Nietzsche's "will to power" projected to infinity.[38] Indeed, a sense of fated predestination by an arbitrary god would have also sounded familiar in Caesar's city. But that is no mark in its favor.

In addition to problems for God's goodness, other troubles show forth in Piper's glory-driven determinism. First, God's eternal self-sufficiency

---

[35]Piper, *Justification of God*, 121n28. It is to Piper's novel definition of divine righteousness that Wright is responding with his claim that "if there is complete disjunction between God's justice and everybody else's, it would be better not to use the term at all." Wright, *Romans*, 639. Edwards spoke of everything as depending on the "arbitrary divine constitution" in his treatise *On Original Sin*, in *WJE*, 3:399. See again chap. 8 for my own look at Edwards's metaphysical speculation.

[36]Piper, *Justification of God*, 201.

[37]Piper, *Justification of God*, 220.

[38]To this point, Piper would no doubt respond that we should be grateful that God predetermined to save anyone at all. Unfortunately, this defense fails since it is God who appears to be the active agent behind our actions.

and perfection are compromised since God's life would seem to be deficient apart from the "arbitrary" display of certain attributes (wrath and mercy), which Piper claims are "the essence of what it means to be God."[39] Questions abound: Must God engineer evil to be fully glorious!? Was he not fully glorious before creation? How can wrath and mercy be the "essence" of God's character if evil is not eternal? After all, the life of God within the Trinity is characterized by holy love, not wrath and mercy.[40]

Second, there is something approaching a contradiction in Piper's odd assertion of what God "must" do in order to be free. For Piper, "the ultimate aim of God is to show mercy. But to do this he *must* place it against a backdrop of wrath."[41] This definition of divine liberty (which is hardly the only option within the broad and venerable tradition of Reformed theology[42]) turns out to be a straitjacket that requires God to cause all manner of horrors to maximize and "externalize" his grace and freedom. That argument finds resonance in Romans. Unfortunately, it is that of Paul's imaginary opponents who define "freedom" by a need to "go on sinning so that grace may increase"! (Rom 6:1 NIV 1984).

On the other hand, as a Wesleyan myself, I often feel that "those of my own [theological] race" (Rom 9:3) have hardened their interpretive hearts to the way Paul is cutting off some of the very branches we attempt to sit on in Romans 9. For instance, it seems obvious that the passage is dealing—at certain points—with eternal destinies, and not merely with election to service. Otherwise, Paul would not be so aggrieved that he is willing to be damned for other Jews![43] Second, it seems unavoidable that Paul is dealing—at some level—with individuals and at least the question of determinism. Otherwise, the queries "Is God unjust?" (Rom 9:14) and

---

[39]Piper, *Justification of God*, 219. The worry over Piper's doctrine of aseity (that is, God's eternal self-sufficiency and perfection) is expressed by Thomas H. McCall, "I Believe in Divine Sovereignty," *Trinity Journal* 29, no. 2 (2008): 205-26.

[40]See also Joshua M. McNall, *The Mosaic of Atonement: An Integrated Approach to Christ's Work* (Grand Rapids, MI: Zondervan Academic, 2019), 223-36.

[41]See Piper, *Justification of God*, 220 (emphasis added).

[42]For the helpful move to broaden our understanding of Reformed theology, see Oliver D. Crisp, *Deviant Calvinism: Broadening Reformed Theology* (Minneapolis: Fortress, 2014).

[43]Pace Cranfield, *Epistle to the Romans*, 2:492.

"Why does God still blame us?" (Rom 9:19) would not arise at all. (Recall, no one would ask the former question of the Edomites.) Despite its faults, Piper's methodical analysis of Paul's logic does a better job of noting the force of these questions than do many Wesleyan-Arminian interpreters. So where does this leave me?

God of Incomplete Sentences

My speculative suggestion involves the need to take more seriously the grammar of Romans 9:22 precisely as an unanswered question and an incomplete sentence.[44] What if it is designed not as an assertion of what is true but as a rhetorical device (an argumentative trap) to put Paul's opponents on their heels before clarifying that our status as ingrafted human "branches" is not all predetermined (Rom 10 and 11)? Allow me to explain.

Recent scholarship focuses on Paul's use of "diatribal" rhetoric by which he engages in imaginary conversations with hypothetical questioners (say, a Judaizing Christian, an anti-Jewish Gentile, or a Corinthian libertine who misunderstands God's grace).[45] Romans 9 contains just this sort of back and forth. But in Romans 9:22-23 there is no "answer." The apodosis ("then . . .") that completes the thought is missing.

Douglas Moo suggests that Paul leaves the sentence hanging in order to have the audience complete the thought (i.e., "Yes, I suppose God does craft certain individuals for the purpose of destruction and damnation").[46] But this speculative conclusion seems less than obvious. What if an unanswered question is precisely that . . . ?

John Barclay agrees with Reformed and Augustinian scholars that Paul seems intent on treading the "risky path" that leads "toward a form of determinism" through the use of "shock tactics."[47] Yet, just when it

---

[44]"Notoriously, the whole sentence is syntactically incomplete, lacking an apodosis that would clarify exactly what God will do in relation to these two kinds of 'vessel.'" Barclay, *Paul and the Gift*, 534.

[45]See Stanley Kent Stowers, *The Diatribe and Paul's Letter to the Romans* (Chico, CA: Scholars Press, 1981).

[46]Moo, *Epistle to the Romans*, 604.

[47]Barclay, *Paul and the Gift*, 532-33. All this points to the "incongruous" nature of divine grace, a grace that does not depend on the work, worth, birth, or moral uprightness of the recipients.

appears that Paul must topple over into what I have dubbed a "trashcan theology," Barclay notes how he stops short of the precipice, in mid-sentence (Rom 9:22-23). Paul therefore moves "from the prospect of a double predestination to the hope of a singular mercy on all [i.e., in Rom 10–11]."[48] In Barclay's opinion, "God's plan is not a blueprint, but a promise. Those whom God calls are the product not of a pre-determined past, but of a purpose" that allows us "to imagine a future in which even the excluded can be integrated again ([Rom] 11:11-32)."[49] In other words, there is hope, even for "vessels of wrath" now fit for destruction.

The problem with Barclay's brief explanation is that it leaves the reason for Paul's rhetorical about-face unclear. Why propose the possibility of a double predestination in Romans 9 before disavowing it in Romans 10 and 11? Why does he suddenly break off his most controversial line in midsentence (Rom 9:22-23)? To be sure, Paul is highlighting the "incongruity" of divine grace as something that comes apart from status, merit, or ethnocultural identity. But why shift gears so suddenly without asserting that the deterministic prospect is true?

Douglas Campbell offers an intriguing suggestion. In his view, Romans 9 is designed as an argumentative trap that mirrors the claims of Paul's opponent, a hypothetical Jewish "Teacher" who thinks Paul's gospel implies unrighteousness in God. In mimicry of the Teacher's position, Paul notes that God's choice was that of Isaac over Ishmael, Jacob over Esau, Moses over Pharaoh, clean pots over common ones. In so doing, Paul has probably brought forth an amen from his Jewish opponents.[50] But then the trap springs shut in Romans 9:24, as the imaginary conversation partner anticipates the apodosis ("then") that never comes. The questions are a setup. Or to quote Admiral Ackbar from *Return of the Jedi*, "It's a trap!"

The twist occurs when Paul suddenly asks if the vessels "prepared in advance for glory" may include "even us, whom he also called, not only

---

Incongruity is one of the six "perfections" of grace/gift language highlighted by Barclay (73), yet this incongruity need not imply that no response is necessary.

[48]Barclay, *Paul and the Gift*, 556.

[49]Barclay, *Paul and the Gift*, 534-35.

[50]Campbell, *Deliverance of God*, 776.

from the Jews but also from the Gentiles?" (Rom 9:24). To answer in the negative would require Jewish objectors to "take their stand with the boorish Ishmael and Esau, whose descendants were later enemies of Israel, and with the great oppressor of Israel, Pharaoh."[51] In other words, Paul does not finish his deterministic train of thought because its function was not to affirm a trashcan theology at all but to show that divine grace has always meant some strange reversals and strange fruit, brought forth by God's hardening mercy.[52]

The least likely people often find themselves as recipients of God's surprising grace. Campbell highlights the significance of Paul's rhetorical strategy in a crucial endnote:

> The suggested rereading frees Paul's notion of election from a strong sense of double predestination, because the key statements establishing that dynamic are primarily argumentative entrapments more reflective of the views of Paul's opponent, the Teacher, rather than his own position.[53]

The advantage of the reading is that it acknowledges the strengths inherent within the Augustinian-Reformed perspective as affirmed by Barclay. Yet the approach also explains why "Paul does not follow through on the merciless determinism."[54] Repeatedly in Romans 9, Paul seems to be intentionally marching toward a robust affirmation of God's sovereign right to do whatever he wishes with vessels he has made. The Creator *could* even craft some vessels specifically for damnation, but Paul never asserts that God *does* so.[55]

---

[51]Campbell, *Deliverance of God*, 776.

[52]See again my prior point that it is the incongruous nature of divine grace that causes hardening in prideful hearts.

[53]Campbell, *Deliverance of God*, 1132n34. An acceptance of this reading of Romans 9 does not commit one to the unconvincing parts of Campbell's bold proposal. These include his claim that vast swaths of Romans (especially Rom 1–4) do not represent Paul's thought at all, but rather that of the aforementioned "Teacher." That Paul employs diatribe to mimic and defeat opponents is uncontroversial, but that he rejects what Campbell calls "justification theory" is dubious. For elaboration, see again my *Mosaic of Atonement*. For a critique of Campbell's slippery definition of the "apocalyptic Paul," see N. T. Wright, *Paul and His Recent Interpreters: Some Contemporary Debates* (Minneapolis: Fortress, 2015), chap. 9.

[54]Luke Timothy Johnson, *Reading Romans: A Literary and Theological Commentary* (New York: Crossroad, 1997), 163.

[55]This is apparently what Barclay means by the "prospect" of double predestination, but without the straightforward assertion that this is actually what God does.

Paul's point shows that God has the right to bestow grace in a way that subverts our sense of merit, which is precisely what God has done by welcoming tax collectors, Gentiles, and former persecutors. Paul uses his opponents' strong theology of predestination against them. Still, the brilliant trap need not imply a rejection of the biblical idea that God desires the salvation of "all people" (1 Tim 2:3-4). To say otherwise can result in a divine schizophrenia in which one of God's competing wills desires salvation while the other (God's dark side?) crafts certain individuals for the express purpose of damnation.[56] In the words of Lesslie Newbigin, "The whole passage makes clear that God has *not* done what he might have done. He has not made some for honor and some for destruction. What he has done is to consign *all* [humans] to disobedience in order that he may have mercy on *all*" (Rom 11:32).[57]

I do have, however, one quibble with Campbell's theory. I disagree that Paul's argumentative entrapment in Romans 9 works only against a Torah-loving Jewish Teacher. Like many parts of Romans (e.g., Abraham in Rom 4), it works just as well as a pride-obliterating salvo against anti-Jewish Gentiles. By placing the widespread Jewish rejection of the gospel against the canvas of divine sovereignty—and then reassuring his audience that hope for Israel is not lost—Paul avoids the anti-Judaic implications of putting excessive blame on Jews themselves. In other contexts, Paul is perfectly happy to emphasize human responsibility, but as Leander Keck perceptively notes, to do so here "would have abetted the very attitudes that he is trying to thwart" (i.e., a prideful sense of ethnic or moral superiority on the part of Gentiles).[58]

Paul's rhetorical "what if" is meant not to endorse a full-on determinism but to shut the mouths of those who would boast in anything except the cross. Only once this entitlement is quashed, for both Jews and Gentiles, can Paul go on to give the hope of yet more strange

---

[56]This is the unfortunate theological result in Schreiner, *Romans*, 520: "There is a sense in which [God] truly desires the repentance of all people, yet he ordains that only some would be saved."

[57]Lesslie Newbigin, *The Gospel in a Pluralistic Society* (Grand Rapids, MI: Eerdmans, 1989), 83 (emphasis original).

[58]Keck, *Romans*, 241.

reversals to come (Rom 11), even for "vessels of wrath."[59] The shocking revelation is that "God has bound everyone over to disobedience so that he may have mercy on them all" (Rom 11:32). In the words of Barclay, the divine will "initially appears equally set to harden or to save, but turns out on closer inspection, and in the end, to harden only in order to save."[60] Here too a familiar pattern pokes up its thorn-scarred head: redemption via hardening mercy, salvation by catastrophe.

Conclusion: *Timshel*

All this brings us back to *East of Eden*. What would Paul say to Steinbeck's claim that "the free, exploring mind of the individual human is the most valuable thing in the world"? I assume he would have harsh words for such a foolish, human-centered notion. Indeed, the undirected mind of the individual (if there could be such a thing!) is not "the one thing that separates us from the beasts,"[61] but the thing that threatens to make us like them! (Rom 1:21-22).[62] East of the biblical Eden, any freedom we have comes only as a gift of grace, through the Holy Spirit.[63]

But not every intended lesson in Steinbeck's tale is nonsense. At the end of *East of Eden*, we find ourselves at the beginning, mulling another line from Genesis. The LORD asks Cain some more unanswered questions: "Why are you angry? Why is your face downcast? If you do what is right, will you not be accepted? But if you do not do what is right, sin is crouching at your door; it desires to have you but you ['must'; 'shall'; 'may'?] rule over it" (Gen 4:6-7). Within this passage resides an issue of Hebrew translation. Clearly, Cain is to "master" [*timshel*] the Sin that crouches near him.[64] But is this mastery

---

[59]Cf. Paul's words in 2 Timothy 2:20-21.

[60]John M. G. Barclay, "Unnerving Grace: Approaching Romans 9–11 from the Wisdom of Solomon," in *Between Gospel and Election: Explorations in the Interpretation of Romans 9–11*, ed. Florian Wilk and J. Ross Wagner, WUNT 257 (Tübingen: Mohr Siebeck, 2010), 109.

[61]Steinbeck, *East of Eden*, 131.

[62]See G. K. Beale, *We Become What We Worship: A Biblical Theology of Idolatry* (Downers Grove, IL: InterVarsity Press, 2008).

[63]See McNall, *Mosaic of Atonement*, 300-305.

[64]Both Genesis and Paul personify Sin as a destructive, enslaving, killing "power" (hence my capital "S") rather than treating it as merely a human infraction against a divine standard of righteousness (see esp. Rom 6–8).

1. a **command**—you *must* master it,

2. a **promise**—you *will* master it, or

3. a **possibility**—you *may* master it?

Commentators are divided.[65]

Steinbeck's entire novel hinges on this single word (*timshel*). And it is Lee—the idiosyncratic Chinese Presbyterian—who undertakes the Hebrew word study:

> Lee's hand shook as he filled the delicate cups, He drank his down in one gulp. "Don't you see?" he cried. "The American standard translation *orders* men to triumph over sin, and you can call sin ignorance. The King James translation makes a promise in 'Thou shalt,' meaning that men will surely triumph over sin. But the Hebrew word, the word *timshel*—'Thou mayest'—that gives a choice. It might be the most important word in the world. That says the way is open. That throws it right back on a man. For if 'Thou mayest'—it is also true that 'Thou mayest not.' Don't you see?"[66]

In some ways, the three interpretive possibilities of *timshel* correspond to three lands detailed in this book (doubt, dogmatism, and perhaps). The divine word is not an impossible "ought" that mocks us (doubt), or a "shall" that predetermines everything (dogmatism), but a "may" accompanied by grace.[67]

The interpretation proves crucial since the saga ends with an adult son (Cal) standing like a cloven Cain and Esau before the bedside of his dying father (Adam Trask). The son is wracked with guilt since in jealousy he goaded his brother to go off to the "field" of war, where he was killed. His father never recovered, and he fell mute with a stroke upon reading the telegram. The question with which the novel ends is this: Might there be fatherly forgiveness for such a shattered vessel fit for wrath? Is there still hope for a "son of Adam," whose faults were partly preconditioned by genetics, environment, and choices made? On cue, an aging Lee

[65]See, for instance, Victor P. Hamilton, *The Book of Genesis, Chapters 1–17*, NICOT (Grand Rapids, MI: Eerdmans, 1990), 228.

[66]Steinbeck, *East of Eden*, 301 (emphasis original).

[67]Thanks to Jerome Van Kuiken for this insightful connection.

approaches with two unanswered questions and a word that is by now familiar in this book on theological perhapsing: *maybe.*

> "Does a craftsman, even in his old age, lose his hunger to make a perfect cup—thin, strong, translucent?"
>
> "Cal, listen to me. Can you think that whatever made us—would stop trying?"
>
> "Maybe you'll come to know that [we can be] refired."

Cal approaches his father's bedside. And recalling the Hebrew word from far back in the novel, Adam opens his mouth one last time to bless his hardened son with just one word: *timshel*—"thou mayest."[68] One's status as a wrath-deserving vessel need not be final.[69]

---

[68]Steinbeck, *East of Eden*, 601.

[69]Steinbeck's interpretation of the Hebrew has scholarly merit since, as Victor Hamilton notes, "Cain does have a choice. He is not so deeply embedded in sin, either inherited or actual, that his further sin is determined and inevitable." Hamilton, *Book of Genesis*, 228. See also Walter Brueggemann, *Genesis*, Interpretation (Atlanta: John Knox, 1973), 63.

○

12

●

After the End

The Marriage Supper
and The Great Divorce

Do not ask of a vision in a dream
more than a vision in a dream can give.

C. S. Lewis, The Great Divorce

Is a classic work of Christian fiction any less prophetic if it opens with a lie? In his preface to *The Great Divorce*, C. S. Lewis begs readers to remember that "the trans-mortal conditions [that follow] are solely an imaginative supposal: they are not even a guess or a speculation at what may actually await us." The disclaimer is important since the "last thing" Lewis says he wishes to arouse is "a factual curiosity about the details of the after-world."[1] In many respects, I believe him. I do not think Lewis is suggesting that the grass blades of heaven are literally as hard as diamonds (as they are in his story). Nor is he supposing that the damned will be ferried between hell and heaven by way of a celestial bus. Fair enough.

But on other matters, Lewis protests too much. For the arousal of anything less than "factual curiosity" about the afterlife would make *The*

---

[1]C. S. Lewis, *The Great Divorce: A Dream* (1946; repr., New York: Harper, 2001), x. To eliminate excessive footnotes, I will hereafter cite page numbers parenthetically.

Great Divorce a bit of pointless moralizing. Make no mistake, the book has serious theological proposals to explore, however couched in fiction. Lewis intends to awaken our imaginations to new possibilities. Hence, the truthfulness of the preface hinges on two words: *details* and *speculation*. Just how much detail and what kind of speculation are profitable when we consider what happens after death?[2]

My third and final case study involves *The Great Divorce* precisely as a bit of imaginative supposing if not detailed speculation. Lewis situates his view of final states in a kind of sacred middle ground between two extremes: on the one side, a rigid exclusivism that asserts confidently that all who have not responded to de facto altar calls are damned, and on the other side, an equally confident universalism that flies in the face of Scripture and tradition. Was Lewis right to say perhaps as he did?

Beyond this question, I am also interested in the *kind* of writing that awakens healthy (as opposed to unbiblical) speculation. On this point, Lewis is heralded as the twentieth century's most famous exemplar of the Christian imagination, even if one laments how he is sometimes appealed to by evangelicals with something approaching a doctrine of infallibility.

Lewis's creativity flourished because, in his words, "The imaginative man in me is older . . . and more basic than either the religious writer or the critic."[3] He never lost a childlike willingness to be enchanted, which, of course, means being open to saying perhaps. In later years, when German bombs fell and his closest relations either died or descended into alcoholism, Lewis became more childlike than ever. "When I was ten," he wrote, "I read fairy stories in secret and would have been ashamed if I had been found doing so. Now that I am fifty I read them openly."[4] But *The Great Divorce* is not a children's story. And

---

[2]To recall, Origen believed that speculative theories on what happened before history's "beginning" and after its "end" were fair game since the church had not yet ruled on these matters (see chap. 2). Despite affirming some things in Origen, my own claim was that he could have benefitted by some more substantial guardrails (see chap. 3).

[3]Lewis made this confession in a statement to the Milton Society of America in 1954. Cited in Alan Jacobs, *The Narnian: The Life and Imagination of C. S. Lewis* (New York: HarperOne, 2005), xxiv-xxv.

[4]Cited in Jacobs, *Narnian*, xxii.

to satisfy any readers who are not familiar with it, the briefest summary is in order.

From the Grey Town to the Distant Mountains

The tale begins at a bus stop with a line of grumpy travelers. The location is Grey Town. And despite the absence of fiery torment, we soon learn that it is hell. In Grey Town, shoddy and deserted houses spread toward the horizon as the inhabitants quarrel to increasing "social distancing." Loneliness and boredom pervade. But in place of white-hot coals, there is only White flight, exported to every tribe and tongue under perdition.

The trouble in Lewis's hell involves the unrestrained and misdirected nature of human desire. "You can get everything you want," says one ghost, though "not [of] very good quality" (13). This false form of freedom only expedites the alienation, since the hellions' wants are perverted terribly. (This insight would have delighted Jonathan Edwards, though much else in the book would have horrified him.) Thus hell's inhabitants spread ever further from communion, and from the bus stop that is their escape.

The damned in *The Great Divorce* are allowed to take holiday excursions to the borderland of heaven (67). Lewis adapts this idea from the ancient notion of the *refrigerium* (a period of refreshment or "cooling off") that was said to be granted to the occupants of hell on Easter Sunday. The fictional Lewis—for he himself is the main character—now finds himself on one of these excursions. After boarding the bus, he is shocked to watch it rise above the gloomy streets toward an expanse of "greenness and light" (23) that is the "Valley of the Shadow of Life" (68). It is here that the majority of the tale plays out.

The hellions are but "Ghosts" and "phantoms" in comparison to the heavenly solidity (20). This paradise is not a wispy realm of clouds and spirits but a solid country populated by ever-thickening entities, including plants and animals. Lewis, it seems, entertained views similar to John Wesley and Julian of Norwich about the eternal possibilities of non-human creatures. The ultimate end for Christians is not less physical than our current earthly existence but more so. Our fallen world is the Shadow-land; God's redeemed creation will be reality itself.[5]

As in Dante and Bunyan, the insights in *The Great Divorce* come in interactions with the travelers Lewis meets along the way. Among the damned, there is an entrepreneur who journeys to heaven only to find commodities to sell in hell. There is a liberal bishop who boasts of the Theological Society "down there." There is a tousle-headed poet who jumped under a train because no one recognized his genius. And there is an embittered mother who departs heaven—leaving behind her long-lost son—because she cannot love a God who allowed the boy to die in childhood.

Each ghost is met by someone from his or her past. These "Bright Ones" sacrifice the joy of moving closer to the mountains (the heavenly throne) to evangelize their loved ones by imploring them to make the holiday permanent. Lewis's ghost is guided by the nineteenth-century Scottish writer George MacDonald (1824–1905). The real-life Lewis knew MacDonald only by his books. But the relationship was no less deep for that.[6] When Lewis was still an atheist, MacDonald's faerie romance *Phantastes* awakened in him a spiritual longing that he would name "Joy"[7]—a piercing, almost painful, pleasure that is "the scent of a flower we have not found, the echo of a tune we have not yet heard."[8] MacDonald's fiction reignited the ache for transcendent joy in Lewis and nudged him toward the Christian faith.

But MacDonald, like Origen, was a universalist. One purpose of *The Great Divorce* is therefore to rehabilitate him through a kind of post-mortem penance whereby the Scotsman recants his belief in universal

---

[5]There is, however, an unfortunate tendency for Lewis to conflate our spiritual existence after death with our ultimate resurrected, bodily existence in God's new creation at the eschaton. For a corrective, see N. T. Wright, *Surprised by Hope: Rethinking Heaven, the Resurrection, and the Mission of the Church* (New York: HarperOne, 2008).

[6]"I am a product," Lewis once wrote, "of long corridors, empty sunlit rooms, upstairs indoor silences. . . . Also, of endless books." C. S. Lewis, *Surprised by Joy: The Shape of My Early Life* (New York: Harcourt, 1955), 10.

[7]C. S. Lewis, *The Collected Letters of C. S. Lewis*, vol. 1, *Family Letters 1905–1931*, ed. Walter Hooper (San Francisco: HarperSanFrancisco, 2004), 169. Cited in Jacobs, *Narnian*, 63. See also Lewis's later recollection in *Surprised by Joy*, 179.

[8]C. S. Lewis, *The Weight of Glory* (San Francisco: HarperCollins, 1949/2001), 31

salvation. In this way, the book implements some guardrails to eschatological speculation: "Ye can know nothing of the end of all things," MacDonald quips in Lewis's book. But he also holds forth hope that God's mercy may be wider than we fathom: "It *may be*, as the Lord said to the Lady Julian, that . . . all manner of things will be well" (140, emphasis added).

In this exchange resides the whole spirit of *The Great Divorce* in miniature. It is both cautious and daring, both traditional and innovative, both fictional and open to theological facts that may be different from those we expected. In this perhaps of the heavenly MacDonald is Lewis's eschatological imagination, bounded by orthodoxy yet open to being surprised by joy.

The story ends with a warning: "Do not ask of a vision in a dream more than a vision in a dream can give" (144). With these words, MacDonald's character reveals that the book's journey is different from the tales of people claiming to have actually gone to heaven. It was all a dream. The fictional Lewis awakes on the floor of his study with "the clock striking three, and the [air raid] siren howling overhead" (146).[9] He is clutching a blotting cloth that he falsely took to be the hem of George MacDonald's garment. Yet even in this misconception a certain healing has taken place (cf. Mk 5:27) by way of fantasy and fiction.

Against Eternal Both-Anding

What should we learn from Lewis's heavenly perhapsing? A first lesson is a word against eternal both-anding. And it is especially important for my own book.[10] Lewis defines the error as a belief that "reality never presents us with an absolutely unavoidable 'either-or'" (vii). In contrast, he claims that there must be a final distinction between good and evil, truth and error, salvation and damnation.

---

[9]This, like so many of Lewis's greatest works, is a war story, though the threat of eternal damnation is more menacing than even the German *Luftwaffe*. For an in-depth look at how World War II served as a catalyst for Lewis's Christian humanism, see Alan Jacobs, *The Year of Our Lord 1943: Christian Humanism in an Age of Crisis* (Oxford: Oxford University Press, 2018).

[10]See my prior borrowing of this phrase (in chap. 9) from Alan Jacobs, *How to Think: A Survival Guide for a World at Odds* (New York: Currency, 2017), 100.

I do not think that all who choose wrong roads perish; but their rescue consists in being put back on the right road. A sum can be put right: but only by going back till you find the error and working it afresh from that point, never by simply going on. Evil can be undone, but it cannot "develop" into good. Time does not heal it. The spell must be unwound, bit by bit, "with backward mutters of dissevering power"—or else not (viii-ix).

The starkness of this "either-or" must not be missed, especially since *The Great Divorce* floats some imaginative noncontrastive notions on the afterlife. In the dream sequence at least, Lewis attempts to bridge divides between Protestants and Catholics, universalists and traditional Christians, fantasy and theology. But the both-anding cannot last forever. Despite the dreary banality that pervades Grey Town, Night is coming. "It will be dark presently," remarks one spirit, and "no one wants to be out of doors when that happens" (15).

This either-or should also be noted in a book like mine, in which I have often sought to find a middle ground between modern doubt and religious dogmatism. As I have noted, the eternal via media is not a road that Christ endorsed. Hence, Lewis claims that the poet William Blake's quest to officiate *The Marriage of Heaven and Hell* must face the irreconcilable differences between the broad and narrow ways.

A Dog in Heaven's Manger

Lewis explains why his fictional perhapsing steered clear of universalism: "It has a grand sound to say ye'll accept no salvation which leaves even one creature in the dark outside. But watch that sophistry or ye'll make a Dog in the Manger the tyrant of the universe" (136).

The metaphor may be confusing since the only manger some of us register is a reference to the Christmas nativity. But for Lewis the image refers to a barnyard occurrence in which the family dog would often sleep upon the dry food inside the cattle's trough. The hound has no interest in consuming what lies beneath him. But if his freedom to lounge upon it is not disturbed, the cattle will go hungry. Jerry Walls sums up Lewis's point with a pair of questions: "Should hell have the power to veto heaven? Should those who have chosen misery have the power forever to destroy or undermine the happiness they will not accept for themselves?"[11]

One wonders if Lewis has not presented a false choice with this analogy. Why must the two groups, the damned and the redeemed, be pictured in such close proximity, sharing a postmortem barnyard, as it were? And why must their respective happiness be a zero-sum game? Still, there is biblical precedent for both (1) the metaphorical nearness of the two groups and (2) the penchant of the damned to attempt to exert a tyrant's will on the saved. We find both themes in Christ's parable of the rich man and Lazarus (Lk 16:19-31).[12]

In Jesus' teaching, the rich man and Lazarus appear in the same vicinity, despite the chasm separating them, and despite the odd fact that the rich man seems unable to see the chasm since Abraham must inform him of it. In the parable, the three parties are close enough to speak, and to create the illusion that Lazarus might dip his finger in water to chill the rich man's tongue, a request that reveals the rich man attempting to play the tyrannical "dog" to Lazarus's "manger." Even in the afterlife he is still ordering the former beggar (not to mention Abraham!) around.

Lewis is attuned to these themes from Christ's parable as he creates his own fictional narrative, and he also adapts the chasm separating the rich man and Lazarus. In *The Great Divorce*, the great "gulf" that loomed large from the omnibus is in fact a tiny crack in the soil of the solid country. That is why the saints of heaven cannot cross the gap: "Only the Greatest of all can make Himself small enough to enter Hell" (139).[13]

But other elements in Jesus' story do not fit so well with Lewis's dream sequence. As father Abraham explains, no one may "cross over from there to us" (Lk 16:26). And there is no mention of holiday exceptions.

---

[11]See Jerry L. Walls, *Heaven, Hell, and Purgatory* (Grand Rapids, MI: Brazos, 2015), 157-58.

[12]Some question whether it is a parable since Luke does not explicitly name it as such. Without going into this debate, I will side (for now) with the majority of the tradition that sees the teaching as a fictional narrative designed to convey certain truths about the kingdom of God.

[13]For a critique of the notion that Christ descended into hell rather than the place of the righteous dead, see Matthew Y. Emerson, *"He Descended to the Dead": An Evangelical Theology of Holy Saturday* (Downers Grove, IL: IVP Academic, 2019).

It would likely be foolish to take either parable (Christ's or Lewis's) too literally. As with *The Great Divorce*, I do not think the intention of the story of the rich man and Lazarus is to describe the geography or temperature of our final abodes. It is rather a stern warning to rich oppressors that justice will one day "roll on like a river" (Amos 5:24), even if cool water is withheld from fiery, flapping, and oppressive tongues. There will be a final either-or. And regardless of particulars, the damned will not doggedly prevent the saints from enjoying the marriage supper (Rev 19:9).

On Evolution in the Afterlife

A third lesson to be gained from Lewis's postmortem perhapsing involves the possibility of human evolution (that is, transformation) in the afterlife. For Lewis, there is no reason to assume that death automatically alters our desires, nor must it suddenly render our personhood immutable. Why shouldn't growth and change have at least the possibility of continuing after death?

On the first point (death and unaltered desires), Lewis again finds support in the story of the rich man and Lazarus. The rich man is as selfish and demanding in Hades as he had been in earthly life. And the same is true for the ghosts in *The Great Divorce*. One example exists in the vindictive phantoms who make the painful journey to heaven's borderland only to spew forth a single word of hatred (82). The goodness of the solid country can be experienced only as a cruel joke by them because the ghosts are just like their earthly selves, only more so.

But the ghosts are not necessarily identical to their former selves. They have continued on a trajectory. For Lewis, "everything becomes more and more itself" (132), even after death. A painful example involves the ghost of a famous artist who cannot appreciate the solid country's beauty as anything other than a means to express his artistic talent. When his bright guide cautions him that "looking comes first," the artist despairs and then departs for hell. The scene occasions a warning that the real-life Lewis felt personally:[14] "Every poet and musician and artist, but for

---

[14]Jacobs details the spiritual danger that Lewis felt with regard to his becoming a famous apologist: "Nothing is more dangerous to one's own faith than the work of an apologist. No

Grace, is drawn away from love of the thing he tells, to love of the telling till, down in Deep Hell, they cannot be interested in God at all but only in what they say about Him." The solution is for the famous artist to grow "into a Person" so that he loves "Light" more than the paint and talent he uses to express it (85).

For Lewis, to be redeemed is to become a true and full person.[15] Thus the growth toward heavenly fitness continues for the saved forever. For the hellions, however, devolving has a terminus. To be fully damned is to have the last flicker of humanity snuffed out by a hardening of one's own heart so there is nothing left to redeem. This sounds like a version of annihilationism, though the thing that ceases to exist is the image-bearing humanity of the reprobate individual. The person's post-human "remains" continue on, perhaps even in torment.[16] If this is so, then Lewis has again offered an intriguing, noncontrastive solution to the old conundrum over texts that seem to teach eternal torment and those that sound more like annihilationism.[17]

On Purgatory and Postmortem Opportunity

Because some occupants of hell retain a flicker of humanity, *The Great Divorce* suggests provocatively that some may be saved after death. This hope raises questions of purgatory and postmortem opportunity.[18] Lewis's fictional suggestion can be seen in the ghost of a complaining old woman. "The question," states MacDonald, "is whether she is a grumbler, or only a grumble. If there is a real woman . . . it can be brought to life again. If there's one wee spark under all those ashes, we'll blow it till the

---

doctrine of the Faith seems to me so spectral, so unreal as the one that I have just *successfully* defended in public debate" (italics his). Cited in Jacobs, *Narnian*, 229. It was partly this worry that led Lewis to turn from apologetics to fantasy and children's literature. See also Jacobs, *Narnian*, 237-42.

[15]See also John Behr, *Becoming Human: Meditations on Christian Anthropology in Word and Image* (New York: St Vladimir's Seminary Press, 2013).

[16]Lewis entertains this stance in *The Problem of Pain* (New York: Harper, 1996), 127-28.

[17]For more on the biblical basis for these two positions, see Gregory A. Boyd and Paul R. Eddy, *Across the Spectrum: Understanding Issues in Evangelical Theology*, 2nd ed. (Grand Rapids, MI: Baker Academic, 2009), chap. 17.

[18]See James Beilby, *Postmortem Opportunity: A Biblical and Theological Assessment of Salvation After Death* (Downers Grove, IL: IVP Academic, 2021).

whole pile is red and clear. But if there's nothing but ashes we'll not go on blowing them in our own eyes forever. They must be swept up" (77).

Despite this opportunity, only one ghost accepts the offer to remain in heaven. Lewis chooses for his "rescued sheep" a degenerate sexual sinner who is chained to a lizard representing his lust. The ghost finally allows an angel to slay the reptile, at which point the animal is not eliminated but transformed into a stallion that the man rides into the mountains. The tale communicates several important themes. First, our fleshly appetites must not be repressed but crucified and resurrected since "the Lord finds our desires not too strong but too weak."[19] Second, the final occupants of heaven and hell may surprise religious people (cf. Mt 25:31-46). And third, Lewis crafts a fictional portrayal of a purgatorial second chance at salvation.

Biblical support for Lewis's hope has sometimes been sought in the passage that inspired his first book: *Spirits in Bondage*. The title is a play on 1 Peter 3, which some read as claiming that, after death, Christ was "quickened by the Spirit" so that he "went and preached unto the spirits in prison" (1 Pet 3:18-19 KJV). This was dubbed the "harrowing of hell" in medieval theology, and a line from the Apostles' Creed ("He descended to the dead") has given rise to several interpretations.[20] For Lewis, however, the possibility of postmortem repentance came primarily from presuppositions about God's character rather than prooftexts. Our loving Creator is, in his view, committed to extending grace as long as there is something left to redeem. So if hell's doors are locked, perhaps they are "locked on the *inside*."[21]

None of this means people may actually leave hell. Instead, Lewis's fictional suggestion is that the difference between hell and purgatory is determined retroactively. "You have been in Hell," remarks MacDonald, "though if you don't go back you may call it Purgatory" (35).

Like Paul in Romans 9–11, Lewis does not give anything like an exhaustive explanation about how this all makes sense. And in my view,

---

[19]Lewis, *Weight of Glory*, 26.
[20]See again Emerson, "*He Descended to the Dead.*"
[21]Lewis, *Problem of Pain*, 130 (emphasis original).

this portion of *The Great Divorce*—with its metaphorical description of time, eternity, and human freedom—is the least successful portion of the work. Confusingly, it whisks us out of the solid country to highlight the both-and of divine sovereignty and human freedom by way of a giant chessboard on which humans are moved about by our immortal souls, which simultaneously inhabit both the present and the future (143-44). Origen would have been intrigued, but few others are likely to find it very helpful.

Lewis himself believed in purgatory as a merciful allowance that our souls will "*demand*" as a means of being cleansed.[22] But in *The Great Divorce*, he entertains the possibility of a purgatorial second chance at salvation. Since the work is fiction, it is hard to know quite what to do with this "imaginative supposal." It deserves some further thought.

Walls and Bridges to the Solid Country

One of the few evangelical Protestants who has attempted to affirm something like Lewis's view of purgatory and postmortem opportunity is Jerry L. Walls.[23] Walls begins by arguing that passages often taken to forbid the notion have been misread. Hebrews 9:27-28, for instance, proclaims that judgment comes "after" death, but it does not say that this judgment is immediate or always final. Likewise, Christ's parable of the narrow door depicts some people being shut out of salvation despite their later pleading (Lk 13:23-30), but Walls sees it as applying only to those who had ample opportunity to know Christ in this life since these people say to Jesus, "We ate and drank with you, and you taught in our streets" (Lk 13:26).[24]

Prooftexts aside, Walls is similar to Lewis in rooting purgatorial hope in assumptions about God's character: "The deeper question," he writes, is "does [God] truly love all persons and sincerely desire the salvation of

---

[22]C. S. Lewis, *Letters to Malcolm: Chiefly on Prayer* (1963; repr., New York: Harcourt, 1992), 139; 108-9 (emphasis original).

[23]Walls explores these views most thoroughly in his trilogy on heaven, hell, and purgatory. Jerry L. Walls, *Heaven: The Logic of Eternal Joy* (Oxford: Oxford University Press, 2002); Walls, *Hell: The Logic of Damnation* (Notre Dame, IN: University of Notre Dame Press, 1992); and Walls, *Purgatory: The Logic of Total Transformation* (Oxford: Oxford University Press, 2012).

[24]Walls, *Heaven, Hell, and Purgatory*, 204.

all, or is his primary concern only to provide sufficient grace so that those who are damned are without excuse?"[25] These questions bring Walls to what he identifies as two different views of grace: "sufficient" versus "optimal."

"Sufficient grace" is said to be aimed solely at justifying God's condemnation of those who have not heard a coherent version of the gospel.[26] In contrast, Walls proposes "optimal grace." And it is this proposal that leads him to Lewis's hope for a purgatorial opportunity. In optimal grace, God loves all people and does everything short of overriding our freedom to bring about our salvation.[27] Since many people do not hear a compelling presentation of the gospel in their lifetimes, however, the question for Walls is whether a perfectly loving God might do anything "to level the playing field." If God could provide optimal grace for all, would God do so? Walls thinks the answer is yes, and he then asks whether there is "room to speculate" about a purgatory that looks something like the kind described in *The Great Divorce*.[28]

The Perhaps of Purgatorial Salvation

This conclusion provides an interesting case study for when and how one should say perhaps in theology. Personally, I find it refreshing that Walls is willing to admit theology has a place for speculation—even if not all versions of the practice are praiseworthy. The real issue, then, pertains to the extent to which one *should* speculate beyond, though not against, the clear teachings of Scripture.

Walls's reasoning bears a similarity to what takes place within so-called perfect-being theologies. Following Anselm, this mode of

---

[25]Walls, *Heaven, Hell, and Purgatory*, 203.

[26]As an example, Walls considers the moderate Calvinism of Terrance L. Tiessen, *Who Can Be Saved? Reassessing Salvation in Christ and World Religions* (Downers Grove, IL: InterVarsity Press, 2004), 25. Tiessen speculates that all people will meet Christ personally upon death, whereupon they will respond in a way that corresponds to how they have responded to God's general or special revelation in their lifetime. However, the "sufficiency" and "accessibility" of this grace may be misleading since Tiessen maintains that the grace is not sufficient to save apart from the application of a further grace that is given only to the elect.

[27]According to Walls, the reason God does not transgress our freedom is that he is Love, and "the essence of salvation is a freely chosen relationship." Walls, *Heaven, Hell, and Purgatory*, 200.

[28]Walls, *Heaven, Hell, and Purgatory*, 200-201.

theologizing affirms that God is, by necessity, the maximally perfect being. One cannot possibly conceive of any being that would be greater.[29] This conclusion is then taken to entail a host of attributes: God must be all-knowing, all-powerful, unchanging, and utterly "simple" (i.e., not composed of parts) since all these beliefs may supposedly be extrapolated from assumptions about perfection.

But perfect-being theology has fallen on hard times. Some worry that it proceeds too much by speculation based on our fallen intuitions. Thomas McCall summarizes the critique: "Perfect being theology, they say, encourages us to sit back and imagine what God ought to be like if God were really going to meet our standards of goodness." But "why should we, as fallen sinners, think that we can theologize from our own intellectual resources and come up with anything other than idolatry?" The need, therefore, is for theologians to "repent of . . . speculation and hope for the renewal of [their] minds."[30] There is something to be said for this critique in certain instances. In fact, one could argue that faulty intuitions regarding the "maximally perfect Messiah" kept many first-century theologians (like Saul of Tarsus) from recognizing the incarnate Christ.

What does this have to do with Walls and Lewis? The critique might be that Walls especially imports extrabiblical assumptions about what an optimally perfect grace *should* do. And if so, then speculation regarding things like purgatory and postmortem conversion represent a transgression of God's warning from the whirlwind: "Thus far shall you come, and no farther, / And here shall your proud [words] be stayed" (Job 38:11 ESV).

But the danger runs both ways. McCall notes that some use of intuition in theology is unavoidable, and there is no reason to conclude that it must always run counter to divine truth. What matters is that our intuitions be "correctable" by God's revelation.[31]

---

[29]See Anselm of Canterbury, *Proslogion, with the Replies of Gaunilo and Anselm*, trans. Thomas Williams (Indianapolis: Hackett, 1995/2001), chap. 15.

[30]Thomas H. McCall, *An Invitation to Analytic Christian Theology* (Downers Grove, IL: InterVarsity Press, 2015), 47. To reiterate, McCall is summarizing this critique, not necessarily endorsing it.

[31]McCall, *Invitation to Christian Analytic Theology*, 48-50.

Imaginative openness to new ideas is not always a vice. Its absence can be just as problematic. How much Spirit-baptized imagination was required to fathom a Jewish God-man who, though sinless, was crucified and resurrected? Indeed, it seems possible that one reason the gospel caught on more widely with former pagans, as opposed to Torah-observant Jews, was a Gentile willingness to think beyond the "box" of old assumptions about Yahweh's plan and presence. For while the New Testament church retained far more of Hebraic thought than it did of pagan sensibilities, the more free-wheeling pagan imagination proved more pliable to being surprised by a joy that both shattered and fulfilled its wildest dreams.

Still, I must confess that I am far more compelled by Lewis's fictional narrative than I am by Walls's analysis of "optimal grace." To speak of grace as optimal—like the performance of a car engine or the productivity of an employee—has a squelching effect on my imagination of "what dreams may come" beyond the grave.[32] Dissecting optimal grace nearly kills my sense of its future realness. And this makes Walls's analytical defense of Lewis's fiction seem (at least to me) more speculative and less alluring than *The Great Divorce*.[33]

Herein lies a point toward which my entire book has been building.

Inspired works of art (I have focused here on poetry and fiction) must complement our analysis and our apologetics because the intellect is not the only aspect of our fallen personhood that stands in need of redemption. We need both imagination and analysis. So while I am not dismissing logical rigor in favor of what Richard Rorty called "strong poetry,"[34] I do think we should be open to the ways works of poetry and fiction may be "Egyptian midwives" (Shiphrah and Puah [Ex 1:15-21];

---

[32]William Shakespeare, *Hamlet*, 3.1.65-66.

[33]This is not so much a critique of Walls's conclusions as it is a comment about the most effective medium by which to convey such hopes. Analytic reasoning can be essential to test the truth-value of ideas. And I have engaged in a fair bit of it in this book. It is also worth noting that some of the more creative "imaginative supposals," to use Lewis's words, in recent years (fictional scenarios designed to test the coherence of various positions) have come from the burgeoning field of analytic theology.

[34]Richard Rorty, *Objectivity, Relativism, and Truth* (Cambridge: Cambridge University Press, 1991), 7.

Steinbeck) in our exodus from the Shadowlands of doubt and dogmatism.[35] It's time to reclaim the other hemisphere of our minds at a time
of mental division and cultural polarization.

The Great [Remarriage] of Fiction and Theology

This may be one reason Lewis's works of fantasy have outlived, in some
respects, his apologetic treatises: certain truths are best awakened
through poetry, fantasy, and fiction. In *The Great Divorce*, an imaginative
portrayal of the afterlife allows Lewis to communicate biblical hope more
effectively than do many works of theology, while also avoiding the more
"vicious"[36] side of speculation.[37]

The same is true of Christ's parables. In the famous example of the
sheep and the goats (Mt 25:31-46), Jesus challenges conceptions of who
may be in and who may be out of his kingdom. The determining factor
that separates "eternal punishment" from "eternal life" (Mt 25:46) is one's
response to the Messiah. But the twist comes when we learn that some
disciples respond to Christ as he appears incognito in the form of the
poor, the migrant, the sick, and the imprisoned. In this way, Jesus uses
fiction (parable) to challenge the false certainty of religious dogmatism,
and to convert our eschatological imaginations.

So too with Lewis. His own conversion involved not only reasoning
but the preparatory work of "faerie stories"[38] like that of *Phantastes* by
George MacDonald. These stories awakened a longing for transcendence

---

[35]The poet Samuel Taylor Coleridge contended that "deep Thinking is attainable only by a [person]
of deep Feeling." Thus he dared to utter that it would take the souls of five hundred Isaac New-
tons to make up a single Shakespeare or Milton. This is not the tired Romantic smear that pits
heart against head in simplistic opposition. Indeed, in the next breath, Coleridge notes how he
has committed himself—with aid of "hourly prayers"—to devouring the whole of Newton's
works. Carl Sagan, eat your heart out! See Samuel Taylor Coleridge, letter to Thomas Poole,
March 23, 1801. Cited in Malcolm Guite, *Mariner: A Theological Voyage with Samuel Taylor
Coleridge* (Downers Grove, IL: IVP Academic, 2018), 218-19.

[36]See again John Webster, *The Domain of the Word: Scripture and Theological Reason* (London: T&T
Clark, 2012), chap. 10.

[37]As Austin Farrer claimed at Lewis's funeral, "His real power was not proof; it was depiction."
Austin Farrer, in *C. S. Lewis at the Breakfast Table and Other Reminiscences*, ed. James T. Como
(New York: Macmillan, 1979), 243.

[38]The definitive treatment of this elusive genre was provided by J. R. R. Tolkien in his famous essay,
"On Fairy Stories."

within him. In the words of one of Lewis's biographers, "He became a Christian not through accepting a particular set of arguments but through learning to read a story the right way."[39] *Phantastes* was an inoculation to the modern plague of *Pale Blue Dot* (see chap. 8). In other words, good fiction may be a conduit of prevenient grace.[40]

What's missing in our age of doubt and dogmatism is a biblical variety of enchantment and imagination. This is precisely what Lewis sought to reinvigorate with books like *The Great Divorce*. And we need it more than ever in our current state of busyness and digital distraction. "Do you think I am trying to weave a spell?" Lewis once asked his audience. "*Perhaps* I am; but remember your fairy tales. Spells are used for breaking enchantments as well as for inducing them. And you and I have need of the strongest spell that can be found to wake us from the evil enchantment of worldliness which has been laid upon us."[41]

Conclusion

Now to answer my initial question in this chapter: Is a classic work of Christian fiction any less prophetic if it opens with a lie? My somewhat radical claim is that the lie (though that is not the best word for it) is actually required.

The partly disingenuous demurral that *The Great Divorce* is "solely an imaginative supposal" serves to set the rational and critical faculties of both doubters and dogmatists at ease. The lie (or rather, the fiction) is necessary for weaving redemptive spells. "This is *just* a fairy tale," we say. But that is nonsense. It is untrue, not because faerie tales should be read with wooden literality, but because the literal world is inhabited by spirits in bondage. "The kingdom of God is like this"—says the weaver of parables and faerie fiction—"if you have ears to hear."

---

[39]Jacobs, *Narnian*, 238.

[40]In Wesleyan theology especially, prevenient grace is the preparatory work of God that comes before salvation by the Holy Spirit. It does not overpower but enables human capacity to accept or reject God's gift of salvation. See Joshua M. McNall, *The Mosaic of Atonement: Toward an Integrated Approach to Christ's Work* (Grand Rapids, MI: Zondervan Academic, 2019), 300-305.

[41]Lewis, *Weight of Glory*, 31 (emphasis added).

ET IN ARCADIA

Latitude: 0° 00′ 0.00″ N
EQUATOR

Junior year.

The old tortoise came to the home of Frank and Ethel Mercer in the same way Sophie and Eliza had—through a series of unlikely events.

Ethel initially encountered the creature during a yearlong Fulbright scholarship at the *Estación Científica*, a research outpost in the Galápagos islands, far off the coast of Ecuador. She was there in 1959 to study the local fauna. But her true goal was to figure out her future. Should she marry the handsome Black preacher she had marched beside in Alabama? Could she marry the disparate poles of her affections: science, faith, a longing for justice?

She needed time to think it over. The rest is history.

A smaller version of Wilbur first limped up the front step of Ethel's bungalow one Sunday morning on a wounded leg. She found him crushing and eating a carton of eggs that had just been delivered for Ethel's breakfast. Frank now joked that the event foreshadowed how all of their "adoptables" were ushered into the Mercer home.

Decades later, Ethel maintained contact with an old friend at the *Estación Científica*. And after hearing from Sophie how Eliza was struggling with school and family and life, the old woman pulled some strings. A fully funded internship was arranged. A semester in the Galápagos for college credit. Eliza accepted.

Two years prior, desertion had been the plan, and the Galápagos sounded even more remote than England's Lake District. She had her opportunity.

The goal, at least officially, would be for Eliza to explore the intersections of the island's biodiversity and her chosen field of poetry. "An unlikely marriage," Ethel called it. But that, she reminded Eliza, had always been her style.

Then, not long before the flight, another curveball. Eliza had stopped by Frank and Ethel's to do a load of laundry. And while there, the old woman mentioned that another young lady—once connected to the college—had been accepted for a scientific internship in the Galápagos.

"Oh! So you know Claire," Ethel said with delight as she told Eliza about the biology major who would be joining her.

Eliza tried to wipe the appearance of having tasted sour milk from her face. She hadn't seen Claire since freshman year, when the preacher's daughter responded tersely to Eliza's roommate-breakup email: "No problem. I'm not coming back."

Claire was what they called a "legacy student" at the Christian college, going back to biblical times through her father and her father's father all the way to Moses and the Prophets. So Eliza had been surprised at her abrupt exit.

Now two years later, Eliza was incensed that her long-awaited flight would include a stowaway (or perhaps a chaperone). The line from Virgil, by way of Evelyn Waugh's *Brideshead Revisited*, came suddenly to mind: *Et in Arcadia Ego*. It was uttered of death, but it had other applications.

The past is an invasive species. It always clears customs.

The two girls finally glimpsed each other across the airport terminal before boarding the Boeing 757 that would soon point its nose toward the equator. Eliza tried to be polite. Claire looked different somehow. Smaller almost.

"Eliza! I'm so glad you're here! I've been trying not to chicken out all morning."

"Me too," Eliza said. "I haven't flown much."

"I'll sit by you," Claire remarked. "It's open seating in Coach." She appeared to be knitting, nervously, with several spools of yarn in a plastic Walmart sack. "You can help me work on my security blanket."

"I brought mine too," and Eliza gestured to her grandmother's quilt that had formerly draped her dorm-room bed.

Then the aircraft started boarding.

It was hard to quantify what happened on that lengthy flight—crossing hemispheres and continents. It was as if an invisible barrier broke between the two young women.

Perhaps, for Eliza, it had something to do with the two bloody marys consumed to calm anxiety. Or perhaps it was a phenomenon that she had felt previously with her brother, Jeremy. It was striking how a person who had once been, at best, a cause of annoyance could become a source of comfort merely by being the one familiar face around. Familiarity bred contempt, until one lacked anything familiar.

The cloud billows out the window looked like mountains rising from the deep. And the sun sank in the horizon. Eliza finally worked up the courage to ask, "So why'd you leave?"

Claire paused for several seconds.

"I got pregnant," she said, without looking up.

Eliza's mouth fell open, and she dropped her crochet needle.

"I didn't tell anyone," Claire went on.

A cascade of confession followed: the clandestine drive to an abortion clinic on the other side of town, then turning around in the parking lot. The miscarriage. The sense—ubiquitous among sixteen-year-olds—that she had never belonged to the community in which she looked completely at home.

Claire continued: "I met Ethel through the crisis pregnancy center. They have a program that gives free counseling and ultrasounds. I started coming to the knitting group and Bible study Ethel leads for women at the center."

"Sounds riveting," Eliza responded in an awkward attempt at a joke.

"It was what I needed," Claire said. "After the miscarriage, Ethel and Jesus were the things that got me through."

"I always wondered why you left," Eliza responded seriously.

"I just needed to get away."

"I get it," Eliza replied.

But before she could elaborate, a voice came over the plane's loudspeaker to inform them that they had crossed the invisible line of the equator.

Conclusion

Latitude: 0.7423° S

Longitude: 90.3038° W

GALÁPAGOS

TOWARD THE END OF EXODUS is a sad story about a lack of patience and a lack of trust. We know it as the story of the golden calf
(Ex 32). But it is also a tale about what God's people still do when our
mediator seems slow in returning from a higher elevation. We find a
mouthpiece to tell us what we want to hear, we fashion idols, and false
worship tides us over in our boredom and our fear that we have been
abandoned. In Exodus, the mediator (Moses) returns with stones in
hand and hell to pay. But once the culling is complete, we hear a word
of hope amidst the carnage. "You have committed a great sin. But now
I will go up to the LORD; *perhaps* I can make atonement" (Ex 32:30,
emphasis added).[1]

My book has focused on this little word (*perhaps*) between the
extremes of secular doubt and religious dogmatism. I have described it

---

[1]A look at the Hebrew word choice (*'ûlay*) reveals a construction that often expresses a hope
(Gen 16:2; Num 22:6, 11; 23:3; 1 Sam 6:5; Jer 20:10), but occasionally a fear or doubt (Gen 27:12;
Job 1:5). As such, it fits quite well with the meaning I have sketched throughout this book. See
Francis Brown, Samuel Rolles Driver, and Charles Augustus Briggs, *Enhanced Brown-Driver-
Briggs Hebrew and English Lexicon* (Oxford: Clarendon, 1977), 19.

as faith seeking imagination, not merely on matters of academic debate but on questions that haunt the hearts of everyday people. Perhaps there is still hope for the divided tribes called evangelical, though we elevate unhelpful mouthpieces (often Aaron-like, because they are blood-relatives of our Moses-figures), with the sad result of God's name being defamed among the nations.

The hope in Exodus 32 involves a familiar theme. Moses goes back up the mountain, like Abraham before him (see chap. 1), with his mind on sacrifice. He takes no animal, no son, no daughter. Instead, the mediator offers himself to be blotted out (Ex 32:33), despite being the one Israelite who was not present in the sinful camp. Moses reasoned (cf. Heb 11:19) that a human self-offering might be the way of atonement. He was both wrong and right. That is often the case with sacred speculation. But his hopeful perhapsing, and his journey, was important nonetheless. "I will go up to the LORD; perhaps . . ." renewal is still possible (Ex 32:30).

Understanding Perhaps

"To believe in providence," says N. T. Wright of the apostle Paul, means learning how to say perhaps—and especially if your past life as a zealous Pharisee proved to be a painful adventure in having missed the point.[2] But that does not mean that a chastened form of sacred speculation is a panacea for the fractured Pangaea of evangelicalism. No human stratagem can knit our divided lands together. And the theologians who view *speculation* as a shame word are not wrong to note its dangers. We must learn from Scripture (chap. 1) and tradition (chap. 2) how to say perhaps, and we need guardrails for the journey (chap. 3). With these in place, a certain form of speculation can lead not to heresy or oddity but to a more robust orthodoxy, or to matters of orthodox indifference (adiaphora) that are nonetheless important for the wrestling match of faith. Cultivation of a redeemed imagination is intensely practical in an age beset by crippling skepticism and strident certitude.

---

[2] N. T. Wright, *Paul and the Faithfulness of God* (Minneapolis: Fortress, 2013), 1351.

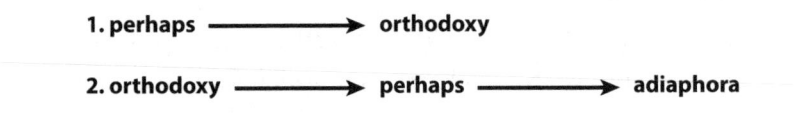

Figure 3. Beginning with perhaps or orthodoxy

Against Dogmatism

The posture of perhaps exists apart from the prevailing winds of dogmatism (part 2), which is defined by tonal shrillness (chap. 4) and a projection of false certainty onto complex questions (chap. 5). While the dogmatic posture may seem warranted when faith is under attack, the result is often an Absalom-like assumption that a militant platform-building is the way to construct the kingdom (chap. 6). Not so, says the Messiah. "Better he kill me than I learn his ways." Better not to practice "the ways that cause kings to go mad."[3] The prophetic imagination weeps over Jerusalem rather than try to conquer it by flame of war.

Against Doubt

Perhaps also stands distinct from pervasive skepticism and deconstruction (part 3). Though some have sought to valorize doubt as a good thing, the Scriptures speak often against it. In the Bible, problematic doubt is not uncertainty or honest questions but the cultivation of a divided heart that fosters divided allegiance to our King (chap. 7). By listening to a personal story (Science Mike; chaps. 8–9), I sought to empathize with doubters while simultaneously rejecting the smear that says *Cogito, ergo* None. Despite the hemispheric drift of our split brains, the Spirit works to heal divided hearts when we open ourselves to supernatural experience, embodied discipleship, and relational connectedness in Christ's body, the church. A sanctified imagination works against both doubt and dogmatism.

---

[3]See again Gene Edwards, *A Tale of Three Kings: A Study in Brokenness* (Carol Stream, IL: Tyndale House, 1992), 36.

Practicing Perhaps

The final portion of the book (part 4) practiced some perhapsing on three topics that bridge the divide between academic theology and questions that haunt the modern mind in general. I affirmed the goodness of both God and science in the face of Darwin's "dead animal" dilemma (chap. 10). I reimagined the interplay of human freedom and divine sovereignty in Romans 9 (chap. 11). And I sought to learn from C. S. Lewis about the place of fiction and imagination when pondering "what dreams may come" beyond this earthly life (chap. 12). My conclusions are all tentative since it is risky to tread into these blank spaces.

A final claim of my book is that pastors, professors, and laypeople need to have not only our minds but our bookshelves expanded. This shelf space should include not just Augustine, Aquinas, and Scripture but Shakespeare, Steinbeck, and Marilynn Robinson (to name a few). *Tolle lege* is an eleventh commandment for those hoping to ignite a Christian imagination: "Take up and read."[4] It is high time to turn off Cable News, put down social media, and allow our storied world to be renarrated. If this happens, we may recognize with Karen Swallow Prior that "books [can be] the backwoods path back to God, bramble-filled and broken, yet, but full of truth and wonder."[5] In the fault line between doubt and dogmatism, this path needs treading, overgrown though it may be. Fiction may be a prevenient grace. "All things are yours," remarked the apostle (1 Cor 3:21). Now for one last story.

ERUPTION

Summer, before senior year.

The biodiversity of the Galápagos emerged because the islands rose up from the sea as mountainous byproducts of underwater eruptions. They were never in contact with surrounding continents. Nor were they part of the great Pangaea that would fragment via fault lines.

---

[4]Augustine, *Confessions*, 8.11.29.
[5]Karen Swallow Prior, *Booked: Literature in the Soul of Me* (New York: T. S. Poetry Press, 2012), 11.

For the Galápagos, the same molten fissures that drove other lands apart created rather than divided habitat. And despite their isolation, life found its way there in long ages immemorial. Wind brought seeds and birds and tiny organisms; waves carried marine creatures, including Wilbur's ancestors, to an environment of unmolested grandeur.

Claire tried to explain these mysteries to Eliza throughout their year of study. "Science for English majors," she called it. During these tutorials the girls sat perched on bunks inside their seaside bungalow. Eliza pondered how odd it was to find herself again in a small room, next to the same roommate, atop the same quilt from freshman year. The only thing missing was the New Testament homework with the fateful line, "not peace but a sword."

But the Bible was not absent.

Claire's well-worn copy sat on an eclectic bookshelf, lined with science texts, poetry, and novels by a host of authors.

Much had changed in three years. And soon would change again with the internship approaching its conclusion. Eliza's faith remained a question. But she felt increasingly that there was another option alongside the noisy extremes of unbelief and religious certainty. That dichotomy no longer meshed with the biodiversity of her experience. Folks like Frank and Ethel Mercer, Claire, and even Sophie (whom she now texted daily) were like islands thrust up in the sea, driven by a force that Eliza couldn't see and didn't understand. "Faith for dummies" didn't begin to cover it.

Less than a month to go in her internship, a call came from home. It was Jeremy, Eliza's brother. He relayed the news about her father. "Heart disease." "A year or two to live." Stubborn as always, her father insisted that she stay and finish the program.

Eliza had been alone when the phone rang, finishing (at long last) Evelyn Waugh's *Brideshead Revisited*. Sophie had mailed it in a care package with Lucky Charms and a photo of herself with what looked to be a thousand-year-old tortoise. In the book's conclusion, the main character (Charles Ryder) finds himself at the bedside of a dying man who has stubbornly refused last rites. An ardent atheist, Ryder implores the devout family to stop pestering their dying loved one, only to be horrified to catch himself praying, inwardly: "O God, if there is a God, forgive him his sins, if there is such a thing as sin."

Claire came home and found Eliza crying.

They talked long into the night. Finally, Eliza switched off her lamp and lay there in the humid darkness. She recalled the dream from three years prior: the tiny boat, the two receding beaches, the stitched-together quilt blocks in her hands. She recalled the sense that she was drifting in the sea, about to capsize.

She still felt like that sometimes. But she wasn't alone. And she sensed now that the eruptions driving things apart were not the only forces at work. The earth itself was moving—a giant heaving, breathing thing, suffused with mystery. And the islands thrown up around her gave a sense that there are indeed more things in heaven and earth than can be dreamed in mere geology.

Eliza did not pray, *"O God, if there is a God . . ."* But she understood the sentiment. It was an intimation not of faith but of aching hope: an eruption beneath the surface, a blank space on the map, a rock thrust upward in the sea that might one day become a mountain. Then came to mind Waugh's famous lines from *Brideshead Revisited*:

> Perhaps . . . perhaps all our loves are merely hints and symbols; vagabond-language scrawled on gateposts and paving-stones along the weary road that others have tramped before us; perhaps you and I are types and this sadness which sometimes falls between us springs from disappointment in our search, each straining through and beyond the other, snatching a glimpse now and then of shadow which turns the corner always a pace or two ahead of us (348).

This flickering intimation was not itself sufficient. It was not the goal. But it was not nothing. It was itself a creature crawling slowly from the waters—a start to bind things together, like stitching between quilt blocks, clutched tightly between fingers.

Name Index

Subject Index

Scripture Index